there were such a thing as a dream anthropologist, you'd find
rson Vaughan at the top of the profession, helping us understand
w some dreams become traps—become cages—and how sometimes
hen a dream dies, it kills everything around it. I truly feel that
aughan's chronicle of Royal, Nebraska, and its heartbreaking zoo is
an Americana masterpiece."
—Bob Shacochis, National Book Award–winning author of
Kingdoms in the Air and *Easy in the Islands*

"Dick Haskin's dream of starting a primate research center in his tiny
hometown in Nebraska is the kind of crazy notion that would be easy to
mock or deride, especially when everything spins absurdly and tragically
out of control. But Carson Vaughan recognizes something deeper. With
**Willa Cather's eye for the countryside and the Coen brothers' ear for
dialogue**, Vaughan reveals Haskin's story for what it really is: a strange,
ineffable, and heartbreaking emblem of what it means to live in—and
feel circumscribed by—the narrow bounds of a dying town. **This
amazing book of good intentions and bad outcomes reminds us that
no place is too small for big ideas or devastating consequences.**"
—Ted Genoways, James Beard Award–winning author of
This Blessed Earth: A Year in the Life of an American Family Farm

"In the finest John McPhee tradition, Carson Vaughan has picked his
spot on the map; described its surface in careful, evocative detail; and
then drilled deep, revealing the dreams, ambitions, frustrations, and
failures of the citizens of Royal, Nebraska, who hoped to put their
town on the map by opening a zoo. The product of meticulous research
and reporting, *Zoo Nebraska* **has a narrative drive and a collection
of complex characters that few books, fiction or nonfiction, can
match. It's a remarkable achievement.**"
—Larry Watson, author of *As Good as Gone* and *Montana 1984*

PRAISE FOR *ZOO NEBRAS*

"**A marvelous, meaningful book**, full of deep reporting, f̶ and big questions about the nature of community, of li animals, of challenging values. **Zoo Nebraska will surp engage you and make you think.**"

—Susan Orlean, author of *New York Times* bes *The Library Book* and *The Orchid*

"**Zoo Nebraska is the kind of delightfully unexpected book t comes along once in a blue moon.** The subject, the bittersweet an hilarious collapse of a once-charming zoo in a once-charming Midwes town, is as unlikely as it is wonderful. The chimpanzees run wild, and away we go. Carson Vaughan writes with eloquent meticulousness. He has a novelist's eye. **The overall impact is stunning.**"

—Buzz Bissinger, author of *Father's Day* and *New York Times* bestseller *Friday Night Lights*

"Reading like a sustained segment of *This American Life*, in a tone at once dryly comic and doleful, this account of bizarre events in northeastern Nebraska paints a portrait of the entire region and suggests a metaphor for mankind in general. **Well observed and crisply written.**"

—Alexander Payne, Academy Award–winning director of *Nebraska* and *The Descendants*

"*Zoo Nebraska* is Great Plains Gothic, **Fargo meets S-Town meets Alexander Payne**, a riveting tale of quixotic hopes and dreams and bad blood, all of it carefully, knowingly, sympathetically told."

—Kurt Andersen, author of *New York Times* bestsellers *Fantasyland* and *Heyday* and host of *Studio 360*

"With the deft touch of a novelist, **Carson Vaughan brilliantly weaves an intricate, intimate, in-depth look into the heart and soul of a small Nebraska village**. But along the way—from a tapestry of mischievous characters, memorable scenes, and machine-gun dialogue—he illuminates a much larger landscape chockablock with haunting questions: Can you ever know who you are if you don't understand where you are? What happens if you lose the ability to dream? And in the end, what does it mean to be human? So read this real-life story carefully. Think about it lovingly. Handle it gently. Because **this is a gem**."

—Joe Starita, author of *A Warrior of the People* and *I Am a Man*

"**There is a movie here, in this thrilling, crisply reported, and altogether wonderful book**, but despite the chimps romping around and terrorizing a tiny Nebraska town, it isn't *Planet of the Apes*. No, *Zoo Nebraska* would ideally be codirected by Werner Herzog and John Ford as a story of obsession and folly leading to tragedy while at the same time leaving its characters, who seem as integral to the place as the dusty winds that blow through it, with their dignity intact. **Carson Vaughan, like a young Truman Capote, takes us into the points of view of a multitude of characters who, like the roadside zoo at the book's center, provide a menagerie of strangeness and possibility;** but despite the temptation to caricature, he inhabits these people so fully and honestly on the page that he brings them and their story fully alive."

—David Gessner, *New York Times* bestselling author of
All the Wild That Remains

"Here is a real-life small-town drama, literary journalism that reads like a novel—heartbreak, dreams, bad luck, loss on a 'local level,' where pain can be seen and heard. It's also sometimes very funny. *Zoo Nebraska* **resides in the bull's-eye of good literature: it's about heart, soul, and grit**—all made tactile. Vaughan, just out of the chute with his first book, has hit his stride already. **This book will keep you up way past bedtime—reading to find out what could possibly come next, and next, and finally next. And if you were lucky enough to be raised in a small town, you will ever so clearly recognize lives, events, hopes, and fears that are so eloquently opened to you."**

—Clyde Edgerton, author of *The Floatplane Notebooks* and
Walking Across Egypt

"This **wild, beautiful** book is so inventive and genuine, full of insight into life on this earth and particularly in the teeming microcosm of Zoo Nebraska. **Who could guess that what happened here could so thoroughly and strangely explain our times?"**

—Rebecca Lee, author of *Bobcat and Other Stories*

"Vaughan catapults into the sphere of my favorite writers by rooting out and unfurling this nearly lost but epic story of an American back road. This book howls to life and delivers a tale of people and critters like none I've ever heard. I was instantly lost in the fascinating story of an eccentric achievement and its violent, then slow grind into obsolescence. **A brilliant writer and researcher, Vaughan dazzles when he turns all his talents to his home state, which in his hands, is flyover country no more."**

—Devin Murphy, national bestselling author of
The Boat Runner and *Tiny Americans*

"From the very first sentences, this story grips you with such rich detail and passion for place and character that you won't be able to put it down. Writing in the tradition of investigative work such as Susan Orlean's *The Orchid Thief*, Carson Vaughan explores the tale of a small zoo in Royal, Nebraska, and the well-intentioned people whose untenable dreams are lost at great expense to the lives around them. Beginning with the calls to police, the story brings us into obsessions that drive the human heart beyond the boundaries of reason, leading to the inevitable tragedy that follows. **This is a book not only for animal lovers but also for readers who want to experience the many corners of worlds we build through sheer will and imagination, the kind of private dreaming that is a hallmark of our culture.**"

—Jonis Agee, author of *The Bones of Paradise*

"Carson Vaughan's *Zoo Nebraska* is the real-life story of a struggling zoo improbably located in the dwindling farm town of Royal, Nebraska, population eighty-one. But it is also the tale of a hapless would-be primatologist, four doomed chimpanzees, and the fractious and eccentric community that both supports and destroys them—**a narrative of obsession, yearning, and human frailty worthy of Melville and his white whale. By turns sweet, sad, funny, and tragic, *Zoo Nebraska* digs deep into what makes us human—and why we can't stop making monkeys of ourselves.**"

—Robert Anthony Siegel, author of *Criminals: My Family's Life on Both Sides of the Law*

"**A vivid evocation of a place and its people**, *Zoo Nebraska* traces the rise and fall of a small zoo—concluding with the gripping narrative of the desperate efforts to capture escaped chimpanzees and the aftermath of that event. **Carson Vaughan has written a fascinating tale from beginning to end.**"

—John Biguenet, author of *The Torturer's Apprentice* and *Silence*

"In *Zoo Nebraska*, Carson Vaughan traces the beauty and terror of one man's dream to create a haven for exotic animals amid the fossil beds and farmland of rural Nebraska. What follows is **an epic of small-town America**, an all-too-human story where the dreams of men run wild of their aims and unlikely beasts break loose on city streets. **Like Cather, Vaughan has an eye for the grace and folly of the pioneer heart against the vast, stern beauty of the American plains.**"

—Taylor Brown, author of *Gods of Howl Mountain*

ZOO
NEBRASKA

ZOO NEBRASKA

THE DISMANTLING of
an AMERICAN DREAM

CARSON VAUGHAN

Little
a

Published by Little A, New York

www.apub.com

Amazon, the Amazon logo, and Little A are trademarks of Amazon.com, Inc., or its
affiliates.

ISBN-13: 9781503901506 (hardcover)
ISBN-10: 1503901505 (hardcover)
ISBN-13: 9781503901490 (paperback)
ISBN-10: 1503901491 (paperback)

Cover design by David Drummond

Printed in the United States of America

First edition

For Mel

I should like to stress the idea that if you know and understand the story of your community you will know and understand a great deal about the story of man, anywhere.

—*Mari Sandoz, 1959*

Contents

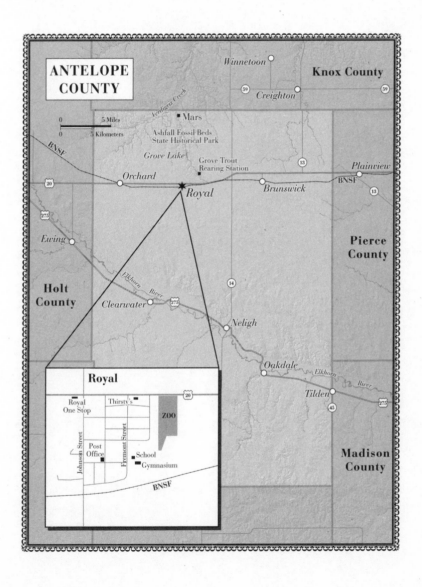

PROLOGUE

The wind bolted for open doors and whistled through window-panes. It stole crumpled Powerball slips from the gutters—feed sacks and greasy napkins and leftover baling twine. It rolled cigarette butts down Main Street. It whipped the dust—fine and buff—from the hoods of worn-out pickup trucks. September 10, 2005. A typical day in Neligh, Nebraska. The sun hammered the plastic sign above Daddy's Cafe, blurred the candy stripes racing up the tin exterior. Inside, cafeteria silverware clanked on ceramic dishes while coffee burned on the warmer. Occasional gales shook the glass like a Freightliner passing at full speed. An American flag hung prominently from the wall beside a shadow box of country trinkets and antiques.

Brian Detlefsen and Darrell Hamilton sat at a table near the center of the room. They were an odd couple: Detlefsen a square-jawed, rosy-cheeked, twenty-seven-year-old state trooper and Hamilton a pudgy, slow-moving, fifty-year-old county sheriff. One in blue, the other brown, both easygoing and optimistic. They placed their hats on the table and surveyed the room: familiar faces all around.

Detlefsen grew up chasing the goats around his parents' farm behind the Dodge dealership on the west edge of town. He had wanted to be a cop or a rodeo clown.

"My mom said she would disown me if I became a rodeo clown, so I became a cop."

He'd enrolled at Wayne State, a small college wrestled from a corn-field sixty miles east. He studied criminal justice with "a little bit of psychology thrown in there," he says. After graduation, he spent six months training with the Nebraska State Patrol in Lincoln, which then stationed him with the Carrier Enforcement Division back in his home-town, weighing and inspecting semitrucks with a portable scale. And two years after that, he'd transferred to the Field Services Division, where the job aligned more with his original vision: racing to the scene, issuing citations, clocking highway travelers, grabbing lunch with the county sheriff. He was hardly one to brag, but the whole process had seemed almost too smooth. All the patrolmen he'd known as a kid had been old guys with a mustache and a gut, and here he'd come, fresh out of the academy at just twenty-two years old, already back home with his boots on the ground.

Their meals had just arrived when the sheriff's pager lit up. **Animals loose at Royal Zoo. Need 10-49. Traffic control.** Hamilton sighed and set his pager back on the table. Royal was a twenty-minute drive. Detlefsen kept eating. Neither sat up. Neither rushed out the door. A loose goat, most likely. Potential roadkill, or soon to be. Maybe the donkey slipped its pen. Hardly a pressing case either way. Hamilton took another bite, wiped his mouth, and drew a deep breath.

"Well," he said, shaking the table as he stood.

"Let me know," Detlefsen replied.

Detlefsen watched as Hamilton replaced his hat and stepped into the sunlight, wind rushing in through the closing door. He hadn't thought about the zoo in years. He used to visit when he was just a kid—they all did—back when the zoo was still a trailer home off the highway, a chimpanzee in a corncrib, a few petting goats. Not so dif-ferent from the farm, really, save for Reuben, "that stinker throwing his feces." Detlefsen and his family would make a day of the trip: first the zoo, then Ashfall Fossil Beds State Historical Park, the trout hatchery, sometimes the Gavins Point Dam up north along the Missouri. He'd lost track of the zoo over the years, grown out of it, maybe, though by the time he returned from Wayne, Zoo Nebraska had grown up, too, with tigers and lions now stalking the cages and Reuben's three new roommates: Ripley, Tyler, and Jimmy Joe. Still a novelty, perhaps, but no longer a joke.

A few minutes later, as Detlefsen eyed the last fries on his plate, dispatch called.

"They need you up there now. They need guns."

The cab of the cruiser was static and warm. Detlefsen cracked the window as he backed onto Main Street and steered toward the highway, past the redbrick courthouse with the golden antelope perched on top. He sped north, cutting through a vast sea of corn, green and undulating, past crooked telephone poles and drooping lines, past long, thick rows of shelterbelts dividing one field, one property, one farmhouse from the next, the road so familiar after all these years he could practically drive it blind, every dip and swell expected. The sky offered blue and more blue without a single cloud mooring on the horizon, nothing to count, nothing to question. Just endless blue, and a yellow streak of bug juice glued to the windshield. He hadn't even turned on his lights. *I'll get there,* he thought, *when I get there.*

By the time he met the juncture at Highway 20 and turned west, he could hardly remember the last fifteen miles, as if he'd simply materialized at the intersection where the Yum Yum Shack used to sling burgers and swirl soft-serve ice cream in the dog days of summer. Three miles more and the Royal water tower crested above the trees, a giant tin can on stilts, silver and blinding in the sun. Irrigation pipe scalloped above corn tassels like the bones of a sea serpent, and a yellow haze drifted across the road. Detlefsen kept his eyes peeled for an escaped goat or an injured animal on the shoulder as he passed the cemetery and its white vinyl fence, the zoo just a quarter mile ahead.

But the ditches were clean. The road was open. Only the sheriff's vehicle hinted at distress. Detlefsen stalled briefly behind the mileage sign for Plainview and Sioux City before slowly pulling closer to the zoo's front gate, shaded by a row of trees bowing in the wind. Detlefsen flipped on his dashcam. The radio crackled in the cab, the equipment jostling with every divot in the dry dirt parking lot, as Arvin Brandt, an off-duty county patrolman, drove past him.

"Is Arvin upset or what's the story, four-seven-eight?"

"I just got here," Detlefsen replied.

"Ten-nine?"

"I just got here when Arvin was pulling out."

Detlefsen noticed a black mass in his periphery, slowly moving on all fours outside the old church-turned-activity-center, its back flat as a two-by-four, rump naked and pale. A smaller one shambled around the corner. A white golf cart emerged from the tree line and sputtered toward the animals, a hulking man behind the wheel, his arm outstretched, revolver in hand. Two shots rang out, but the animals didn't stop and the golf cart didn't slow down, and State Trooper Brian Detlefsen, badge number 478, stared in utter disbelief, hands clutching the wheel tight, as the bigger chimp galloped down the fence line at full speed, limbs a blur, a sci-fi-cum-Western, a shootout at the church. This wasn't the petting zoo he remembered. They hadn't covered this at the academy.

"It wasn't like I could just get out and tackle this thing," he says. "There ain't no way you're going to get out and talk to a chimpanzee and say, 'Hey, how's your day going?'"

So Detlefsen sat there sweating in his patrol vehicle, watching the wildness before him, this macabre circus, an active shooter and two bleeding chimpanzees—maybe more—blitzed on a double shot of adrenaline and chase. It was the most surreal thing he'd ever seen, on duty or off. Behind him, a semitruck barreled down Highway 20, oblivious to the mayhem. Ahead, a shriek lifted from the trees and carried across the yard, a shriek so wild, so primal it seemed to rise from within, a shriek so desperate he would remember that precise pitch for the rest of his life.

The bigger chimp kept running, kicking up dust, until he mounted a bank of cinder blocks in a single fluid skip and rested in the shade of a lone tree on the zoo's eastern fence line. The whole tree warped and yawed as if battered by a tropical storm. And just as two pickup trucks thundered past him and punched into the parking lot, elbows hanging out the windows, his cell phone rang out with the digital cannon fire of Tchaikovsky's *1812 Overture*. His wife was calling.

"Hello?"

"I'm telling you . . . where are you at?"

"Royal—why?"

"Our washer is flooding again."

"Okay, shut it off. I . . . I've got a situation here. I've got to go."

PART I

EVERYTHING MUST GO

They don't talk about it much anymore—the day the chimpanzees broke loose—though at night, when Diana Wavrunek slips into bed with her husband, Dean, and drifts off to sleep, the images rush back like water from a broken levee: the gate swinging forward; the chimps screeching and slapping the windows; the tranquilizer darts slipping from her trembling fingers. She hears the muffled *pop-pop-pop* of distant gunfire. She sees the director in his golf cart and the chimps trailing close behind. She sees the windows in the old minivan, broken and blood smeared. She sees the look in Jimmy Joe's eyes, the judgment, the knowing, and everything that comes next.

"The dreams vary," she says, "but they always end the same."

Except for one.

Sometimes, all she sees is Tyler, perched atop the door to his cage, rocking back and forth and gripping a handful of wires. He used to sit like that all the time, waiting for her to surprise him. Tyler was the youngest of the chimps, loved games, the *gotcha* antics, the high jinks of hide-and-seek. In the dream, something's different. It's difficult to translate in waking life. Nothing happens, really. Tyler just sits there, watching her from the shadows. His eyes are heavy. He looks tired. Older. Despondent. "Kinda like, *How could you let this happen?*"

Before the great escape, busloads of schoolchildren would flock to Zoo Nebraska every week. They couldn't wait to step inside the gates;

couldn't wait to watch Reuben, the star chimpanzee, speak with hands so remarkably similar to their own; couldn't wait to watch the macaques frolic and the lemurs bound. Since the late 1980s, the zoo had been a key attraction for northeast Nebraska, the ultimate field trip for students within a hundred-mile radius. Staking the eastern end of tiny Royal, Nebraska, the grounds were neatly kept, the lawn trimmed short, the trails maintained, the signs freshly painted with the species and their scientific names: chimpanzee (*Pan troglodytes*), mountain lion (*Felis concolor*), whitetail deer (*Odocoileus virginianus*). After visiting, kids would write letters to their county papers describing their favorite animals. They'd beg their parents or grandparents to take them again. At least one family timed their visits according to the train schedule, thrilled by the chimpanzees' reaction, the way they swung their arms and pounded their chests, hooting at the noise on the tracks.

But now, on June 28, 2010, everything must go: the cages, the signs, the old Church-of-Christ-turned-visitor-center, the dust-caked aquariums, the maintenance equipment, even the wooden fence posts and the seven acres they enclose. Five years ago, the USDA revoked Zoo Nebraska's license. The buses stopped coming. The parking lot emptied. Prairie grass reclaimed the walking paths, and the director begrudgingly relocated the animals that remained. Several years later, the Nebraska attorney general deemed Zoo Nebraska's malfunctioning board of directors unfit to liquidate itself and appointed a lawyer to wind up the whole affair. After years of petty litigation, all the cages lie empty and rusting, stalks of ragweed and big bluestem jutting through their concrete foundations. The impending auction is the last act, the coup de grâce, the final farewell.

"You gonna pay for sixteen, and them other ones just gonna be kind of a little bonus deal for ya, right there," explains the auctioneer, Colonel Darrell L. Crabtree, a seventy-year-old man from nearby Brunswick with a pencil-thin mustache and straw cowboy hat. "Do I hear ten?"

The colonel starts slowly.

"Twelve and a half here, twelve and a half here! Fifteen, fifteen!"

And he's off, spitting numbers like bullets from a semiautomatic weapon, landing on "Twenty!" or "Do I hear twenty-five?" only to reload and fire again. It's "The Sound That Sells," according to his red Chevy Scottsdale. The contest began at 1:00 p.m. It's a clammy summer afternoon, eighty-five degrees, and the mosquitoes are scouting fresh blood. A crowd of nearly one hundred area residents, predominately thick-armed farmers wearing sleeveless T-shirts and dusty ball caps, follows the colonel's pickup as it rolls from one article to the next, the colonel himself chanting his cattle rattle into a bullhorn from the bed of the truck. A handful of blond-haired Amish men stand among the crowd. Trailing twenty yards behind, the county sheriff monitors the event, hands resting on his belt, peering out from the shadow of his campaign hat. Time and again, the colonel describes an item as "functional" or "handy," waits for a bid, confirms there is none, makes a lazy joke, and sells for dirt cheap. An elderly woman pokes her head out from the service trailer. The highest bidder claims his number.

"It's bittersweet. This was a good zoo, and it was good for the area," says sixty-seven-year-old Valda Young, wife of Marvin, the last acting zoo board president. She's been keeping tabs on the auction from her post in an aluminum lawn chair, totaling the bids. She's wearing black sunglasses, a turquoise flower-patterned top, and black sweatpants that fall just below the knee. She's a sturdy woman and looks young for her age. "Too bad the community lost it," she says, echoing the whispers of many, "but that's just the way it is."

Like Diana, she's anxious to forget, to rise above the turbulence and breathe again. And she's nervous that with the end so near in sight, the locally notorious Jensen family, whose questionable legal maneuvers have already prolonged the whole affair, might make yet another move to complicate things, still insistent that a public attraction should remain. Valda personally requested the county sheriff patrol the grounds, "in case there was any difficulties."

"The Jensens have filed lawsuits against the zoo board and against my husband," she says, "and so we weren't sure how they would handle today."

Valda slides her shades down the bridge of her nose, heedfully scratching a few digits in her notebook: *Neck Yoke $10, Bear Stand $15, Marten House $17.50.* Grasshoppers spring from the paths of half-hearted participants. The meadowlark sings from its perch.

NOT RESPONSIBLE FOR ACCIDENTS, the hand-drawn signs say. WATCH YOUR STEP. LOTS OF HOLES.

In a starched white button-down, pleated khakis, and a bright pastel tie, Mark Fitzgerald, the state-appointed custodian, looks out of place. His assistant stands beside him in dark shades and a white tank top, recording each sale in a black leather notebook, her wavy brown hair falling just past her shoulders. Regarding the property as "dilapidated" and finding little to no value in the zoo's assets—mostly scrap metal, in his opinion—Fitzgerald estimated a total return of little more than $6,000 in what he'd originally proposed as a silent auction. He guessed the eight-foot-high fencing around the zoo would sell for more than the land itself, and he doubted whether a regular auction could generate enough revenue to hire the auctioneer. But the board claimed there was plenty of interest in the lots, and, in spite of Fitzgerald's misgivings, the judge approved the open-outcry auction.

Fitzgerald, who has now rolled up his sleeves, shed his tie, and loosened his collar, has already spent weeks working with the state and the IRS to withdraw their tax liens on the zoo—a total of roughly $100,000—to ensure the best possible results at the auction. But he's never quite mastered the art of corralling the Jensens.

"I thought they might say something to cast an issue concerning the quality of the title that can pass to the buyers here," Fitzgerald would later say. "I was concerned that might queer the deal a little bit, particularly in regard to the real estate."

But Valda and Fitzgerald's worries expired with little fanfare. Earleen Jensen did make an appearance at the auction, her burly husband, Marlowe, and forty-five-year-old son, Justin, by her side, but they left shortly after losing their bid for the land to Chris Williby, a Royal native. When the bidding reached $12,000, Earleen trashed her bidding card, unlocked the station wagon, and drove home, convinced Williby and the Realtor had conspired.

By the end of the auction, the sun has shifted farther to the west, and the colonel has left few items untagged. With the day's total well over $6,000, Fitzgerald is pleased. The board made a smart move—*the first in a long time,* he thought—by scrapping the silent auction. But, for some, this isn't about money or tax liens or government procedure; it isn't about a cheap fence or a pair of feed barrels. For some, today is about paying respects, saying goodbye to something they loved, something they once believed in.

Eighty-three-year-old Jim Haskin stands in the shade of an elm tree and remembers feeding the chimps peppermint leaves as the sun rose each morning, tickling Reuben's tongue—"they like that, you know"—and the years he spent here with his family, helping his son, Dick, maintain the zoo. The auction is a reminder of what once was and what could have been. And it's a reminder of his wife, Lucille, who died just one year ago, serving on the board until she passed.

"It hurt, when I seen the zoo go down, because our family had so much in it," Jim says, his beige bucket hat throwing shade down his cheeks. "The day that all ended"—his soft voice quavers a bit, then drops a decibel—"that hurt, real bad."

Jim knows the story well. He's part of it. He remembers donating the zoo's first two and a half acres, the land he's standing on now. He remembers when Nu Home in O'Neill donated a trailer for Reuben when Reuben was still an infant, living in a corncrib halfway to Neligh.

He remembers when the first lemur gave birth. And, of course, he remembers the short string of Dick's successors and the winds of change so discordant with his son's grand vision.

"This was something that could have been going for years and years and years," he says, the sun drawing attention to the white stubble on his chin and neck, his bushy blond eyebrows, and small red liver spots. "It hurt my wife and me both. Of course, she's gone now."

The colonel just sold the owl house for twenty dollars, the hawk cages for sixty, and across the highway, less than fifty yards away, Kenneth Schlueter Jr. sits alone in his machine shop, shades closed, smoking a cigarette. He lives there, in an apartment in the back, the last director in Zoo Nebraska history. More than once since the shootings took place, he's crawled out of bed to find the words *Reuben Killer* spray-painted in red across the shop windows. He doesn't talk about it—doesn't talk about much at all anymore. Doesn't open the shop for coffee and doughnuts in the morning. Doesn't keep the door unlocked like he used to, his friends say, in case a traveler broke down and needed refuge, a telephone, a place to warm up. His body's failing. He's suffered two heart attacks since the shootings took place. He underwent quadruple bypass surgery. He's heavily medicated. He's broke, ignoring one creditor to pay off another.

"After this all took place, it was just like he was in another world," his sister Kathryn says. "It hurt him when he had to shoot them. And now I've got a brother who is wholly opposite because of it. I don't think he ever will snap out of it."

As for Dick Haskin himself, whose childhood dream perverted itself into the creation of Zoo Nebraska, he's ignoring the sale altogether. He couldn't have known, when he first moved back to Royal more than twenty-five years ago, that his life's passion would come to this: a country auction, a fractured community, an empty zoo, and a career he'd rather forget. All the anger, the grief, the remorse that would have undoubtedly surfaced had he chosen to witness the auction, he's kept at bay by retreating to the dig site, an archaeological cat's cradle seven miles north of Royal where he recently began searching for evidence of Mars, Nebraska, a pioneer settlement founded 130 years ago by his great-great-grandfather. Digging. Sifting. Dusting. Today's just another day in the dirt, another day without Reuben, his best friend, his surrogate son, the embodiment of everything he'd once hoped for.

A pale-yellow light peeks through the trees. When the last few items sell—two cat skins for $7.50 apiece, the calf shed for $385, and what the Realtor listed as "stick" for $4.00—the grand total is $25,379.50, land included. A certain tranquility returns to the zoo, like a park after the children have gone home. A warm breeze parts the grass, and the few remaining attendees load chain-link fence onto a flatbed trailer. This skeleton has been picked clean. The vultures have fled.

"I guess you'd say I'm sad to see this happen, but it's got to happen," Jim says. "Maybe we can all get back to normal lives."

WELCOME TO ROYAL

There is no welcome display, just a quiet green highway sign that reads ROYAL: POPULATION 81. Motorists passing through on Highway 20 are prone to mistake it for a cluster of old sheds and broken farm equipment—just another memento mori stitched into what author Willa Cather dubbed the "loose hide" of the Great Plains. Some thirty miles below the South Dakota state line, the village of Royal idles in northeast Nebraska. From an aerial perspective, it's a tiny box with a slanted southern edge, a glitch among the perfect circles of center-pivot irrigation. When the eastern wall of the post office collapsed a few years ago, petrifying Mrs. Carlson, the postmistress, inside, residents started picking up their mail in Orchard, a town six miles down the road.

Unlike the Sandhills farther west, where the land heaves and swells and vast, untouched miles separate one community from the next, northeast Nebraska is perforated with small get-togethers: Plainview, Brunswick, Orchard, Neligh, Clearwater, Oakdale, Ewing, Creighton, and others—each one founded by optimistic pioneers. Faint silhouettes of old church steeples and grain elevators can be seen from the highway, staking their claims against barbwire and disked earth. Corn and soybeans blanket 65 percent of Antelope County. For miles in every direction, the view is open, flat, plain. The name *Plainview* is not a coincidence.

But Royal is the smallest of these foregone aspirations and withering further all the time. To pass through it is easily forgettable, unless one takes the time to stay awhile. Talk. Explore on foot and feel the peculiar silence of the streets, the crunch of gravel underfoot, see the billow of plastic over broken windows. It's difficult to distinguish, standing among Royal's modest homes, whether residents are just inside or miles and years removed. On those rare occasions when the wind calms and the trees steady, the creak of a screen door can carry from one end of town to the other. One might imagine, if not for the muffled signs of activity—a distant engine clap, say, or the low hum of a power drill—that pulling a single string could leave the homes splayed flat and empty, like a film set after the final shoot. The city itself is 0.1 square miles, a grid of twelve blocks wedged between the highway and what was once a passenger branch of the Fremont, Elkhorn and Missouri Valley Railroad. Now freight trains pass through several times a day, filled mostly with corn and ethanol from Plainview and Brunswick. Like the vehicles on Highway 20, they never stop. Not anymore.

But Royal is not a ghost town. The stilted water tower still carries its name in capital letters, announcing itself from miles away, the sun gleaming off the steel above the treetops. And the locals don't hesitate when talking about its future. *It'll be here,* they say, *just like it is now.* But the median age is forty-five, according to the latest census data, and that figure is surely rising.

"Population wise, we're dribblin' all the time, we're goin' downhill," says Mayor Max Heiter, who cannot remember how long he's held the position. His best guess is about a quarter of a century. "There's nothing here for the young kids. Some farm, but . . . in the last month, we've lost two young people right here, one thirty and one forty-six. And there's nobody to replace them."

As in most of these towns, heritage is mixed—German, Dutch, English, Irish, a few Scotch-Irish—but overwhelmingly white. It's a sleepy town of veterans and GEDs, hardy and hardworking. They chew

17

a rural vernacular and steady their speech, and on Saturday nights their trucks fill the lot at Thirsty's, the only bar in town, where a fluorescent sign casts a hard glow on the highway and the gossip slowly percolates.

"A few days before Roger died, he told the postmaster in Brunswick, 'If I should die, investigate the matter,'" says forty-five-year-old Justin Jensen, who occasionally works for his father crafting buggy wheels for the Amish. The Jensen family carries an incendiary reputation, which it touts like a merit badge. "About a month before that, Roger was in the bar there, and we were sitting at the stool. He took off his hat—he had beautiful hair, and it was just fallin' out in mats. He said, 'You ever see your hair fallin' out in mats like that?' And my cousin Virgil Wilcox from Ewing goes, 'Your wife's poisonin' ya! Figure it out, Roger!'" Murder. Embezzlement. It rarely matters—most Royalites reject their outlandish claims out of hand, long past numb to their stories.

The street names outside—Ponca, Fremont, Ryan, and Johnson—are hand-painted on plywood signs posted on steel poles at the intersections. The old two-story brick school building, buzzing with children in 1912 and silent by the end of the century, still stands—abandoned—on Fremont. When visitors ask, locals say two million kids graduated from the Royal school: Emma Hergert Million in 1930 and brother Fred Million in 1932. The United Methodist Church across the parking lot chained its doors three years ago. A sign posted in the front yard whispers the epitaph: ROYAL CHURCH. EST. 1890. CLOSED 2007.

The Royal Public Library, a tiny clapboard cabin with a stone chimney and a pitched brown roof, crouches alone at 3rd and Ryan. A CLOSED sign hangs permanently from a suction cup between the screen and the soot-glazed window, the WILL RETURN clock frozen at 6:30. Dead and dying flies litter the sill, and if you look closely, you can barely make out the Care Bear theme that decorated the children's room in 1981. Down the street, the bricks of the decommissioned post office pile up at the foundation, mounting higher every year.

Jim Haskin was born and raised in Antelope County. He is the oldest man in town, a veteran, and lives alone in a small white home across from the war memorial. A 1953 Ford Jubilee tractor sits in his driveway, fully restored. Sixty-seven years ago, on his eighteenth birthday, he enlisted in the army, said goodbye to his sweetheart, Lucille, and spent the next two years fighting in World War II in the Philippines. "I was one of the lucky people," he says softly. "I had someone to come back to." He and Lucille married two years after his return. But after sixty years together in Royal, Lucille passed away. In her wake, he tinkers around the house and with his Jubilee, opening his door for anyone willing to visit.

"You notice around town you don't see many sidewalks," he says. "I love a sidewalk. It isn't home to me without a sidewalk."

Eventually, Jim laid his own. It runs the length of his front yard and cuts off abruptly on both ends.

"We're down to about sixty people, about a hundred and ten when we came to Royal," he continues. "But a lot of our kids left—there wasn't anything here to hold them. There was three Pettijohn boys up there, they all left. One's in Indiana, one's in Ohio, one's in Alaska. Mitteises all left. The Montgomerys, they left. Mike Michaelson, he's back in town. I don't see Royal to grow, but it can't lose much more."

By sheer necessity there is a filling station here, too, skirting the highway. Managed by Jim for nineteen years, it is aptly named the Royal One Stop and is widely considered the local coffee shop, diner, and what fifty-one-year-old Arvin Brandt calls "the hub of what's going on." It's where farmers like Marvin Young and Chris Williby go to bitch about the weather and damn the market. It's where Arvin grabs his coffee before heading out to his next field assignment for the Nebraska Motor Vehicle Industry Licensing Board. It's where Doc Pedersen, bovine veterinarian, comes to escape calving season, if just for a minute, and where the Jensens come to stir the pot.

The fact that Royal is still on the map at all seems almost counter-intuitive. When the town first sprouted along the tracks in 1890, they begrudgingly named it Savage for a railroad man in Sioux City, a doctor who promised to build a new school for any settlement named in his honor. That's the prevailing history, anyway, and yet there is no record of a Dr. Savage in Sioux City during said time. Even Royal's history, it seems, is unsure of itself. Nevertheless, by the early twentieth century, after the mysterious namesake had failed to build a school, the locals reverted back to the name of the original post office one and a half miles north of the town: Royal, named for Royal Thayer, an early settler and Civil War veteran.

Counterintuitive because in September 1902, the whole village burned to the ground. Only the Short Line depot and the grain elevator escaped, divorced from the blaze by the railroad tracks. The flames rose under a midnight moon, licked from the lumberyard by an angry southern wind, barreled down Main Street like a drunk behind the wheel. First the pool room, then the blacksmith shop and the dry goods store, the hotel, the post office, five barns, three icehouses, and more. When it finally burned out, Savage lay in ashes, twelve buildings consumed, a total loss of roughly $20,000—more than $520,000 today. Some said it must have been a couple of tramps taking refuge for the night at the lumberyard. The rest claimed spontaneous combustion. Either way, for the two hundred citizens who called Savage home, there was little question of what to do next. "The town will be rebuilt at once," wrote the *Plainview Republican*.

Twenty-one years later—after Savage begot Royal, and the city's electric lights flickered on for the very first time, and the streets were finally paved in clay—it burned again. This time it started in a restaurant kitchen, discovered by Mrs. Charf, the night operator, around 1:00 a.m. The flames had already consumed the restaurant. Fifteen miles south, residents in Neligh reported seeing "plainly" the orange glow in an otherwise-black night sky. Running water hadn't yet been installed, and the flames were too strong for chemical retardants. Instead, Royalites and their neighbors—dozens of them—formed a bucket brigade, hauling water until daybreak to keep the remaining buildings wet.

And yet they rebuilt again, certain the future unfolded right here in this tiny pocket of the globe, the southern terminus of the Verdigris River, right here where the earth leveled out and the spidery veins of the valley shriveled up and the oaks and the elms gave way to an oblivion of bluestem. And, of course, it did. And like every history, the gravity of the mundane occasionally pressed itself into a shining exception, conjured something from nothing, spawned a novelty or three among the daily litter of humdrum activity: a runaway carriage; a crackerjack baseball team; a lightning strike and a whole family electrified, the baby flying from the mother's arms. The latter occurred in June 1919. The dog died. The mother's stockings singed. The list goes on.

The same day Royal installed its first water fountain, April 17, 1925, the Ku Klux Klan lit a cross between the school building and the Methodist church. And in 1928, Art Watson, working on the road north of Royal, found the bones of a mammoth animal, origins unknown—a leg, a jaw, some teeth—nearly twenty feet below the surface. When he dug them out, they crumbled apart. In the Dirty Thirties, Roosevelt put thirty local men back to work through his New Deal programs, a trio of nudists stopped through en route to California, and a truck hauling forty-five dogs puttered up and down the streets of Royal looking for more.

"Although the driver was evasive," the *Orchard News* reported, "a boy in the truck said they were bound for an Indian reservation where dogs were worth about $2 each."

When World War II broke out, fifty-two local men registered for the draft. At least twenty-one served, their names displayed beside their overseas addresses at the Rundquist Store, a reminder to send greetings from home. The town sold bonds, constructed a war memorial in the park, purchased subscriptions to the local newspaper for every soldier.

On July 28, 1944, word reached home of the first local casualty. Fred Million had been killed that June in Normandy. (The joke didn't work in reverse.)

No doubt the early settlers were tough stock: thrifty, resourceful, inventive—uncanny. A cast of gamblers and misfits, innovators and entrepreneurs, each one with a knapsack of stories in tow. Old Charley Johnston, who filed a homestead claim in Royal in 1885, saved Mary Todd Lincoln from a runaway stagecoach in Washington, DC, during the Battle of Gettysburg. The coachman had been thrown from his seat. The horses had spooked. Standing nearby, Johnston and his comrades witnessed the events and sprinted into the street to corral the horses. Later that afternoon, President Lincoln himself tracked the men down to thank them.

Frank Salisbury worked in North Platte, Nebraska, for nine years as the foreman of Scout's Rest, Buffalo Bill Cody's 4,400-acre ranch, before moving to a farm east of Royal with his wife. For decades after, Salisbury kept the Mexican horsehair bridle Cody had gifted him. In 1913, a Royal man named Elias Luther Clark laid his own telephone line, borrowing cash to purchase three thousand pounds of wire and string it seventy-five miles across the surrounding hay country. By 1928, he carried forty-five subscribers and ran the switchboard with his wife and two daughters. Outlaw Jesse James taught Royal resident Charles Howard how to play the bones when they clowned around together as kids in Missouri. And longtime resident Ed Helmer, born in 1852, spent his limber years touring the country as a dancer and singer with both P. T. Barnum's Circus and the May Fiske Blondes, who billed themselves as the "25 Most Beautiful Women in the United States."

"If I wasn't crippled up now," Helmer told a local reporter in 1936, "I'd dance like a fairy and sing like a canary, and I wouldn't be sitting here swatting flies, I can tell you."

Like every town, Royal is an epic. But it's easy, looking at it now from the highway, to imagine the whole place missing, covered by the sandy loam and wild bluestem it was built on, as if the fire of 1902 had had the last word; the silence would feel more natural. It's easy to picture this divot of land as the first white frontiersmen encountered it nearly 150 years ago, covered by the skeletons of buffalo; easier still to picture the buffalo alive, roaming this freckle on the face of the plains, aerating the soil with their hooves. Nor does it take much to imagine the prehistoric rhinos, called *Teleoceras*, raised from the volcanic ash that filled their lungs and buried them here, alive, ten million years ago. Early explorers certainly had their doubts. Writer Rufus B. Sage, who wrote *Scenes in the Rocky Mountains* after traveling through the area in 1841, wrote, "That this section of the country should ever become inhabited by civilized man, except in the vicinity of large water courses, is too preposterous to be entertained for a single moment."

In many ways, Royal is like every other small town, at least in the West, defying the odds of the "Great American Desert," forcing fertility onto the plains and reinhabiting this long-ago wilderness after the Poncas, Omahas, and Pawnees were nearly stamped out. Unless one considers Zoo Nebraska, the only national news this town ever produced, once the pride of contemporary Royal and the tragedy that nearly unraveled it.

MEET DICK HASKIN

They never would have guessed that in ten years' time, Dick Haskin, the lone wolf of Neligh-Oakdale High, would return with an adolescent chimpanzee caged in the bed of his father's pickup truck. When he did, it was the first time most of his old classmates had thought about him in years, since their graduation day in May 1979. Dick was easy to forget, frankly, easy to ignore, the white noise of their teenage years. Remarkably unremarkable. He slipped through high school like a fly on the wall, quiet, focused, respectfully indifferent to popular opinion. He rode the bus with a book in his hand, cared less for sports than science and social studies, the type of kid who wrote the group paper himself. Former classmate Mark Strassler remembers working on a project with Dick: "Alternative Methods of Eliminating Pests."

"I built a bug zapper, and he wrote the paper for it," he said. "I just unloaded all the books on him. I knew he could write it better than I ever could."

In high school, Dick sported a full crown of auburn hair, straight and loose, neatly parted—left over right—for his senior portrait. Dark jacket, white shirt, wing collar suited for takeoff. When it came time for the ritual of class predictions, his classmates noted not his intelligence or his quiet independence but the fit of his pants, the inch of white tube sock peeking out beneath the cuffs. In ten years, they predicted, Dick Haskin would still be "waiting for a flood." His chin protruded like a small granite outcrop. Bright cheeks, heavy eyes. He rubbed them constantly, palm to eye socket. Allergies, mostly. Dust and dander. He banked on Benadryl. He loved *Star Wars* and *Blazing Saddles* and Kenny Rogers. He read Cather and Mari Sandoz, authors who, as fellow Nebraskans, knew that bitter, beautiful landscape as intimately as he did.

Born August 3, 1961, Dick was the youngest of three children, the only son, eleven years younger than his sister Bettie. The oldest, Bonnie, graduated college the same year Dick graduated kindergarten. And so, while he had "the benefit of having siblings," he says, he "also had the benefit of being an only child." All three were raised on a mostly self-sufficient farm outside Wausa, Nebraska, a community of six hundred about forty miles northeast of Royal with a conspicuous Swedish heritage: a Dala horse hanging outside the door of the public library, an annual "Swedish Smorgasbord" celebration, every athlete a Viking. Apple trees grew outside his parents' farmhouse, and his gray-haired mother, Lucille, tended a sprawling garden, lush with vegetables and melons. In addition to roughly three hundred acres of corn, oats, and alfalfa, his father, Jim, raised chickens and a rotating congregation of livestock, from milk and stock cows to pigs and—Dick's favorite—sheep; he loved to bottle-feed the lambs. Come shearing time each spring, "they'd put me in the great big bag, and I'd have to jump up and down and pack the wool." Bettie and Bonnie merely lived on the farm, they later told him, but he *experienced* it.

The isolation, the quietude—they fit Dick like a tailored suit. With his sisters already off to college, he found a certain freedom on the farm, in the frankness of the landscape, the candor of an open field, the birdsong in the old shelterbelts. And especially in his work with the livestock. He woke every morning before sunrise to help his father milk the cows, sneezing and rubbing his eyes. He developed a comfort with the animals—a rapport, even—far beyond anything he found in humans. Before she died, his mother often told the story of Dick and the robin, a story he only vaguely recalls, just fragments and flashes. A robin once flew into the window, she began. Dick heard the sudden *thwump* against the glass, watched the tiny, limp body fall to the dirt. He ran outside, gently picked it up, and, after a brief inspection, began performing mouth-to-mouth resuscitation. Before Lucille could say a word, the bird jolted back to life. After that, she said, every time Dick left the house, the robin followed somewhere close behind.

"I understood the animals," he says, "and they understood me."

He took refuge in their companionship, especially because he never felt comfortable with his peers in Wausa. With humans, he was always too shy; "Too weird," he says. He was the only kid at school without Swedish ancestry—the only one he knew of, anyway.

And though he loved both his parents, their relationship was often rocky. He admired his father, a short man with a barrel chest and military mien, but came to loathe his often-explosive temper. In public, Jim "never met a stranger," Dick says. But at home, with a cigarette balanced between his fingers, he was someone else.

Dick tried his best to soothsay, to predict his father's orders, to blunt the mounting rage, but no matter where he stood, it was never the right place, always too late or too early, yards ahead or behind. The cattle churned up clouds of dust from which Jim soon emerged, fists clenched and spit flying, the bridge of his nose bright red and burning in the sun.

"Get your goddamn ass over where it's supposed to be! Damn it, anyway!"

"If that's how you're gonna talk to me," Dick whined, angry and a little put out, "I'm going back to the house."

Dick turned his back and walked away, his sisters incredulous, certain they'd have seen the belt already. But Jim simply returned to the cattle and kept barking orders. What they didn't know, Dick says, what they weren't around to see, was that when Jim finally returned to the house later that day, the cattle secure in their pen, he found Dick in his room, whipped out his belt, and beat him anyway, not the kind of man to let transgressions slide. Not the kind of man to raise a feeble son.

"Dad didn't want to have a son that couldn't break a horse. He'd put me on the horse and of course, I would get bucked off. I'd cry, he'd spank me and put me back on the horse, and again I'd get bucked off," he'd later write, describing his experience with a Shetland-Appaloosa cross at five years old. "This happened over and over until I didn't care if I ever got back on another horse as long as I lived, and the poor horse just got so tired, she stopped bucking."

He mellowed over the years, Dick says, but the treatment was hard to shake—harder still when he began to notice that same temper in himself. Unlike his mother, who seemed to never lose her cool, Dick found that his anger would often consume him as a young boy. Sometimes he would injure himself in the process, bashing his head into walls. He could flush red and furious in a heartbeat, a rage he compares to the Incredible Hulk's. A rage his parents worked steadily to extinguish.

"I still work to control it. I always have," he says. "That temper scares the hell out of me sometimes."

In the late 1960s, Jim took a second job working cattle at the sale barn in Creighton, where Dick was born, another small community about twenty miles west of Wausa. But the writing was on the wall. The rising cost of inputs, the new regulations—all of it was conspiring to price him out. With little more than an eighth-grade education, Jim studied for the US civil service exam, hoping to become a postmaster or a milk inspector for the USDA. He envisioned starting over, moving west to an old cowboy town in the crook of the panhandle.

Dick had rarely seen his father as happy as the day he passed the test, but before he could start applying for federal positions, a cousin from Royal paid them a visit. He'd bought the filling station on the edge of town, Dodd's Oil Company, and he needed a man to drive the fuel truck.

Dick, a ginger-haired boy with a pencil-thin upper lip, a creeping grin, and thick black glasses, was twelve years old when they left the farm and moved to Royal. In the shadow of the moon landing, he dreamed of becoming an astronomer. He attended seventh and eighth grade in the old yellow-brick schoolhouse at the corner of 4th and Fremont, the only student in his class, and though he made several good friends, he was initially skeptical about "city life," unsure how he'd handle the transition. But they lived on the north edge of town, and they brought two horses with them, and if he looked out the back windows, he could still see the horses and the windbreaks and the empty, studded farmland. He could still peer up at the stars, that black, braille sky. And when he did, the anxiety of his new life would ebb, and he would settle again into that familiar comfort of the land, something he would accept—many years later—as the touch of god, the warm hand of spirituality.

During Dick's second year in Royal, Mrs. Klabenes, who taught grades six through eight on the second floor, the rooms always flooded with light from the big west windows, drew the shades. She turned off the lights, loaded the film, and asked Dick to run the projector, neither of them remotely aware of the consequences.

"Determined to uncover the secrets of the chimps, in 1960, Miss Goodall arrives in Tanzania," narrator Orson Welles began in his suave and swashbuckling timbre. As the camera bobbed up and down, a young Jane Goodall, just twenty-six years old, sat on the prow of a small wooden dinghy in the teal waters of Lake Tanganyika, hair tucked behind her ears, a few loose strands dancing in the wind, surveying the patchy green mountains of the Gombe Stream National Park. "Her discoveries here will startle the scientific world and lead to the possible redefinition of the word *man*." The brass and timpani drums of the familiar *National Geographic* theme song crashed in as a rainbow crowded out the mountains, and the title, *Miss Goodall and the Wild Chimpanzees*, shot to the forefront. Dick watched, spellbound, as Goodall threaded her way through the dense jungle foliage in khaki shorts and Converse sneakers, through the palm trees and alpine bamboo, skipping streams and climbing mountains, pausing on a grassy knoll to scan the valley with her binoculars. "She's been told how a frightened chimp once ripped away a man's cheek. She has also been warned, 'You'll never get near them,'" Welles continued. "But any thought of personal danger is diminished by Jane's determination to find and study the elusive chimpanzees."

Dick leaned forward in his seat, eyes wide and mouth agape, as the camera settled on two chimpanzees swinging through a sun-filtered canopy. He watched how the apes constructed their beds high up in the trees and how Goodall tested one herself, how at first she observed the animals from afar, but ultimately worked herself into the troop, playing and feeding them bananas. Dick smiled as one of the infants, whom Goodall had named Flint, clumsily stumbled through her camp, rolling down the canvas roof of her tent, and learned how the chimps utilized leaves to soak drinking water from the trees and long stems of grass to fish termites from their holes. Their behavior astonished him, their intelligence, how similar they were to humans, *to him*, and how little we really knew about them.

It was the land of dreams—*his* dreams—so eerily similar to the world he imagined while reading *Tarzan*. "When I arrived at the Gombe Stream Reserve, I felt that at long last my childhood ambition was being realized. Always, I had wanted to go out into the field and study animals," Goodall said. *Me too,* Dick silently replied. She had given voice to his desires, direction to his interests. Suddenly his future had an outline, and it looked a lot like Africa.

Royal didn't offer more than an eighth-grade education, so when high school arrived, Dick had a choice between two larger communities nearby: Neligh to the south or Orchard to the west. Though several miles farther, Neligh offered college-prep courses, and Dick was determined—now more than ever, with Africa in his sights—to enroll at the state university in Lincoln just like his sister had. Dick fit in better with his class at Neligh-Oakdale High. There were cliques, to be sure, but he was never bullied or made to feel dumb. In fact, though Dick himself often claims otherwise, his peers considered him bookish, one of the smarter kids in their class. "I didn't want to do sports. It was all I could do to keep my grades up," he says. "I didn't need any extra activities to get in the way of that because I'm not a smart person." But he *was* an animal person, with a touch of the farm boy still in him, and so, after the final bell rang and the rest of his class hit the locker room or palled around town, Dick rushed home to feed the pigs his brother-in-law Gary kept penned across the highway.

"All through high school, Dick took care of them hogs," Jim recalled decades later, still proud of Dick despite all their differences. "All those years he never lost one pig."

Beyond the animus Dick already possessed for his father, he felt increasingly stifled by his parents, he says. By the outset of high school, Dick knew he wanted to study primates in Africa, and he knew college was the next step to get there. He stayed focused, studying hard, taking care of the hogs, and sometimes—usually for noble goals like raising funds for the tiny Royal Public Library—he performed amateur magic shows. Eccentric, perhaps, but hardly irresponsible. Drugs held about as much intrigue for Dick as sports did; the Budweiser his peers were shotgunning on the weekends held even less. His only confrontation with the police stemmed from a science experiment concocted with his biology teacher. With a few dry cleaner bags, some aluminum foil, and a little rubbing alcohol, they jerry-rigged a small fleet of makeshift hot-air balloons. When Neligh residents saw the blue orbs hovering over Main Street, they called the sheriff's office to report a series of UFOs.

"I hadn't done anything to show my parents they couldn't trust me, but they were so restrictive in high school. They told me who I should be hanging out with, who I should be dating. I couldn't wait to get away from that," he says. "I just wanted to try things. I was putting on magic shows and stuff like that. They were just totally against it. They were so scared I was going to fail."

After he graduated in May 1979, Dick enrolled at the University of Nebraska–Lincoln, the state's flagship school. He majored in life sciences—one of the few students in the department not preparing for medical school—and minored in anthropology and psychology with a focus on animal behavior. UNL didn't offer a primatology degree, but he figured his cocktail of studies would suffice. With textbooks in hand, Africa felt closer already, though in many ways he had just begun a primate study of a different kind.

He lived in the middle of campus, just blocks from downtown Lincoln. He'd always considered himself a country boy, but he loved the cosmopolitan atmosphere, "the mix of all different cultures," the theaters and the museums and the general acceptance he felt in the city. Attractions far more provocative, he thought, than any basement kegger or killer high, both of which he viewed with astonishing aloofness, neither wagging his finger nor partaking himself. He seldom went home, and though he dated some, his receding hairline soon vanished altogether, undercutting what little confidence he had to begin with.

But while Dick was testing the waters of a more social environment, he was simultaneously submerging himself in the habitat of nonhuman primates. He ravaged the library. He read about Louis Leakey and his paleoanthropological discoveries, his influence in shaping the way science interprets human evolution and primate ancestry. He filled his queue with the works of "Leakey's Angels": Leakey's protégés, Jane Goodall and Dian Fossey and Biruté Galdikas. He studied nonstop to finish his degree and he worked several jobs to pay for it—in a biology lab, where he helped breed hydra and shrimp, and at the Super 8 Motel on the edge of the city.

While Dick was enduring a material technology course, a guest lecturer named Robert Hitchcock, newly hired as a physical anthropologist at UNL, visited the class and briefly addressed his work with indigenous populations in Africa. Dick perked up. Based off nothing more than a mutual interest in Africa, Dick started building a relationship with Dr. Hitchcock, whom he would later call his "mentor." Only after their first meeting did they discover a second mutual interest in primatology.

"I didn't have very many students at UNL that I thought had a passion. That's not to say anything about Nebraska students," Hitchcock says. "It's just a lot of them were still trying to figure out what they wanted to do. Dick knew what he wanted to do, and I thought that was pretty unusual."

In May 1983, Dick graduated with his bachelor's degree, moved to a small flat in an old two-story house in the shadow of the Nebraska Capitol Building, and set about finding a job working with nonhuman primates, a task that proved exceedingly difficult for a newly minted college graduate without any firsthand experience. Nor did it help that Dick hated zoos, considered them morally perverse. He sent inquiry letters to nearly every primate facility in the country, from the Gorilla Fund to the Oregon National Primate Research Center to the Primate Foundation of Arizona and several more abroad, anywhere that might provide a gateway to Africa. He wrote to the Karisoke Research

Center in Rwanda, founded by primatologist Dian Fossey, and to Jane Goodall's Gombe Stream Research Centre in Tanzania.

Most facilities ignored the letters completely. A few sent applications, only to reject him shortly thereafter. But when the Yerkes National Primate Research Center in Atlanta invited him to its facility at Emory University for an interview, he went all in. He broke his lease, packed everything he owned into his 1968 Ford Galaxie, and hit the road. He took the scenic route, took his time, south to Oklahoma, east to Arkansas. He even toured the ranch of his country idol, Loretta Lynn, in Hurricane Mills, Tennessee. But when he finally made it to Emory University, the interview lasted just minutes.

"They just came out and told me there was no chance of getting a job working with primates because I had no experience," he says. "My dreams were dashed."

When he left Georgia, he'd resigned himself, at just twenty-three years old, to washing dishes for the rest of his life. He felt "utterly destroyed." He returned to the cafeteria in Lincoln, head hung low, and asked for his old job back. And while he was at it, he asked the food services director, half-jokingly, almost involuntarily, if he knew anyone who worked at the zoo in Lincoln, as if his dream, like a tom turkey minutes after the blast, were still flapping its wings in the dirt.

"I'm a friend of the director. Why?"

"Maybe I can work with *their* primates," Dick suggested.

He hated zoos—truly, viscerally *hated* them. Hated the guilt he felt just looking between the bars. But without more experience, his dreams were dead in the water, and more than anything he wanted to feel alive, wanted to feel that primal rush of freedom that he'd first felt as he watched Jane Goodall projected on the wall of his eighth-grade classroom. He wanted to fight for the apes. Study them. Save them. He was desperate.

—w—

When Dick arrived for his interview the next morning, it was only the second time in his life he'd stepped foot inside a zoo. He was just seven years old the first time, visiting his sister Bonnie in Lincoln with his parents. They toured the city's Ager Zoo on a warm spring afternoon, the crab apple trees flowering pink and white in the sun, a den of vines slithering up the old limestone WPA building. Tourists crowded the walkways and clumsily organized for family portraits. Dick marveled at the animals inside—at the birds and the monkeys and the alligators—unlike anything he'd ever encountered on the farm, especially the chimpanzee. Dick leaned forward on the gate, standing on his tippy toes, craning his neck toward the animal. But the longer he stared, the worse he began to feel. The chimp lurched around his cage, shook the bars, threw fistfuls of straw at gawkers like himself. The chimps he'd seen on television, in picture books—they seemed buoyed by their human counterparts, not oppressed and certainly not indentured. He felt heartsick, and then he felt angry, and for the first time, he seemed to understand what freedom was and, more importantly, was not.

"He appeared miserable. I hated it. I thought it was so cruel," Dick says. "That experience has remained with me my whole life."

At the time, neither Dick nor his parents had any idea there was another zoo, this one privately funded, just out of eyeshot farther down the street, a zoo that would quickly outshine Ager in both size and reputation: the Folsom Children's Zoo. By the time Dick arrived for his interview in the summer of 1984, Folsom had developed a reputation as one of the premier children's zoos in the country, boasting sixty-five species—from petting goats to a sixteen-hundred-pound Kodiak bear named Gentle Ben, who had starred in the *Grizzly Adams* TV show.

Despite the Children's Zoo's prestige, Dick couldn't staunch the feelings of anger and sadness cropping up as he passed through the gates, past the tulip beds and the railroad tracks and the small stream meandering through the park. He'd spent the better part of his child-hood among wildlife, at the farm, at Grove Lake, in the hills north of Royal, and he'd seen what freedom looks like: a herd of whitetail deer bounding effortlessly across a barb-wired fence; a bobcat slink-ing through a grassy meadow; a fox trotting along the banks of the Verdigris; a family of raccoons crossing the road, one by one, under the cover of night.

Everything for Africa, he told himself. Just another stepping-stone. Despite Dick's hesitations, Al Bietz, a self-declared "animal egghead" with a thick salt-and-pepper beard, a booming voice, and a pearly white smile, liked him immediately. Like Dick, he was a kindhearted man who understood what it meant to be wholly consumed by another spe-cies. The board of the Folsom Zoological Society had appointed Bietz director of the Children's Zoo in 1973, and in the decade and change since then, he'd developed something of a sixth sense for identifying fellow eggheads.

"He didn't come in like so many people do and say, *I want to work in a zoo because I love animals.* That almost disqualified anybody that came in," Bietz says. "He impressed me as somebody who was just con-sumed, almost obsessed with the subject. He had a dream and a goal, and that was to work with great apes."

Even then, Bietz wasn't about to let Dick step into the chimp enclo-sure on day one.

"They'll kill you," Bietz said. "But I tell you what: we've got a snow monkey that was raised as a pet that we're trying to integrate into the group. I'll hire you to work on that."

The Super 8 had recently offered him the title of assistant manager, a position with upward mobility and an honorable income. When Dick chose the meager-paying zoo job instead, his father's temper returned, a stark reminder of why he'd been so eager to leave home in the first place. But with more miles between them now, the pressure was easier to brush off. Dick worked with Skokie and the other snow monkeys until the current chimp handler left the zoo a few months later, and Monica, the pinch hitter—like a bad transplant—never quite took. So Bietz, who'd spent many long hours discussing primate behavior with Dick, letting him regurgitate everything he'd learned through his compulsive self-directed studies, asked him to shadow Monica. A few days later, Dick delivered his final diagnosis as if he'd been studying apes his entire life.

"She's scared of them," he told Bietz. "Everything she's doing is causing problems. The way she's moving—she's scared of them, and they know she's scared of them. You've got to get her out."

Dick had studied Monica's posture, her gestures, the way she flinched and blinked, and the way the chimps responded, taking advantage of her hesitation. Bietz took notes, and though he didn't necessarily disagree, he wasn't ready to remove her either. One week later, Bietz approached Dick again. Monica had been attacked the night before. She was currently in the hospital, bruises all over, stitches but no broken bones.

"You're going in," Bietz said.

Just hours later, Dick began his first real work with great apes, and the animals he'd long dreamed of, the animals he'd first seen projected on the wall of his eighth-grade classroom, the animals he'd obsessed over throughout his college career, huddled up in his dorm room so late at night with so many books spread over the foot of his bed—here they were, sizing him up, waiting to be fed.

"Everything he learned on paper . . . all of a sudden was right there, like discovering King Tut's tomb," Bietz says. "I think Dick—if there is such a thing—was born into it. It filled all the niches in his personality, and the chimps and the orangutans—they reciprocated."

When the Children's Zoo first acquired three-year-old chimps Kumi and Cousteau through a Saint Louis Zoo breeding loan in May 1982, they were the only captive chimps in Nebraska. In time, Bietz hoped the two would mate. "Everything suggests they're in for a real tough road ahead, depending on what we can do for them," he told the *Lincoln Journal Star*, noting their status as an endangered species. Less than a year later, the zoo acquired Chewbacca, a two-and-a-half-year-old Sumatran orangutan they nicknamed Chewy. And on July 15, 1984, a scorching hot Sunday just a few months after Dick was hired, the Saint Louis Zoo delivered one final gift: Kumi's brother, a chimpanzee named Reuben, this one just sixteen months old, eighteen pounds, and eighteen inches tall. The son of Joe and Annie, two chimpanzees captured in Africa in the late 1960s and early 1970s, Reuben carried a burlap sack wherever he went, like a toddler with his blankie.

"The first time you're around great apes and they give you one of their babies, and you hold it," Bietz says, seeming to lose himself, "um . . . you see in that face the word 'pet' doesn't come into it. And if you're like Dick, from that moment on, you feel a responsibility for another being that doesn't deserve to be caged up in some small cage and bananas thrown at him. You get an internal feeling that the rest of the population doesn't get to have because they'll never see it. They'll never experience it. They'll never understand it until they do."

As Bietz tells it, the honeymoon moment—the shock and awe, the starry eyes—lasted scarcely a heartbeat before Dick, now the primate specialist, snapped out of it, cracked his knuckles, and set to work. He fed, he cleaned, he socialized. He controlled diets and took urine samples and coordinated research projects with a crew of interns from the local colleges. And he went to great lengths to enhance the primates' captive environment at a time when environmental enrichment was still a zoological afterthought, a practice Bietz wholeheartedly endorsed. In fact, amendments to the Animal Welfare Act providing for the psychological well-being of nonhuman primates weren't even passed until 1985, well over a year after Dick had arrived.

Dick experimented with different climbing mechanisms, found the chimps preferred old cotton or nylon fire hoses over just about anything else. He set up a television set and recorded the apes' preferences: Cousteau loved sports, Kumi the soap operas, Chewy the Clint Eastwood films, and Reuben the cartoons. He hid sunflower seeds in the straw and placed burlap sacks and other innocuous items in the cage, items they could get creative with, keeping them constantly engaged.

"There's no good facility for them," Dick told the *Journal Star* in October 1985, never wasting an opportunity to broadcast his distaste for captive environments. "They're all too small. And a small zoo like ours can't afford a four-acre facility. If they get bored, they get psychotic. And if they get psychotic, they get dangerous."

By the mid-1980s, the Folsom Children's Zoo was in the midst of something like a renaissance. Beyond the growing popularity of Chewy and the chimpanzees, the zoo was also garnering national acclaim for its work breeding the golden lion tamarin, a small Brazilian monkey threatened with extinction. In just four years, the zoo had produced thirty-two babies, an unparalleled success at a time when fewer than 150 golden lion tamarins lived in zoos nationwide and perhaps even fewer in their native habitat of Brazil's coastal forests. As one of his thirteen concurrent research initiatives at the zoo, Dick and his interns studied the tamarins' parent-infant relationships, and—following orders from the Smithsonian Institute—the effects of a subdermal contraceptive.

"He was extremely conscientious," Bietz says. "I don't think he ever missed a day of work. If anything, you'd have to tell Dick to go home. It was his life. He would have rather been working at the zoo than doing anything at home. He just relished the job."

Locally, however, it wasn't his work with the tamarins that brought him notoriety, but his work teaching American Sign Language to the apes, a practice Dick considered another form of environmental enrichment. It landed him on the front page of the city's largest newspaper. CHIMPANZEE GOES APE OVER SIGN LANGUAGE, the headline reported, beneath a photo of Dick tickling Reuben, the infant's limbs so long and twisted one could hardly distinguish where one began and the other ended. Though Bietz claims he had nothing to do with it, Dick says Bietz suggested teaching Reuben how to sign as a gambit to draw more visitors to the zoo. Opposed to humanizing animals, Dick compromised: rather than teaching them for entertainment, he would teach them to sign for their own health, to express pain or illness before they grew too sick to recover.

To reach that level of dialogue, however, he began with the basics: *sit, give to me, look at me, tree, water, ball,* and *tickle me,* Reuben's favorite. Adjusting for their short attention span, Dick kept the lessons short, usually no more than six or seven minutes at a time. While Reuben, much younger and a more social species, caught on right away, Chewy resisted. Or so Dick thought, until one day, he says, standing out of eyesight, he watched Chewy pick up the ball in his cage and sign *ball,* point to the water and sign *water.* He knew the field was controversial. He knew many were skeptical and some believed Reuben was merely mimicking Dick, that no real communication had been achieved.

"Yeah, there were people like that. However, watch it. Watch him. Watch him do the signs unsolicited. This chimp does know what he's saying. People are gonna doubt. They have their opinions, but just watch him . . . When Reuben was losing his baby teeth, he'd show me which tooth was loose. If he was sick, he could tell me he was sick. There's no doubt in my mind, they know what they're saying."

Dick worked such long days, remembers David Kilcoyne, a physics professor and Dick's upstairs neighbor, that his apartment smelled like the zoo.

"He just had this devotion to them. And it was infectious in a way," he says. "If his apartment smelled like the zoo, it's because he wanted it to smell like the zoo. He was a genuine person in many ways. He was super devoted to something that sparked his imagination, his purpose."

Despite sharing an address, Dick and Kilcoyne—now a research scientist at the Lawrence Berkeley National Laboratory—rarely found time for small talk; when they did, often late at night over a gin and tonic, the topic quickly turned to Dick's work at the zoo.

"There was a seminal moment where the primate slapped Dick in the cage while he was trying to teach him. And Dick's instinct at that point was to slap the chimp back—which he did—as a matter of saying who's boss. That was one of the things he did to gain their respect."

Well after business hours on a nose-biting winter night, Dick invited Kilcoyne to meet the primates. They drove from their duplex to the zoo, the streetlights casting a soft orange glow on the pavement, the previous week's snowfall weighing down the branches and softly lining the streets. To Kilcoyne, an Australian graduate student new to Nebraska, the whole scene looked surreal, the animals quiet and asleep in their cages, his own breath rising into the night sky, the zoo dark and empty. When they first arrived, Dick vocalized to the chimps, and one of the chimps vocalized back. Then he brought out Chewy.

"He actually said for me to be very quiet in the middle of the Lincoln zoo, but no one else was there. And he took out the orangutan for me, and he just told me not to move. He said as long as you stay still, everything will be fine. And that's what I did," Kilcoyne says. "He wasn't trying to show off or anything like that. I think he just genuinely considered the primates part of his family."

Over the years, Dick gradually opened up. Part of his role at the Children's Zoo entailed educating the public about the animals under his care, and according to Bietz, he enjoyed the task. He'd often sit in the middle of the zoo's green space with Chewy as the kids and their parents gathered around. He taught them about the orangutan's natural environment and deconstructed Chewy's behavior in real time. When he waved, Chewy waved, too, and hundreds of kids waved back. He trusted the primates enough to climb into their cages as if he were one of them, grooming them and being groomed in return, Chewy carefully combing through Dick's remaining hair and beard. Those who only knew Dick within the context of the zoo often thought of him as sociable, an extrovert well-suited to public presentation. What they didn't know, Dick says, is that he learned how to perform from the apes.

"People didn't see it, but I was reading their behavior. I was predicting what they were going to do next and modifying their behavior and such so that they [wouldn't] hurt me or the public. And it taught me that, when I'm doing presentations, I'll just concentrate on something else. It allows me to do something I couldn't normally do because I'm so shy."

Dick so zealously wanted to master his work with the apes that he coaxed his friend Robert Gearhart, an amateur photographer, to film him at work. For the first month on the job, Dick spent his nights analyzing the footage like an athlete studying his game, scrutinizing the apes' movement and his own reactions: the gestures, the postures, the facial expressions, the eye contact, rewinding and rewinding again.

Though exemplary, his work was hardly without incident. More than once, he'd been slammed against a wall, thrown across the cage, dragged through the dirt, had hair ripped out, clothing torn, jewelry pilfered. In fact, after a year or so on the job, Dick was the only employee allowed to enter the enclosure. "If Dick gets in trouble in there, nobody is to go in after him," Bietz told his staff shortly after he watched Chewy crush a steel bar in his grip. But Dick had grown accustomed to these incidents; if not quite comfortable with the attacks, "comfortable in my abilities to manage them," he says. In fact, the notion that working with great apes would one day maim or even kill him had been steadily crystallizing ever since he first watched the Jane Goodall documentary as a kid. The more he studied, the more he realized just how dangerous and powerful these animals could be. Somewhere along the way, at a fairly young age, he came to accept his own mortality. "I realized that each day I went in that cage, that could be my last day, and it didn't seem to bother me."

Incidents with the public were another story. A cadre of university administrators once toured the zoo during his shift with an Indonesian emissary, "a rather distinguished guy," Bietz says, short and "probably used to having people fan him while he walks." Bietz rushed to the gift shop, filled a basket with guidebooks, key chains, stuffed animals, "all the Americana zoo crap you can find." He shook their hands, one by one, offered the dignitary his gifts, and hatched a plan "to get some mileage out of this." He sent an assistant to notify Dick of their arrival, to grab Chewy and meet them in the green space behind the Animal Kingdom building.

He didn't have to ask twice. A flock of children had already gathered by the time they arrived, screaming and throwing their limbs over the gate like groupies at Woodstock while Dick and Chewy dallied in the grass. Chewy groomed Dick's orange beard. Dick returned the favor. They held hands while Chewy, roughly 130 pounds, scanned the audience, his shaggy russet fur dusty and littered with blades of grass. Bietz broke his own rule and opened the fence to usher the delegation forward, careful not to step too close, the lawn splotchy with shadows from the leafy branches overhead. Dick now sat cross-legged before them, brown slacks, tan shirt, black-and-white Converse just like Goodall used to wear, still holding Chewy's hand. Dick began his orangutan presentation, the same he'd given one hundred times before, the interpreter translating close behind, the dignitary fascinated and staring at the ape, Chewy's arms "five feet long and bordering on ten," Bietz says.

"I had misjudged how close this guy had gotten, and the next thing I know, Chewbacca has reached out and grabbed this guy's ankle. They've got a grip that Arnold Schwarzenegger would die for, and that guy thinks he's gonna be killed and eaten, and I'm just in shock."

The emissary dangled upside down like a fish on the line, twisting and shouting something no one save the interpreter could understand—and the interpreter had gone silent. Bietz had gone silent. The administrators had gone silent. The children had gone silent. Wind funneled through the trees. And Dick, though paralyzed momentarily as well, fearing for his job, walked calmly toward Chewy, placed a hand on his forearm, and softly chided, "No, Chewbacca. Don't worry." Seconds later the emissary was back on the ground, and Chewy was back in Dick's arms, one hand squeezing his shoulder, the other gripping his biceps, Dick struggling to keep that grimace a smile, as if Chewy were harmless, as if the whole incident was little more than a fun prank, an initiation, really, for the foreigner. Through the interpreter, Dick explained that Chewy was only playing, only curious, that he'd never seen the man before and wanted a closer look, nothing sinister about it. Apparently the explanation sufficed. The next day the emissary returned with his coterie of university officials and a pair of carved wooden ducks—a gift to Bietz for the outstanding experience.

But despite his often-rewarding work at the zoo, his many small adventures, Dick never ceased to dream of Africa. He longed to see the pebble-strewn mountain brooks, sleep in a small hut in the rain forest, his gear stacked in crates beneath a dew-slick tarp. He dreamed of a leopard howling from a tree, a troop of baboons ransacking the camp, a local guide baking bread and cooking meat over an open fire. He dreamed of the apes moving freely through the jungle, no keepers or curators or specialists to corral them, to quarantine them from the rest of the troop, to close one shift gate after another and lock them in. Soon, he told himself, he would reapply, this time with some experience under his belt.

And so, in June 1985, when Bietz offered to send him to a primate conference in San Diego focused specifically on "the road to self-sustaining populations," Dick leaped at the opportunity. The five-day symposium featured a veritable who's who of world primatologists, many of whom ran the facilities he'd first applied to: Jo Fritz, administrative director of the Primate Foundation of Arizona; Benjamin Beck, associate director of the Smithsonian Institution's National Zoo; Frans de Waal, scientist and author of the seminal 1982 book *Chimpanzee Politics*, later a director at Yerkes; and perhaps most exciting, Dr. Dian Fossey, recognized at the time as the world's foremost authority on mountain gorillas and fresh off the publication of her bestselling book *Gorillas in the Mist*, which detailed her work at the Karisoke Research Center in Rwanda. The only major name in the field not attending, it seemed, was Jane Goodall.

When he arrived at the Vacation Village Hotel in San Diego, a sprawling forty-three-acre resort in Mission Bay designed by movie producer Jack Skirball and littered with Hollywood relics, he stepped out of the cab on a mild and cloudy day to find a mob of sign-wielding protesters rallying outside the check-in. At the time, headlines worldwide reported the continued fallout from the Lebanon hostage crisis, with Hezbollah still holding forty Americans hostage. But in San Diego, animal rights activists protested what they saw as a hostage crisis in their own country. As Dick began parting the crowd, he was stunned to spot Dian Fossey doing the same, approaching with a limp from the opposite direction. Dick introduced himself on the spot, intimidated by her height, and held the door open as the two of them stepped inside, the protest rallying cries muffled behind them.

They claimed a seat inside the lobby. With thirty minutes to kill before the first presentation, Dick told her he'd followed her work with the gorillas for several years, and that he longed to work in Africa himself. But, in the middle of his pitch, Fossey—who had appeared on *The Tonight Show Starring Johnny Carson* just a week prior—quickly attracted others to the room, and before long their conversation dwindled.

The symposium was everything Dick had imagined and then some, "like being in primatologist heaven." During the day he scribbled notes on heady presentations covering specialized research topics like "Incidence and Consequences of Inbreeding in Three Captive Groups of Rhesus Macaques (*Macaca mulatta*)" and "Modes of Speciation in Primates: Chromosomal and DNA." At night, he ate dinner with his heroes, with Francine "Penny" Patterson and Fritz and Fossey, too, who regaled the table with stories from Rwanda, working with gorillas and scaring off poachers, confirming many of the stories they'd all heard of her brazen work in the field.

"She was telling us a story that night—this was hilarious, just watching her—and she said that just a month or two before she'd come to the conference, [her group had] caught one of the main poachers. She said he told them where [the poachers] were entering the park. She goes, 'I swear—I didn't touch him.' She said he told them where they were shipping these hands and body parts. She goes, 'I swear—I didn't touch the man.' He told them who in the government is involved in the poaching. 'I swear—I did not touch him.'

"She'd shoot at tourists, that is true. She admitted that to me and the others, that tourists would come in and she'd shoot over their heads. She'd try to scare them off. She would torture the poachers when she caught them. She had been known to hang them by their feet. She'd been known to pistol-whip them. She would do all those things. But what she had done to that particular poacher they caught, I don't know, because she kept saying, 'I did not touch him.'

"Sigourney Weaver portrays her as kind of off the deep end. Dian was not that way. Yes, she was passionate. Yes, she was going to save those gorillas. Yes, she would be aggressive toward the poachers. But there was nothing crazy about her."

Though Dick had already risen to a nearly spiritual plane just sitting at the table—the way a young writer might swoon before

Hemingway—he rose higher still when his companions inquired about his work in Lincoln, many of them already aware of the zoo's success in breeding golden lion tamarins. Dick lacked the research experience and the higher education most of the others had obtained, but they all spoke the same coded language of people who have worked firsthand with primates. If the others knew Dick was out of his league, they never let on. In fact, by the end of the week, the whole group began brainstorming the possibilities of a new institution, Dick says, a nonprofit whose sole purpose was to raise funds for the groups sitting around the table. He felt included, an equal player in conceptualizing the hypothetical endeavor.

Before the conference concluded and they scattered to their various corners of the globe, Dick sat alone with Fossey at the dinner table, discussing his work back home, his childhood in Royal, his hopes of crossing the ocean to study great apes in the wild. Throughout the week, she'd had the chance to size him up. What she found must have impressed her. Perhaps, as a self-declared "hillbilly," she saw a little bit of herself in Dick, both of them a little shy, a little awkward, both sustained in their youth by dreams of an African adventure. Before the others arrived and filled the table, she offered Dick an eighteen-month internship at her Karisoke Research Center in Rwanda beginning that August—just two months away. Eighteen months was the longest she'd let anyone stay, she told him, wary of what she called the "astronaut blues," or the dangers of spending too much time in an environment so harsh and isolated. She explained that the job entailed less gorilla research than monitoring poachers and destroying traps, but if he wanted the gig, "it's yours," she said. Without warning, his dream reclined across the table, his for the taking. He was ecstatic—until he thought about Chewy and Reuben and Al Bietz, who'd taken a chance on him when no one else would lift a finger, who'd given him the experience he so desperately needed, who'd sent him to San Diego in the first place.

"I was arguing with myself," he says. "*I should do this. I should just do this. Alan will understand.* But it was like, *I can't do it. I cannot leave the Children's Zoo like this.*"

He volleyed back and forth, weighing the pros and cons, first silently, then aloud, until Fossey settled it for him. She'd find someone else for August, she said. But when the next internship posted eighteen months later, he'd be at the top of the list.

"I thought my dreams were coming true."

Back at Folsom Children's Zoo, Dick tried his best to stay focused, while thirty-five-year-old Wayne McGuire, an anthropology graduate student from the University of Oklahoma, accompanied Fossey in his stead. He continued ASL training with Reuben and Chewy, continued his research with the tamarins and the snow monkeys. The tulips withered and the trees caught fire—autumn suited Lincoln just fine, a potpourri of yellows and reds and every shade between. The breeze turned cool, then crisp, then frigid. The leafy embers died and the trees stood naked, bare branches creaking like old porch swings above. Fossey and the gorillas were always on his mind. He'd been offered an internship in his dreamland with one of Leakey's Angels. Come March, he would officially reapply, and just eight months after that, he'd be deep in the bush, unpacking his bags in a remote cabin in Rwanda, in Parc Des Volcans, taking orders from that giant of a woman.

In the meantime, Dick maintained a loose correspondence with some of the researchers and primatologists he'd met at the symposium—Jo Fritz, Penny Patterson, and more—the same group toying with the idea of an umbrella charity, a fund-raising arm for their various primate initiatives.

By December, the foundation was still little more than an idea, a thought to mull over as he fed the animals and cleaned the cages. On

Christmas Day, Dick volunteered to work what he thought would be a quiet shift. Temperatures had plunged from forty-six degrees just two days prior to single digits that afternoon, and when the Clydesdale fell on some ice, it took a whole crew hours to stand it back up again. It had been an exhausting and chaotic shift, and he returned home late, only to find that his cat had gone berserk, tearing up all the Christmas gifts his family had sent, gifts he'd placed neatly under the tree, still wrapped, and that he had planned to open, alone, later that evening. The whole apartment was a wreck. And just as he dropped to his knees to start cleaning up, the phone rang.

After all these years, he no longer remembers who made the call, but he remembers what they told him.

Someone had killed Dian.

—⚏—

"Sorry," he finally whispers, staring at his kitchen table, tears spilling over. "That was a terrible day."

The details were unclear, but authorities had found a bloody panga knife with a two-foot blade beneath Fossey's bed. Decades later, he still sometimes refers to 1985 as "the Year of the Bad Christmas." If working with primates in Africa had been his dream, surely this was a nightmare. As Christmas rolled into the New Year and families gathered with their loved ones, opening gifts, breaking bread, sipping cider, Dick flailed in emotional quicksand. Depression. Anger. Confusion. Regret. Guilt. His lifeline to Africa had simply evaporated, and he'd lost, if not quite a friend, a great inspiration.

He remembered her stories back in San Diego, so often making light of a grave situation; he'd even warned her, "those poachers are going to kill you someday," and she had admitted that, yes, her life was in danger, but she would return to Rwanda and continue her work nonetheless.

Details of her death slowly emerged as the weeks passed, each one another twist of the knife. Fossey's longtime cook, a local man named Kanyaranga, had found her door wide open as he approached her cabin in the haze of the early morning. The scene inside had sent him rushing down the mountain to fetch McGuire, the Oklahoma grad student who had taken Dick's spot. When McGuire had followed Kanyaranga back to the scene, he'd found sheets and clothes and suitcases strewn about the cabin, everything ransacked save for her two gray parrots, who were unharmed in their cage. And lying faceup on the floor beside her double bed, he'd found Fossey in a pool of blood, still dressed in the sweater and long johns she slept in, slippers still on her feet. The cause of death was three forceful blows from a machete, which had killed her almost instantly.

"One of the blows had hit her right across the mouth," McGuire later told the *Washington Post*. "The skull was split . . . she was cold as ice."

The doors to the cabin had been unlocked, a hole hacked away through the interior wall, and a crawl space opposite the foot of her bed had been notched out with metal cutters, authorities said. No one was immediately charged, and though many suspected poachers, the circumstances of her murder soon raised questions hinting at a deeper conspiracy. How could the perpetrators have cut through a metal wall without giving her plenty of time to defend herself? How did no one in the camp hear her scream?

"It was even more curious that her attackers had managed to find, by accident or design, the one place in the bedroom wall that was not blocked by heavy furniture on the inside," the *Washington Post* reported.

Nearly a year later, the Rwandan government would charge McGuire, of all people, sentencing him to death by hanging in a trial that lasted less than an hour. McGuire had fled the country six months earlier, in July 1986, days before they'd issued a warrant for his arrest. Prosecutors alleged he had killed Fossey to steal the manuscript of

49

her next book, the sequel to *Gorillas in the Mist*, and bolster his own research—a claim most who have studied the events find highly dubious. Because the United States doesn't share an extradition agreement with Rwanda, McGuire is free on American soil. Today, the trial is largely considered a sham—many believe the Rwandan government ordered the hit.

"I don't know the man, so I'm not going to judge. I have no clue what went on—I have my suspicions, but I don't know," Dick says. He makes reference to the Farley Mowat biography *Woman in the Mists*, recapping an account therein of McGuire leaving Karisoke days before the murder under a pretense of dental work, only to meet with officials from the Gorilla Fund instead. By then, a rift had grown between Fossey, who despised tourism, and the fund, which relied on it. "Why did Wayne McGuire meet with them? I just don't get it. He tells her he's going in for dentistry work. It doesn't make sense.

"It's a mystery that we'll never know," he adds. "But there's that deep burning in my soul: If I had said yes to her then, would she still be alive? If it *was* her research assistant that killed her . . . There is that question, and it does bother me."

Dick had planned to attend her funeral, assuming the service would be held in California, where Fossey's parents still lived. But when the Gorilla Fund called back the next morning, offering to make arrangements, they told him she would be laid to rest at Karisoke instead, in a cemetery she had built herself, surrounded by the graves of her loved ones: thirteen gorillas slain by poachers. Even with the fund's support, he couldn't commit to a trip like that, not with Chewy and Reuben at the zoo and no one there to cover for him. And so he mourned his hero alone from eight thousand miles away, and he mourned his dream along with her.

With Fossey gone, Dick feared for the gorillas. He feared for her legacy. He lunged at the scraps, the tiny threads connecting him to Rwanda and to Fossey's work. For perhaps the first time, he considered the foundation he and the group from the San Diego summit had casually discussed a serious prospect. Given none of the others seemed willing to "grab the bull by the horns," Dick assumed the responsibility himself. Desperate to honor Fossey's memory, he plowed blindly forward. He drew up the paperwork necessary to establish a nonprofit in the state of Nebraska. He scraped together a board of trustees and a local board of directors, the latter convincing him to establish a research center as well. Something small to flush the coffers. *Why not Royal?* they'd asked—or had that been Dick's suggestion? Land was cheap, he told reporters, he had a home base there, and with Grove Lake nearby and the Ashfall Fossil Beds soon to open, the center could tap into a new flow of tourism. By May, the UPI wire service had reported—paraphrasing Dick's rosy outlook—that Antelope County residents were already "going ape over the idea."

When Bietz announced his resignation from the Children's Zoo after thirteen years at the helm, Dick, too, began plotting his departure. Without Bietz, Dick was no longer sure the zoo's research goals were intact. And when the zoo announced plans to relocate Reuben and Chewy, Dick contacted the Saint Louis Zoo, requesting custodianship. Given his history with the animals, the odds were better than they may have seemed.

"The thing people on the outside don't realize is that there's a finite space in zoos for animals," Bietz says. "If you have a good breeding program in chimpanzees, what do you do with the extras? Saint Louis did not want Reuben back. He would have taken up an entire exhibit. They would have had to work several years to reacclimate him into the troop he was from. There was no future in that for him."

Orangutans are mostly solitary by nature—the Saint Louis Zoo could easily relocate Chewy. But Reuben, a highly social creature now three years old, had already lost one companion—Cousteau had been relocated the previous fall—and Kumi was scheduled to leave soon. He now relied primarily on Dick for companionship. The Saint Louis Zoo approved Dick's request for Reuben without hesitation. Despite the good news, Dick hardly had time to celebrate as he scrambled to lay the groundwork for a foundation he still hoped (tapping some hidden reserve) would someday deliver him to Africa.

On the morning of August 1, 1986, just two days before his twenty-fifth birthday, Dick packed up his grubby Lincoln flat and joined Reuben in the bed of his father's pickup truck, rain clouds gathering on the horizon. Even then, he says, he could feel it. Even with the local newspapers sweeping him forward, heralding the return of a native son, trumpeting headlines like FORMER NELIGH GRADUATE PLANS PRIMATE CENTER AT ROYAL and PRIMATE ZOO BEING PLANNED FOR TINY TOWN. He watched the cornfields rush past, one row after another, one mile after the next, center pivots spraying great parabolas of water overhead, Reuben wrapping his arms around Dick. Yes, he says, he could feel it even then.

"I started to get the feeling that maybe I was crazy."

Not long after Dick broadcast his intention to establish a research center back home in Royal, the city of O'Neill—thirty miles west—floated the idea of hosting the facility on land adjacent to its city park, eager to host a zoo. But the city council had yet to finalize the lease—their own fund-raising efforts had apparently stalled—and Reuben needed a home. So Dick had improvised. For the first several weeks, Reuben spent his waking hours in a reinforced corncrib on a farm outside Neligh—the wind rushing through the slats, the sun throwing checkerboard shadows across the concrete—his nights curled up with Dick in a small wooden shed outside his parents' home in Royal, the air heavy with oil and straw.

But winter was fast approaching, and Reuben needed real shelter from the snow and the frigid winds that cut through the plains like a scythe. Dick called Francine "Penny" Patterson, whom he'd met in San Diego and considered an adviser for what he now called the "Foundation for Primate Research and Conservation." He knew she housed her famous signing gorilla, Koko, in a modified trailer home, and he wondered if he might do the same for Reuben. She not only convinced him it was possible, he says, offering directions for specific renovations, but guessed he could get a trailer donated for the cause.

Nu Home Trailers in O'Neill quickly donated the single wide, a Good Samaritan in Royal allowed him to park it on her lot free of charge, and Dick modified the back bedroom to serve as Reuben's winter quarters. Before he'd even finished painting the sign, families and school groups began trickling in to visit Reuben, his reputation far preceding him.

Reuben was three and a half years old, supposedly one of ten chimps nationwide trained in American Sign Language. Travelers on Highway 20 could spot him, small and blithe, hanging by a limb or a digit from the corncrib outside his trailer, puckering his lips, itching his diaper, watching the traffic zoom past beneath him. Dick stood below, twenty-five and gangly in jeans and a threadbare T-shirt, a self-described naturalist. He looked happy, scrappy in the way one does when they jump headlong into their devotion, a slow drip of adrenaline trickling through his veins. Friends used to joke he'd spent so much time with nonhuman primates he was beginning to look like one, with his thick red beard, nose like a poker spade, and shoulder-length hair conspicuously absent on top.

Nevertheless, a single wide was hardly what Dick had advertised. He was gunning for a first-class facility: $2 million, ten primates, twenty-five full-time employees, twenty-five more during the peak tourist season. He stressed the importance of mimicking the primates' natural environment, said he'd been working with an architecture student at the University of Nebraska–Lincoln to design the complex. He said they'd toured the country's preeminent zoos and hoped to incorporate all the best elements back in Royal. In the midst of a hemorrhaging farm economy, good news traveled fast. With the wide-eyed Reuben by his side, just forty pounds and full of life, Dick garnered more front-page headlines than most of the county's governing bodies. And with each new report, Dick's plans seemed to multiply. At one point the figure jumped to $5 million, and by August 1988, Dick was touting plans to incorporate "all the typical zoo animals," according to the *Orchard News*: "bears, lions, tigers, zebras, elephants, birds, etc."

"The possibilities for growth will be unlimited," he said. "Unlike city zoos, we won't be limited by space. We can continue to grow forever."

In many ways Dick's time at the Folsom Children's Zoo seemed years behind him already, swamped as he was in Royal and over- whelmed by the work ahead. And though he'd be forever associated with Reuben, the two of them typecast as something of a Scooby and Shaggy, a homespun comedy duo, Chewy had always been his first love. Orangutans show considerably less affection, are less prone to remem- bering their keepers than chimpanzees, but Chewy had initiated Dick's real-world experience with great apes. Chewy had been the first to break through—to assay Dick's primate passion—and though he may have forgotten Dick, Dick would never forget Chewy. And so—as if Dick didn't have enough worries to juggle with an adolescent chimpanzee, a fledgling foundation, and an existential crisis he toiled consistently to exorcise—he worried for Chewy, who was housed alone in Lincoln without an experienced handler and waiting for a future to reveal itself.

Near the end of August 1986, roughly a month after he'd first returned to Royal, he borrowed his parents' old Ford LTD and headed for the Children's Zoo one last time. They were shipping Chewy back to Saint Louis, and they needed Dick's expertise. He had known the day would come, had been waiting for the call, reserving his sorrow for that final farewell after the sedatives kicked in and Chewy began to drift. Dick left early in the morning, dew still heavy on the grass, haze still burning off the crops. By the time he hit Norfolk, fifty miles down the road, he began to feel light-headed, though he tried to fight it off. He pushed a few miles farther before pulling over to vomit in the ditch, head down, wisps of hair blowing across his forehead. He found a motel parking lot back in Norfolk, rolled down the window, and fell asleep behind the wheel.

"I didn't know what it was, but the muffler had a leak, and I had carbon monoxide poisoning, and I could've very easily died," he says, "which would've solved all my problems at the time."

What so many seemed to recognize but rarely expressed was that Dick, though unquestionably devoted to nonhuman primates, didn't know the first thing about starting a business, let alone a nonprofit. He didn't know how to raise funds. He didn't know how to promote a cause. He didn't know how to pay himself a salary—or anyone else, for that matter.

Unable to afford rent, he moved into a spare bedroom at his parents' house in town, where he kept little more than his clothes and a few toiletries. "Dick's an animal person, not an administrator," Bietz says. "He couldn't administrate to save his ass." And, at just twenty-five, Dick was still green. He hadn't earned or even pursued a graduate degree, hadn't published any research, hadn't logged any significant time in the field. Swimming in the pool of his icons was a heady experience, but more than that, he felt somehow ordained by Fossey's murder, as if by offering him a chance and dying before it was fulfilled, she'd left the mission of primate conservation up to him and him alone. Dick possessed a drive others admired, if never quite understood, and even those who spotted a fool's errand hesitated to step in the way.

"I've never been somebody that wanted to step on anybody else's dream, and his dream was, while maybe not particularly logical—he was willing to make whatever concessions he had to in order to make it work," Bietz says. "His idea was not based on what it was going to do for him at all, but what it was going to allow him to do for chimpanzees.

"I didn't ever see it as being financially viable. But on the other hand, Jane Goodall went out in the jungle and sat for three years staring through rose-colored glasses of the same kind."

Patching together a board of directors took little effort. Dick called in favors from old friends, family members, a former high school biology teacher—the one who'd helped launch his fleet of UFOs over Neligh so many years before. But the board of trustees was another matter. Though Dick often boasted of the support he had from celebrity primatologists, it was perhaps telling that none of them lent their names to the masthead. Instead, he recruited closer to home, enlisting academics whose understanding of Dick's endeavor was limited at best. That fall, for example, Dick scheduled an interview with Dr. Jeff French, a professor in the department of psychology and biology who had established a marmoset lab at the University of Nebraska–Omaha.

"His heart was in the right place, but in terms of zoos and an understanding of primate psychology and primate research, he struck me as a little naive," French says. He was talking to me about the work he'd been doing with sign language, and in academic primatology, the sign language field is really controversial. Do they or do they not have the capacity to communicate with gestural symbols? Some of the best people in the world were working on that at Columbia and at Harvard, and Dick was, at the time, an energetic young man who felt that, like all of us at one point, he had [access to] the answers to everything with a single chimp.

"He wasn't necessarily happy with the kind of feedback I was giving him with regard to things like the need for careful controls, but [we] never [had] any disagreements regarding the broader goal, and that was to promote primate conservation and educate the general public about primates, what distinguishes them from other mammals, the similarities they bear with us, et cetera. So I was always, at least in our initial conversations, very encouraging regarding those goals for the Midwest Primate Center. How could you not be? We're all sort of in different ways trying to row in the same direction."

Dick reached out to James Hayward, too, a biology professor at Union College, a Seventh-day Adventist school in Lincoln. Hayward guesses they first met when one of his students interned at the Children's Zoo, though in truth he can no longer remember, so little was his involvement.

"At any rate, I *do* recall meeting Dick, and that he asked me to serve as a board member for a primate research organization he was initiating. But to be honest, that's pretty much the last thing I remember about Dick and his organization," he says. "I never met with other board members (or knew who they were), never toured the facility, never visited the town of Royal, and never was involved in any decisions involving the organization."

Other members of the board of trustees included Robert Wickert, his college roommate; David Kilcoyne, his former neighbor; Gary Ralston, an employee of the Nebraska Game and Parks Commission; two of Hayward's students from Union College; and Martin Peterson, an anthropology professor at UNL. His old college mentor, Robert Hitchcock, later joined the list as well. Unlike French and many others, Peterson—who earned his PhD at the University of Wisconsin under psychologist Harry Harlow, famous for a slew of highly controversial studies with rhesus monkeys—supported Dick's undertaking without reservation. When Dick stopped by his office looking for support, Peterson gave it to him, few questions asked. He saw in Dick the same thing he'd seen in a budding paleontologist more than a decade before, a professor at Chadron State University named Larry Agenbroad, who was later credited with establishing the Mammoth Site, an internationally renowned research destination in South Dakota. Though hardly analogous, if Agenbroad could do it, Peterson mused, why couldn't Dick, this "very serious, committed, interested" young man in the seat before him?

"Pie in the sky is the closest way I can describe it. But again," he says, "look at Agenbroad, who went from a professor at Chadron State to putting together a national-level mammoth site completely funded. From my standpoint, he could either do it or he couldn't, but golly, there's very few people who try and do things like that."

Even after he visited Dick and Reuben in the trailer, Peterson remained optimistic.

"It was . . . beginning," he says, searching for the right word. "My own view of the world is that until you risk things, you don't get there. So I thought he was off and running."

Royal, for its part, only half subscribed to Dick's grand undertaking, despite what he'd told reporters. His family supported it; his mother, Lucille, and sister Bonnie served on the inaugural board of directors. Despite mocking the venture, his father, Jim, bought and donated the foundation's first two and a half acres on the east edge of town, two blocks south of the highway, where Dick soon relocated the trailer. Other families stood behind him, bolstering his confidence. But the primate center had its share of detractors too. Citizens worried about safety or the noise or simply the change it could bring to Royal. Even those who did support the idea considered it less a boon to the community than a peculiarity.

"They thought he was nuts," says Gary Ober, a local contractor. "Everybody just thought, *What's he doing? How's he going to make this work?*"

"There was one lady whose name I won't mention that lives over there, and Reuben just bothered her," Dick says. "She was so scared the chimp was going to escape and rape her. She would say, 'If that little gorilla gets out and tries to rape me, I'm gonna shoot him.'"

In truth, Dick considered the primate center a regional attraction, not a local one, and he hoped the Foundation for Primate Research and Conservation would eventually operate on a national platform. Royal's concerns didn't factor into his plans. He'd won over the regional press. He'd reaped moral if not yet financial support from surrounding communities. His former boss, director of the Folsom Children's Zoo, served as vice president of the board of directors. And perhaps most importantly, he believed he had the support of a number of top-tier primatologists and other researchers around the world: Russell Mittermeier, vice president for science at the World Wildlife Fund; Jo Fritz, founder of the Primate Foundation of Arizona; Penny Patterson, researcher and keeper of Koko; a number of scientists from Nebraska universities; and of course, the late Dian Fossey, whom Dick still thought of often when the work slowed down. If the foundation never garnered the full support of what he considered the "powers that be" in Royal itself, he wouldn't blame them, and he wouldn't take it too much to heart.

Fund-raising quickly topped the priority list. Over the next few years, Dick swung at every opportunity to make a few hundred bucks, sponsoring more public events than the area could keep up with. Just months after his return, he hosted Reuben's first Christmas party, charging attendees a small fee to meet Reuben and play carnival games at the American Legion Hall in Neligh. In March, he invited Antelope County to celebrate Reuben's fourth birthday in the Royal gymnasium. In June, he hosted a walk-a-thon. In July, an Independence Day turtle race ("Snapping turtles will not be allowed," noted the *Neligh News & Leader*). Talent shows. Zoo jamborees. T-shirts and teddy bear contests. For only five dollars, one could become a member of the "Friends of Reuben Society" and receive a monthly newsletter featuring updates on his sign language training.

He opened the primate center daily, charging guests to walk through a donated trailer home that now bore its title, "THE MIDWEST PRIMATE CENTER," hand-painted in a manic scrawl across the front. Capital letters. Crooked and bold. Though "situated in less than royal facilities," as the *World-Herald* wittily observed, Reuben never disappointed, and Dick's passion for primates always shone through. Four thousand people toured the Midwest Primate Center in its first year—perhaps not sensational, but not bad for a chimpanzee in a trailer home in rural Nebraska. In its second year, after Dick relocated the trailer, the number doubled.

With room now to stretch, and a small clutch of family and friends donating time, Dick slowly expanded the center's offering. Visitors to the new location on Ponca Street, several blocks removed from the highway, could walk a short nature trail, a shady loop cut through a stand of oak and elm, through walnut trees and raspberry bushes, every species identified with hand-painted signs shat on by the sparrows and wrens. He kept Reuben in the trailer, still doubling as the admissions center and gift shop, or outside in the corncrib when the weather cooperated. He stretched every penny, borrowed when he could, acquired new displays whenever luck or opportunity allowed. In February 1987, a "drive-through safari" in Arkansas donated a pair of brown lemurs that gave birth less than two weeks later, quadrupling the zoo's primate total—an impressive feat, Bietz says, given Dick's resources. In September 1988, he purchased a snow monkey and its exhibit—yet another repurposed corncrib, but with a professionally printed sign—with the financial support of a local popcorn farm. He later added two African pygmy goats, several Swedish foxes, pheasants, turkeys, and a variety of smaller, more accessible animals for the kids: guinea pigs, turtles, snakes, and more. He called this group the "Affection Section," an idea transferred from the Children's Zoo, which featured the same. It was all "very primitive and rustic," Dick admits, "nothing fancy," a small but exceedingly eccentric farm, a growing collection of corncribs and makeshift corrals.

He established an adoption program; in exchange for funding a particular animal's food and housing—$700 for Reuben, less for others—adopters would receive a certificate and a sign with their name placed next to the cage. And he initiated a "Junior Zookeeping" program, too, teaching kids animal husbandry in exchange for their help maintaining the rabbits and goats—all of it in service of the research, he says. Though he hated zoos and shied from using the term, he had hoped that displaying more animals and offering more activities would draw more families through the gates and, with them, more donations to the foundation.

By October 1989, attendance had already hit fourteen thousand, nearly doubling yet again, and the property—a vacant lot just two years before—now trembled with life.

THE PRIMATOLOGIST

Distracted by the promotional hoopla—the headlines and the holiday raffles—one could easily forget what the fund-raising was all about: "to undertake and participate in scientific research in furtherance of primate behavior," according to the foundation's own articles of incorporation. When Dick wasn't welcoming guests or singing "Happy Birthday" to Reuben, when he wasn't playing dress up and leading Halloween tours of "Count Royal's Haunted Trail," when he wasn't officiating turtle races or hosting walk-a-thons, Dick was documenting the environmental factors most conducive to successful reproduction in brown lemurs, studying the role of sibling care in Japanese macaques, determining the handedness among different primate species, and developing new modes of environmental enrichment for Reuben—all of which Dick considered serious primatological research. The sign language instruction continued too. By March 1987, Reuben knew sixteen signs, Dick reported.

To publish these "studies," Dick founded and edited *The Primatologist*, the foundation's monthly newsletter. Each issue included news from the Midwest Primate Center, a calendar of events, and a thank-you section acknowledging volunteer contributions. "It was an interesting read," French says, "but not scientific in any sense of the word." Much like Dick himself, the newsletter read both earnest and playful. Most issues, for example, featured a large primate photo on the cover. Reuben playing at the admissions desk. Reuben lounging in the corncrib. A brown lemur gripping a tree branch. But the September 1986 cover careened suddenly toward the dramatic: a large empty frame, a white box. Beneath it, the caption: EXTINCTION. He published pencil sketches of the facility, bush-league essays with titles like "The Obstacles to Action" and "Saving the Primates":

> Without a doubt, we have all seen chimpanzees on T.V., in circuses, or in a zoo. However, many of us do not stop to consider the serious plight of the chimpanzees or animals like it . . . There are many causes of primate extinction, but all of these causes are man-made. Jumans [*sic*] are the ultimate cause of the decline of the number of primates in existence today. Humans cut down trees to make way for farmland or for lumber. Humans populate natural areas causing other primates to leave. Humans hunt and kill many monkeys etc. Humans are inadvertently causing their own extinction through the slaughter of other animals.

Next to his own studies, *The Primatologist* ran articles from far more reputable conservation groups, most often the Primate Foundation of Arizona; the Gorilla Foundation; and the Digit Fund, Dian Fossey's anti-poaching league. Attempting to execute the foundation's secondary goal of "providing financial support to other qualified entities conducting such research," Dick sometimes wrote checks to these same organizations for as little as ten dollars, all of which he noted in *The Primatologist*. Ostensibly for archival purposes, he sent a copy of almost every issue to the National Primate Research Center in Madison, Wisconsin.

And yet, despite a guestbook logging visitors from California to New York, the numbers wouldn't reconcile. Dick charged next to nothing for admission, outright donations dragged—despite Reuben's popularity—and maintenance for exotic animals was and continues to be an expensive enterprise. Though he was always too shy, too awkward to confront him, Dick sometimes blamed his old boss, now his vice president, for his foundation's perpetually broken coffers. He'd seen Bietz effortlessly schmooze donors at the Children's Zoo and trusted he'd do the same for the foundation, allowing his work in Royal to rise above the daily ho-hum of a roadside zoo.

"I was hoping for larger donors, which Alan could've gotten. I've seen him do some amazing things. He could get blood out of a turnip," Dick says. "But it never really happened. I'm not a fund-raiser. It was a struggle [operating out of] an old trailer house and an old corncrib."

Dick's so-called board of trustees played virtually no role at all. Few knew the Midwest Primate Center existed, fewer kept in touch with Dick, and even fewer still had actually toured the facility. Until receiving the first copy of *The Primatologist*, in fact, neither French nor UNL psychology professor Dan Leger knew they were members, had no recollection of being asked. Leger pulled his name immediately, and by the fall of 1987, French wanted out too. None of the primatologists Dick had first associated with the foundation—names French had recognized as distinguished researchers—appeared on the list beside him. In fact, he didn't recognize a single name on the masthead, and as the only credentialed primatologist in the state, he feared association with what he now suspected was a half-baked organization. He wrote Dick a resignation letter—short but overly polite—asking to be kept abreast of the foundation's progress and offering to consult on an ad hoc basis.

"It got a little bit weird," French says. "He sent me some formal letters saying, you know, the board of directors accepts your resignation from the board of trustees. But then he sent this really bizarre letter sort of blaming me . . . and said he was unwilling to accept my resignation until I sent him a valid reason."

Dick first implied confusion, given that "THERE ARE NO OBLIGATIONS TO THE BOARD OF TRUSTEES" and that members are part of the foundation "in name ONLY." But the letter quickly turned hostile. "To put it bluntly," he wrote, "I am rather disappointed." The foundation's first year was a "rocky one," and he often regretted the sudden pivot away from his work in Lincoln, where his duties never extended beyond the animals themselves. No fundraising. No hiring or firing or training volunteers. Nevertheless, he said, his convictions about primate conservation were sincere, and the support of "highly respected" professionals like Dr. French "made me feel more at ease and confident." It helped spur him forward during the most trying times, and finally the foundation was beginning to pay off: memberships were on the rise, the public was growing more educated every day, and they had begun awarding small grants to other conservation groups.

"Then someone like you comes along and promises to help and then says he won't (and doesn't even give valid reasons)—that really bothers me," Dick wrote. "We can protect these animals only if we all work together. So could you please send me (not the Foundation—as the Directors gladly accepted your resignation) a valid reason for your resignation? Thank you."

Though perhaps it should have, the conversation didn't end there. After receiving Dick's letter, French felt unjustly attacked, "a personal insult," he wrote. Pulling off the kid gloves, he swung back, reminding Dick of his professional qualifications, of the twelve years he'd now spent researching captive breeding and the behavior of endangered South American primates. As for Dick's suggestion that he'd withdrawn his support and cut ties altogether, French replied: "Balderdash!! . . .

In my letter of 12 October, I clearly state my willingness to serve the Foundation, and the nature of the help I am willing to provide. I don't understand your reaction."

French continued to detail his concerns, which dealt primarily with the board of trustees. He'd never met any of them, he wrote, and he wondered why some of the previously listed members had been removed from the masthead of *The Primatologist*. He questioned, in particular, the qualifications of Bob Wickert, whom he had never heard of and couldn't find listed in the UNO directory.

"I am left with the opinion that there may be some misrepresentation of the qualifications of the Board of Trustees. I have never met any member of the Board of Directors, other than yourself, I have never been invited to visit the Foundation site in Royal, and other than what is reported in *The Primatologists* [*sic*], I have little knowledge of your operation," French concluded. "How can you, therefore, expect me to feel comfortable serving on the Board of Trustees?"

Three years after Dick's celebrated return to Royal, not only had he failed to garner any serious professional support—at the moment, he seemed to be losing it—but very little of what he once called "temporary" had changed. No zebras. No bears. No customized, state-of-the-art displays. Reuben still lived in a trailer home off the highway, the rest in corncribs and simple corrals. By 1989, the multimillion-dollar facility he'd projected onto his hometown seemed little more than the fantasy of an impassioned college graduate. That third winter, attendance plummeted well below the typical winter doldrums, and the furnace in the trailer couldn't keep up. Electric heaters and a mess of extension cords littered the floor. A tom turkey froze to death in its pen. And, without regular attendance, funding flatlined. He couldn't afford postage for the newsletter, couldn't afford even the most necessary office supplies. They couldn't travel, couldn't pay a phone bill. After three short years, the foundation was running on fumes, and so was Dick.

"At least we now know that The Foundation and the Midwest Primate Center are here to stay," he later wrote in *The Primatologist*, somewhere between delusional and deceptive. "If we can make it through something as bad as that, we can survive through anything!! One thing is for certain, however, we are going to plan things a little differently for next winter . . . just in case."

To make matters worse, Reuben, now a seven-year-old wunderkind, roughly one hundred pounds of muscle and fur, had outgrown his trailer. Dick had drawn up plans for a new enclosure—steel-reinforced concrete, sliding steel shift doors, heavy-gauge wire mesh, approximately 1,100 square feet—but the proposal's $55,000 price tag was completely unhinged from the foundation's fiscal reality. He couldn't afford to print the last three issues of *The Primatologist*, let alone build a chimp complex worth at least double the foundation's book value. If the funds weren't met, Reuben would "more than likely go to AIDS research," he told the *Orchard News*. It was mostly an idle threat, "an attention getter," he would later admit. Still, given Reuben's age and sex and several other factors working against him, he doubted Saint Louis would want him back. Beyond that, anything was possible. Already broke, losing the center's star attraction would effectively nail the coffin shut. As if he'd somehow forgotten how he came to be running the business out of a frostbitten mobile home, his new path to sustainability looked identical to the last one: cross your fingers and throw Reuben a birthday party.

"Fundraising activities will begin (again) this month," Dick wrote in the newsletter in December 1989. "Only the public can keep Reuben here at the Midwest Primate Center. We need your help. Please give what you can to keep Reuben here.

"If the funds are received and the building completed by fall," he continued, drifting helplessly into hypothetical territory, "we will not only be able to keep Reuben, but will be able to bring in another chimpanzee (a female). This is possible with your support."

The birthday parties—he threw two of them—earned the foundation a grand total of $600. He served punch and cake. He set up games for the kids, musical chairs, a ring toss. He organized a puppet show and a silent auction outside the trailer. But despite its admiration, the public wouldn't, perhaps *couldn't* shell out the type of fat donation Reuben needed to keep him in northeast Nebraska, hardly a surprise to any objective bystander, though of course Dick was far from it. Had every citizen living and dead in Royal donated $100, he'd still have come up short. And although the foundation had several staff members, only Dick considered it his full-time job. When the foundation struggled, Dick struggled—and the foundation struggled all the time. In nearly four years as president, Dick had never paid himself. He'd drained his checking account, drained his savings too. He still lived with his parents, and his closest companion was an adolescent chimpanzee supposedly on the cusp of AIDS research. Hardly a show of confidence, he'd even begun to advertise his own position in *The Primatologist*:

> The Midwest Primate Center Zoological Park and Research Center is seeking a qualified person to fill the position of Director. Responsibilities include writing grant proposals, developing budgets, master planning, general promotion, and supervision of all daily activities. Candidates must have excellent oral and written communication skills, must have experience at working with non-human primates, as well as skills in administration, accounting, supervision, and animal care and management.

Too stubborn to admit defeat, he dragged his regret behind him like a harnessed mule. He perked up for the kids, smiled wide for the tours. But after hours, spraying down the pens and feeding the animals, logging what they ate and how much and when, organizing another pointless fund-raiser, sending another notice to the papers, he punished himself. He looked beyond the western tree line, absorbing the blue-black silhouettes of an open field, the wind rustling up the musk of the zoo, and he wondered: *Why didn't I listen to my father? Why didn't I listen to my friends? Why didn't I simply apply elsewhere—anywhere—after Fossey's death, when my future was still unshackled and the slate was still clean? What cosmic gag led me back to the crunching gravel streets of my teenage years?*

"At that time I could have gone anywhere."

He certainly faced better odds than he had fresh out of college. By then he had several years of experience at a small but nationally respected zoo. And he had the full support of the zoo's director, who would have bent over backward—in some ways already had—to elevate Dick's career. With Fossey's murder, he may have lost an opportunity, but if the world had ever been his oyster, it was that moment in the capital city.

"If he'd come to me and said, 'I'd like to try to work for the Smithsonian,' I'd have written letter after letter trying to get him there, and had he made it—which is really hard, don't get me wrong, it's damn near impossible—I would not have been surprised in the least if he had excelled where he was," Bietz says. "They would have had him in a research area with six or eight other long-haired pizza eaters that all talked the same language. It would have been the equivalent of *The Big Bang Theory* with his peers."

But Dick's ambition had gotten the better of him, steering him back to Royal with the goal of raising the profile of primate conservation. After those first three years, broke, exhausted, afraid to lose Reuben, embarrassed to lay claim to the facility—less a research center now than a half-assed zoo, all of it below Reuben's dignity, if not his own—Dick took what seemed like the only exit available: he relinquished control of the Midwest Primate Center to the people of northeast Nebraska, sacrificing his head to save his heart and praying with little faith that with new blood would come new life.

"One thing is for certain: after Dian Fossey was killed, I should have just taken a deep breath and thought the whole thing through a little better," he says. "And Lord knows, I should have never started the Midwest Primate Center. It was just a matter of me operating on impulse and not thinking things through in a clear and rational fashion. A stupid mistake that I now must live with for what is left of my existence."

On the night of April 3, 1990, spring gusts rattling the window-panes, the foundation's board of directors gathered at the chamber office in Norfolk to officially bestow the Midwest Primate Center upon the people of northeast Nebraska. The vote was unanimous—most votes were, the board merely "yes men," says Reverend Mark Richardson, a member of the board who preached at Royal's United Methodist Church. "It was all Dick." Like the board of trustees, the board of directors played a minimal role in the goings-on of the foundation. Dick encouraged anyone with an interest in the research center, or the zoo, or the wildlife park, or whatever the hell they chose to call it—he no longer cared to correct them—to attend the public meeting. Those who heeded the call, whether curious, or killing time, or truly invested in the future of the zoo, elected a new board on the spot.

Just a few years ago, Dick would have scoffed at the whole affair. He'd always hated zoos. He'd had to check his pride and look the other way to accept the job in Lincoln, and the job in Lincoln, he'd told him-self, was only a stepping-stone to Africa. But now here he was, three and a half years after moving back home to start a primate research center, giving the public an opportunity to establish the only zoo within a hundred-mile radius and praying that doing so would allow him to keep the one thing left he truly held dear: Reuben the chimpanzee.

Despite his best efforts—he spent two full days in Reuben's cage in July 1990 in a desperate stunt to broadcast his plight—his fund-raising attempts had failed. Reuben was on borrowed time. He was testing the limits of his environment, too large for the trailer, too strong for the corncrib. Dick remained his sole caretaker, forced to stay within eyeshot should Reuben actually tear through, and he now placed his faith in the idea that a public zoo and a newly elected board of directors could succeed where he had so miserably failed, though in truth he had his doubts, and in fleeting moments of clarity, he would sometimes feel a tinge of relief at the idea of the whole thing crumbling. If it weren't for Reuben, his kid, he might have let it. Instead, he sat stone-faced in that sterile conference room while the new board appointed him executive director—a role he would have gladly declined had there been anyone else half as qualified to work with exotic animals. The board appointed other new members representing a host of communities scattered about northeast Nebraska, a group who would ostensibly face less resistance soliciting donations back home. The zoo was broadening its reach.

The new chairman was Jerry Peterson, a road crew worker for the Nebraska Department of Roads and Vietnam veteran living in Norfolk. He had copper eyebrows and a receding hairline, a patriot with sad and heavy eyes. Originally from Royal, Jerry wore a rotating cast of pearl-snap shirts with a single pen in his breast pocket, polyester slacks, and a bulky Starter jacket in the winter. He walked slowly, a limp to his gait, often with the help of a black wooden cane. After graduating from Royal High School in 1962, he enlisted with the US Army National Guard and received auto mechanic training at Fort Ord in California's Monterey Bay. After his release, he earned his auto mechanic's certificate from Southeast Community College back in Lincoln.

He'd spent more than a decade hopping from one odd job to the next, swapping titles like five-cent baseball cards. Mechanic. Head custodian. Electrician. He drove the bus for Neligh-Oakdale public schools, lurching from one end of the district to the other, picking up kids from their farms long, empty miles outside the city limits. In that capacity, he'd taken notice of one high school student, a wallflower named Dick with messy hair and bright cheeks. Dick always sat near the back, book in hand, always said thanks before stepping off the bus. Jerry dropped him off each day at the filling station in Royal.

Though Jerry had no experience running a zoo or working with exotic animals, he'd long fancied himself a "problem solver," a term he'd been peppering into casual conversation since he first campaigned for the Nebraska legislature six years earlier. By October 1984, a month shy of Election Day, Jerry had raised less than forty-seven of the fifty legislative candidates, less than $1,000 total; so little, in fact, that he wasn't required to report his campaign contributions at all. Jerry lost, but only "as far as the election was concerned," he says.

"I don't really consider it a loss. I learn so much doing things. And likewise, I've been on radio, television, public forums, all over the place. And you can tell by my conversation that I'm used to this talking thing."

He ran again four years later. Filed for office. Campaigned. Shook hands. Touted his problem-solving finesse. He explained his job with the Department of Roads, said he loved it, trudging through fields with transits and steel tripods, measuring and recording distances, setting benchmarks, determining boundaries. One afternoon, he told his would-be constituents, he sat in a monthly safety meeting and listened to his coworkers complain about runaway road signs.

"'Hey, Joe,' I say. 'I got an idea. We'll go ahead and raise those legs so they can't collapse. We'll put a hook up above, a top strap, and let it down to the ground, and get a spike with a hook. It'll hook onto it, and it'll be like a punching clown. Hit it, it'll fall over, come right back up again.' 'Yeah,' he says, 'go ahead, put it together.' So I did. I received an award for that from the state. And I was surprised—I got another letter. They sent my design to Chicago for the national convention, and I won there too.

"I could give you illustration after illustration," he says. "I'm a problem solver."

He lost the second election, too, but by the time he accepted his position as chairman of the new board of the Midwest Primate Center, he still believed in his talent for sparking positive change, still felt a civic compulsion.

"I never done it before, but I knew I could do it," he says. "I knew legal affairs. It's second nature to me."

Jerry's first order of business: a name change. The Midwest Primate Center would henceforth be known as the Northeast Nebraska Zoo—Home of the Midwest Primate Center.

"This name change reflects that 1) the facility is owned by the people of Northeast Nebraska, and 2) the facility is a zoological park," Dick wrote in *The Primatologist*. "This new zoo board has total control of the zoo with final approval of The Foundation Board of Directors. This will allow the local people to have input into the development of their zoo."

During the transition, small contributions to the "Save Reuben" campaign continued to dribble in, donations that—while insignificant in monetary terms—evidenced legitimate public interest. Challenging other schools to match the gift, the student council in Orchard donated $25. The elementary school kids in Niobrara donated $40 by saving their pennies each day. The Norfolk Kmart hosted a bake sale for Reuben, donating $157 in total proceeds. The Alan Baer Foundation in Omaha gave another $100. And the new zoo board sponsored its first fund-raiser that July, a charity auction at the Norfolk Armory, encouraging the public to donate whatever it could: recliners, picnic tables, washers, dryers—anything. Among the donors was Dick's former neighbor, David Kilcoyne, who had been teaching at a scientific institute in West Berlin when the wall fell. He had kept a piece of it, which he then donated to the auction. Dick promoted the fistful of concrete as a "symbol of freedom" to the area newspapers.

"Due to hot weather, poor attendance was observed and many of the items sold for next to nothing," Dick reported in *The Primatologist*. "This was a great setback."

Given the flop, the proclamations soon to follow felt especially contrived. The Antelope County Supervisors officially declared July 7 "Reuben Day," and—at Dick's behest—Nebraska governor Kay Orr proclaimed the entire week "Northeast Nebraska Zoo Week," urging "all citizens to take due note of the observance."

But you can't run a zoo on "due note" alone, and so far as Dick was concerned, the new board proved, if not quite inept, slow to right the ship. It wasn't for a lack of effort. They hosted fund-raisers, encouraged their local schools. They solicited major foundations and every big name they could think of: Michael Jackson, Donald Trump, Johnny Carson, Betty White, Tom Selleck, Dick Cavett. "Name a popular celebrity in the late 1980s—we probably sent them a letter," Dick says. "What was the worst they could say?"

But the few who bothered to respond at all quickly declined. Dick could no longer forestall the inevitable. He'd sacrificed the primate center for a zoo, surrendered his own control to the will of the public, and four months later still had nothing to show for it. The $55,000 chimp enclosure remained little more than a pipe dream, and without proper funding, the Northeast Nebraska Zoo would remain, at best, a slipshod menagerie—the opposite of everything he believed in, anathema to his very core. He'd already stretched his conviction like a rubber band; stretch any more and it would snap. He drafted his resignation. After the centennial celebration at the end of the month, he promised himself, he would deliver the letter and formally recommend the zoo's permanent closure. It was time to find Reuben a new home. It was time to move on. For the first time in years, sprawled out on his bed, parents asleep in the room across the hall, Dick dared to look past tomorrow. And for a tiny fleeting moment, he felt relief.

A few days later, Johnny Carson called back.

A SAVAGE CELEBRATION

The rains came few and far between in Antelope County in July 1990, small pockets of thunder and spit, mornings of fog and fresh-cut, sickly sweet alfalfa. Overnight the clouds had scattered and reconvened again, parishioners between one service and the next. They conferred over Royal on a muggy Friday night, milling about as if waiting for the church ladies to bring out the coffee and crumb cake. Meanwhile, in the streets below, Royal crackled back to life for the kick-off to its highly anticipated centennial weekend, what the posters called "A Savage Celebration." Though Royal itself boasted just eighty-nine residents, nearly twelve hundred people crammed inside the gymnasium for the pork barbecue, their trucks and other vehicles flanking the city's narrow streets and spilling out into the pastures beyond. Shortly before 8:00 p.m., the now-sticky-fingered throng filed outside to watch several F-16 fighter jets with the Nebraska Air National Guard tear through the clouds and shake the earth like a wayward tremor. After the variety show wrapped, headlights flickered on and formed a caravan on Highway 20, back to their homes in the neighboring towns, most to return again the next day.

Though Royal's population had steadily withered since its peak of roughly 250 in 1910, one could forgive a flutter of optimism after a hundred years on the high plains. While the Verdigris was dammed in 1953, Grove Lake had grown ever more popular in the decades since, luring fishermen to its trout-stocked waters, charming campers and romantics with its shady, cattailed shores. And the trout-rearing station nearby was a magnet itself, families flocking to its placid, manicured environs and small holding ponds to watch trout by the thousands shoot through the raceways and battle over fifty-cent divvies of fish pellets, the water churning as if pelted by a summer hail.

In Royal proper, the Northeast Nebraska Zoo had just become a public asset with plans for a sixteen-acre expansion. And though only a handful knew it, a $55,000 check from the Johnny Carson Foundation had recently landed in their PO box, accompanied by a note from the King of Late Night himself: "It is important to help the area kids to have the same advantages and education that larger cities' kids already have and also help the rural area." Though Dick and the board were staying mum until after the centennial to avoid distracting from the long-planned celebration, the funds ensured a new home for Reuben and, if they stretched them thin enough, a long-overdue roommate too.

And twenty years after a paleontologist at the University of Nebraska–Lincoln stumbled upon a baby rhino skeleton protruding from a hill outside town—thirty-seven years after Royal native Donald Peterson first reported a skull to the state museum, his brother Jerry is quick to note—the Ashfall Fossil Beds State Historical Park was scheduled to open the following year. A joint effort between the Nebraska Game and Parks Commission and the state museum, the new park would encompass 360 acres of what *National Geographic*, on the cover of its January 1981 edition, called the "Pompeii of Prehistoric Animals in Nebraska."

"Some of the biggest opportunities to ever hit Royal are really going to help the old town," said Gary Ober, a local contractor and chair of the centennial committee.

The next day, flea market vendors sprouted like mushrooms in an empty lot off Main Street. The Methodists set up a food stand outside the church. Marlowe Jensen performed a wheelwright demonstration in a sleeveless button-down, hot setting a pair of iron tires on wooden wheels at the corner of 4th and Main. An old woman recited a poem. Two trees were planted in honor of Royal's two centennial babies. A steel anvil was shot into the air with black powder—a throwback to simpler times—and a group of tomahawk throwers led by Dean Wavrunek, chief of police in nearby Verdigre, threw their weapons at targets painted on wooden planks. The zoo hit maximum capacity, Reuben's corncrib surrounded by enchanted farm kids and their wide-eyed parents, Dick scrambling to keep it all together. Every Royalite along with their cousins and their friends and their former neighbors mingled in the streets, hot dog and soda in hand. Should they have felt like sending a letter to mark the occasion, the Anson building across the highway offered a one-day-only centennial postmark.

Gray skies lingered above it all, gathering strength, until finally, around three o'clock in the afternoon, the wind picked up, and the clouds rumbled like a truck barreling over some distant bridge, and the tin roofs of Royal's modest homes began to patter, and the gravel softened beneath their feet until small brown puddles formed in the ruts. What should have cast a pall over the entire jubilee hardly registered, farmers overjoyed by the first real precipitation in weeks. The mud racers raced anyway—the muddier the better—the beard judging simply moved inside, and when the rain finally cleared one and a half inches later, nearly doubling the monthly total, they rendezvoused in the park for the free evening dance, boots tapping on glistening pavement.

Reverend Mark Richardson hosted an outdoor worship service the next morning, cooler now after the rain; the flea market picked up where it left off; and the baton twirlers from O'Neill frolicked down Main Street, intermittently flinging their instruments toward the sun. All morning long, participants registered at the park for the Grand Parade, the cherry on top of what had already been—by everyone's account—a smashing success. By noon, the old-fashioned Model Ts, top-down convertibles, and slapdash floats began to line up in the pasture behind the church, their drivers busy checking tires and testing the banners, while across the rodeo grounds, Diana Wavrunek relaxed on a sleeping bag inside her teepee. She and her husband, Dean, both members of a black powder muzzle-loading group, had camped out since Friday, booked for several shows over the weekend. In the distance now, she could hear the engines idling in the field, the muffled murmurs of passersby outside the teepee, the come-hither call of the meadowlark, the wailing of an angry child.

Diana let her mind wander from the past to the present and back again, retracing the steps of a mostly nomadic life. Raised in Verdigre, she couldn't wait to ditch Nebraska after high school. She hated the weather, mostly. The wind and the cold. She spent a few years in Vermillion at the University of South Dakota, then hopped to Iowa and Idaho and Nevada and "almost every state west of the Mississippi," she says, and though of course it only seemed to get colder, it got prettier too. In Boise she worked in "high-security cleaning," employed by a company that cleaned banks and law enforcement offices and health clinics. In Nevada, she enrolled in dog-grooming school, a skill she found useful in every subsequent move. "There's always demand for that," she says. She had a son and was briefly married, but she divorced the father soon after.

She drifted for seventeen years, from 1971 to 1989, until her dad recruited her back to Nebraska, uncomfortable with his daughter roaming the country as a young single mother. Back in Verdigre, she went on a few dates with the local police chief, Dean Wavrunek, and not long after, they married.

"He was the cop when I was in high school," she says. "We dated a couple times, and it was just like, *Are you kidding? This guy's ancient,* you know? It went better the second time around."

She'd always been an animal lover. At ten years old, she'd found a quiet corner in the school library and read Jane Goodall's first article in *National Geographic*, gripping the pages tight. She'd been obsessed ever since, mostly with chimps, but other apes too. Something about the way they looked, the way Goodall described their antics, hooked Diana and never let her go.

At the centennial celebration, the streets were a buzzing hive nearly two thousand visitors strong, easily the largest gathering Royal had ever seen, but Diana was lost in memory until she heard another scream. *The parade will be starting soon,* she thought, and she began to compose herself. The scream came again, but this time it was louder, shriller, more painful. She sat up, fully awake now. She pulled back the flap of the teepee and stepped outside. But there were no signs of a screaming child, no signs, in fact, of any concern at all. The scream came again, high pitched, sadder, angrier still—a truly bloodcurdling scream. *My god,* she thought, only half kidding, *is someone killing this child?*

Music played from the announcer's booth several blocks away. Grandparents fanned themselves in lawn chairs. Teenagers flirted by the food stand. Everything so normal, and yet this scream—was she the only one who could hear it? She followed the noise. Past the gymnasium and the school building. Past the still-shuffling queue of parade vehicles and a cheery couple making a banner from a pillowcase. Around the block, north on Fremont, and east on 3rd Street. She kept walking, under the canopy of cottonwoods and white elms lining the streets of this unfamiliar little town, the screams growing closer and closer and closer and closer still. Until finally, blindsided, she stopped.

"There was Reuben, cowering in a corner, being high-pressure hosed," Diana says. "I didn't even know there was a zoo [in town]. And chimps hate water. I was absolutely flabbergasted. I had walked into this whole thing and I just didn't . . . What kind of maniac would do that?"

She didn't know the circumstances. She likely never would, though she would bottle the memory tight, certain she'd witnessed an atrocity. She came "unglued," Dick says. "She attacked me." Though he'd planned for the influx of visitors, worked with staff and volunteers beforehand to grease the skids, he hadn't predicted this kind of anxiety from Reuben, already so immune to crowds. By that point, he admits, the tin roof of the corncrib "was no longer chimp proof," and as Reuben's anxiety ballooned, he began testing its strength. When Dick spotted him emerging from the crib, he acted fast, already picturing the carnage: a loose chimpanzee in a sea of oblivious parade goers, a Royal disaster. It's true: chimps hate water. Dick grabbed the hose anyway, no time for alternatives. Diana now in his face, Dick tried to talk her down.

"We've got money now for a building," he said, hose still dripping from his hand, Reuben quietly huddled inside the crib. "We're getting a permanent building so he can't do that. But we've got thousands of people here. If he'd got through, somebody would have been injured—probably would have been killed! As it was, he got wet, nobody got injured. Everything's fine."

Like Dick—like millions of Americans—she'd been captivated by Jane Goodall, but Diane had never handled chimps in person. Her knowledge was culled merely from books and television documentaries. Still, Diana felt immediately protective, the scream still ringing in her ears, the hair on her neck standing tall, a cute and completely terrified chimp soaking wet and trembling in the corner. In later years she would soften some, blame the incident less on belligerence than Dick's naivete.

Back in town, the parade would soon commence, the floats slowly crawling past the church and down 5th Street—corn for miles beyond the railroad tracks, a windbreak on the horizon—back on Main, zigzagging up and down, back and forth, east on 3rd, west on 2nd, and finally south on Ponca, past the zoo and its leafy wooden banner above the entrance, the geriatric color guard and the VFW out front, flags hanging limp from their poles, the Orchard High School band marching close behind, trumpets raised, trombones sliding like pistons. Later, the Jensen family would host the buggy show at the ballpark, the Klown Band from Plainview would strike up a tune, the square dancers would do-si-do around the tennis courts, and a projectionist named Elmer would show a free comedy on the side of the old Rundquist grocery— all the staples of small-town Americana, studded with white bread and Jell-O salad.

HERE'S JOHNNY

Though Johnny Carson had asked for his donation to remain anonymous, the news broke immediately after the centennial. The local press covered it. The state press covered it. Even *Time* magazine published a small article detailing Carson's charitable contributions back home in northeast Nebraska.

But for Dick, the donation proved bittersweet. A proper enclosure could now be installed for Reuben, saving his best friend from relocation and paving the way for a female companion too long delayed. But Dick worried little else would change, that months from now, years even, he'd still be living off his parents, living *with* his parents, still be working sunup to sundown, still be too busy and too stressed to meet a woman and start a family. And Carson's donation meant very little in his absence. If Dick left, he worried the zoo would never find a replacement director. They'd be forced to shut down, rendering the donation useless and betraying, as Dick saw it, all the kids who gave their pennies to save Reuben, contributing $2,000 of scrimped donations. After little thought, he trashed his resignation letter. His hands were tied.

"If I leave, I'm letting down Johnny Carson. I'm letting down the people of Royal. I'm letting down those children. I can't leave. There I was. What do I do?" he says. "The support grew and my resentment grew because I felt trapped. I never let on because I didn't want to see the people that had given all that money—I did not want to see them hurt. But that donation was not a benefit for me—it was a benefit for Reuben."

That November, as the wind chilled and the last leaves snapped from the trees overhead, the zoo board dedicated the new "Carson and Northeast Nebraska Kids Exhibit," a twenty-eight-by-forty-foot concrete-and-steel building on the south end of the zoo's two-and-a-half-acre property. Dick had designed the building himself, and he warned the potential contractors up front: "Don't bid Behlen." The Nebraska company manufactures a host of steel products well suited to agricultural work, their sheds and kennels ubiquitous across rural America, but Dick knew their panels wouldn't hold even a half-curious chimpanzee. He ultimately awarded a $62,000 contract to Medallion Construction in Norfolk, but even after his warnings, the contractor was slow to catch on.

"The roof inside the enclosure was tin like this," Dick says, pinching his thumb and forefinger together. "I told them, 'That ain't going to work. He can rip through that.' And he did. We ended up having to cage off the inside because he was ripping up the ceiling. They had no clue the strength these animals possessed. It's hard to explain to people until they actually see for themselves what a chimpanzee can do."

Nevertheless, Reuben would spend Christmas in the new facility. Eighty-five people attended the dedication ceremony, including guest speaker Connie Justis, a representative of the Nebraska Department of Economic Development. She declared herself a "walking billboard" for the zoo and emphasized tourism's standing as the third largest industry in the state, then topping $1.7 billion annually. "I am impressed with the commitment and dedication of you people to develop the zoo," she said. Standing before the new exhibit, Dick described it as "a big step towards future development," and then, as if to distance himself from the whole endeavor, downshifted his tone.

"The zoo can be as big or small as you people make it," he told the crowd. "I am only the director."

For the zoo board, for Royal, for the kids, and for all of northeast Nebraska, the ribbon cutting was an occasion to celebrate, though in truth, the Carson building never was much to look at: a large windowless garage, corrugated steel siding, tan with a dark-brown trim. It was buried on the compound, shaded by trees on the far southern end, several hundred yards off the highway, and if it weren't for the large sign bolted above the door—a close-up portrait of a chimpanzee, mostly eyes and nose—the whole thing could easily have been mistaken for another country outbuilding, a feed shed, maybe, a repair shop. Pragmatic, certainly, but it hardly screamed "state of the art," a far cry from the glitz of an accredited zoo, from artist-commissioned backdrops and ski-lift Skyfaris.

Dick wore a smile, posed for the photographs, shook hands, and scattered thank-yous like birdseed—all of which he was now accustomed to, if not quite comfortable with—but inside he was flailing, genuinely unsure where the hell he was going and what the hell was going on. Though he had transferred control to the board, "I was still the face of that zoo, apparently." He found himself saying things he didn't believe in or agree with to reporters, notions that would have sickened him just a few years before, parroting dreams of growth championed by the board, more acres, more animals, more and more and more, as if he were merely a ghost, disembodied, watching himself talk behind a thin fog of apathy. Any vestige of hope he still carried for conducting primate research simply drifted away. This was no longer a scientific facility, he finally admitted to himself. This was a zoo, now thirty animals strong with a handful of part-time paid staffers—one a veterinary technician, another with a degree in veterinary sciences—and a rotating cast of volunteers. In a whiplash decade of blunder and heartbreak, he may have dropped yet another rung, though of course he had no one to blame but himself, encouraging exactly this kind of growth, both explicitly in the papers and implicitly in his earliest adoption of the Affection Section.

"I just felt hopeless there," he says. "I felt so hopeless."

The winter passed, Reuben gradually warming to his new home in the Carson exhibit. Dick spent the entire first night beside him on the cold concrete floor, trying his best to ease the transition. And just as he predicted, Dick continued to forgo sleep in order to properly care for the animals, to clean and feed and do whatever he could to enrich their captive lives, despite the additional help. That summer, with the opening of the much-celebrated fossil beds nearby and the donation of a new bobcat exhibit from the Lutheran church in O'Neill, attendance at the zoo jumped to unprecedented levels. By the end of the year, Dick estimated nearly twenty-five thousand people would pass through the gates, tripling the previous year's total.

On top of that, the board president and resident "problem solver" suddenly found himself with more time to devote to the zoo's development. In February 1991, following a routine training course at the state lab in Norfolk, Jerry Peterson was speaking with several colleagues at the Department of Roads when he smelled something familiar, something sweet and a bit antiseptic, almost like chloroform. On the table next to them, he found two flasks filled with trichloroethylene, a widely used metal degreaser.

It was not his first exposure. After working long days with the chemical for several weeks in 1981, he reported vision problems, a tingling sensation in his arms and legs, a "weird feeling" in his head. Fearing similar effects, he continued his work but kept a close eye on his symptoms and marked the occasion. At first everything seemed fine, but two days later, on February 23, he told his wife something was wrong. The symptoms returned, the tingling, the light-headedness. Yet, for some reason, he waited nearly two months, until April 19, 1991, to quit his job with the Department of Roads. In May, he consulted with several physicians, two of whom concluded that, as he suspected, his symptoms were the result of exposure to the chemical. One doctor noted a "central pontine lesion," or damage to the central nervous system.

But when Jerry filed for workers' compensation, the judge denied him coverage. At trial, the state submitted its own medical testimony. The Mayo Clinic in Rochester, Minnesota, which Jerry had also consulted with that fall, provided the following summary of Jerry's prognosis:

> Mr. Peterson is a 48-year-old gentleman with a history of two exposures to trichlor-ethelene [*sic*] in 1981 and 1991. He presents now with a neurologic symptom complex. We were unable to find any objective organic disease on this evaluation. Toxicology consultation concluded that Mr. Peterson's history of exposure was not consistent with significant toxic exposure at either time. We were unable to associate Mr. Peterson's current symptom complex to trichlor ethelene [*sic*] exposure and recommended instead further evaluation and treatment of a possible complex somatoform disorder.

The court also questioned why Jerry had waited two months to claim any disability and noted that, just two days prior to filing for workers' comp, the highway department had denied a grievance he had previously filed in regard to a job transfer. In other words, the court questioned Jerry's motives and found no evidence to suggest that his injuries had been work related. In fact, if the Mayo Clinic was right and Jerry did suffer a somatoform disorder, his symptoms may have been phantasmal, the result of a mental illness. Though he had little hope, he appealed the court's decision, "because you have the right to," he said. He lost. And then, at fifty-one, he applied for disability and retired from everything but the Northeast Nebraska Zoo.

And yet, despite the increased attention and what seemed to be a growing legitimacy at the zoo, despite a budding professionalism and serious foot traffic, the Saint Louis Zoo issued a recall for Reuben just

Carson Vaughan

nine months after he'd moved into the new exhibit. The general curator of the Saint Louis Zoo, Roger Birkel, claimed Reuben had been
improperly socialized, that he needed to "learn to be a chimp," and
that after touring the new building, two of his staff members found it
inadequate for the introduction of a second chimpanzee. Dick finds the
latter claim disingenuous; he remembers consulting with Saint Louis
before construction and remembers the two staffers signaling their
approval after inspection.

"The people of northeast Nebraska come here not to see any chimp,
they come here to see Reuben," Dick told the Associated Press. "He's
like family. They know him, they know his personality . . . If they
wanted to pull him before the money was invested, they should have
done that then."

"Without Reuben, it's a worthless building," added board chairman
Tom Colbert, focusing on the bottom dollar. "We could have used the
$55,000 to do other things at the zoo."

The news came without warning. Not once, during all the time
Dick had caged Reuben in the trailer home on the highway or in the
corncrib beside it, had the Saint Louis Zoo expressed any concerns
about their chimpanzee's well-being. And yet, for reasons neither Dick
nor anyone else associated with the Northeast Nebraska Zoo could
fathom, they were now pulling the trigger on his recall just when his
lot had drastically improved. Confused and unsettled, the board called
on Johnny Carson, thinking perhaps his celebrity could help sway the
decision.

"His comment was, 'It doesn't make sense,'" Dick told the AP. "He
didn't know what if anything he could do."

The director of the Saint Louis Zoo, Charlie Hoessle, later wrote
that Reuben's new enclosure "does not contain adequate shifting facilities should separation of individuals be required," an allegation Dick
rejected. The Carson exhibit featured two separate enclosures that could
be used to isolate Reuben and his new mate if necessary.

"I have socialized chimps in the past successfully with a lot less to work with than we have in the Carson building," he said.

Despite the pushback, the Saint Louis Zoo set a September 1 deadline for Reuben's return. Dick and the board drafted a loose "five-tier plan" to keep him in Royal. Step 1: Take it public. Given Reuben's popularity in northeast Nebraska, Dick knew the press would quickly latch on. He was right. Within just a few days of the release, the local papers had covered the recall; the AP and the Saint Louis papers too. And on the heels of the press, the public outcry began. They never made it to step 2.

"When word reached the Royal, Nebraska, community that our Zoo was planning to reclaim Reuben, there was tremendous public outcry," stated a Saint Louis Zoo press release.

In private and over the phone, Hoessle was panicked, Dick claims.

"He calls me, and he says, 'You have got to drop this. Reuben can stay. Our gate attendance is down to nothing.' We could have destroyed that zoo if we'd have gone through all four or five stages," Dick says, likely exaggerating Reuben's effect. "We'd have destroyed the Saint Louis Zoo, and that was not the plan."

Following the uproar, the Saint Louis Zoo did back down, but Dick first agreed to a handful of concessions, later outlined in a Saint Louis Zoo press release: "(1) that he would make immediate remedies and modifications to Reuben's enclosure per the guidelines of Saint Louis Zoo staff; (2) that he would provide a written protocol for the introduction of a companion chimpanzee to provide socialization for Reuben; and (3) that he would apply to join the Chimpanzee Species Survival Plan (SSP) of AZA [Association of Zoos & Aquariums]."

By October, the controversy had passed. The attendance numbers continued their climb, and the board acquired more animals and hosted more fund-raisers and stretched itself thin to keep the Northeast Nebraska Zoo on the map with a handful of part-time employees—an associate director, a curator, a zookeeper, a maintenance man, their various roles often blurred and overlapping—and a budget lucky to reach $50,000. In May 1992, during Johnny Carson's last week as host of *The Tonight Show*, the board voted him an honorary lifetime board member, though he'd still never seen the zoo, which now boasted roughly forty animals and fifteen exhibits, including a newborn two-ounce capuchin monkey. In March 1993, a Royal woman donated four acres adjacent to the original property, and a local family donated funds to purchase one more. In total, the acquisition tripled the size of the zoo and allowed it to expand all the way to the highway, a major boon to its visibility.

Later the same month, the Great Plains Zoo in Sioux Falls, South Dakota, announced plans to raze its cat complex and donate a pair of nine-year-old mountain lions for the new expansion in Royal. Dick told the *Lincoln Journal Star* that plans were underway to acquire a black bear and a grizzly bear, too, in addition to more reptiles and an aviary. They added a pack of gray wolves, on loan from a Canadian couple who once ran the zoo in Grand Island, Nebraska. And in 1994, the board added a rare Przewalski's horse (pronounced "sheh-VAHL-skee"), native to the steppes of Mongolia and the only remaining species of wild horse on the planet. Dick doubted the zoo's ability to provide shelter and socialization for the animal—in truth, he never had been one for horses—but the board pushed ahead and used the horse, one of the first horse species to evolve with a single hoof, as a way to connect the zoo to the Ashfall Fossil Beds, where the remains of ancient three-toed horses had been discovered.

"The Przewalski's horse's attitude is like a zebra. I had no experience with zebras," Dick says. "I didn't think that was going to be good for the horse, or the public, or me."

As the years passed, Dick only bolstered his reputation among the zoo's visitors as a sociable and patient educator, despite all the frustration and fear he'd bottled up inside. Most of the area kids were repeat guests, excited to see what new animals had arrived since their last visit and always eager to greet Reuben, to watch him sign and play with Dick. Kids would recognize Dick at the cafe or the grocery store. They'd point and yell, "There's the monkey man," or "There's Reuben's daddy!"

The new board succeeded in small ways. They helped establish bus tours that ran from Norfolk and Sioux City to Royal and back again, promoting the zoo as just one link in a chain of local attractions. In a one-day package, tourists could visit the zoo, Ashfall Fossil Beds State Historical Park, Grove Lake, and the Game and Parks' Trout Rearing Station a few miles upstream. The board also cemented a reciprocity agreement with the Henry Doorly Zoo in Omaha, which annually drew well over one and a half million visitors and consistently ranked as one of the best zoos in the world. The agreement allowed members of the Northeast Nebraska Zoo free membership to Henry Doorly and vice versa. The vets at Henry Doorly even traveled to Royal on occasion to help administer vaccinations.

And yet, despite all the growth, Dick still failed to secure a companion for Reuben. Six different times he'd identified a possible mate for Reuben, once from the Yerkes National Primate Research Center in Atlanta, he says, which was prepared to send two chimpanzees in the deal. And six different times the transaction fell through at the last minute. "I'd find a companion for Reuben, I'd let the USDA know, and then all at once the facility would back out," he says. None of it made sense to Dick, and though he was hardly prepared to give up Reuben, no one was more aware of Reuben's social isolation than Dick was. It was this very concern that pushed Dick to spend so much time with Reuben in the cage to begin with, trying his best to teach the chimp how to behave like his own species, though of course Dick alone could never quite suffice. In his later years, Dick admits, Reuben "started exhibiting some really weird behaviors I didn't have time to work with him on," constantly smacking his lips and licking the wall.

Still, the area schools kept coming, busloads at a time. And without more help, increased traffic meant more work for Dick, who hadn't seen a paycheck or taken a vacation—not even a weekend—in more than a decade. The volunteers helped when they could, but they were too few and their hours far too irregular. As the 1990s crept forward, Dick lost all sense of purpose, running on little more than Benadryl and copious amounts of Diet Dr Pepper. His family worried he'd grown clinically depressed, and maybe he had, he says. He certainly wasn't optimistic. He was plagued by daily migraines, and his memory seemed to unravel like an old sweater, a little here, a lot there. He rarely ate more than a single can of Campbell's soup in a day. He slept less than three hours a night. Did he lock the cage? Did he feed the bobcats? He wandered the zoo grounds on autopilot, unaware of his surroundings, performing the chores with robotic detachment.

"The crazy kid," says Earleen Jensen, a longtime volunteer. "He used to get up at three thirty in the morning and go down and clean cages and scoop up the yard with a bucket. We offered to get him a golf cart so he could take it to the pile. He said no. So then he started getting up at one thirty, finally twelve thirty. We said, 'Dick, you're not getting any sleep.' Some days he didn't know where he was at."

In 1996, the board finally began to pay him a salary, $4,000 per year, which he would have considered laughable had he not become desensitized to the whole cursed affair. "It was more of a slap in the face than a benefit," he would later say. For nearly a decade already, Dick had maintained the grind: the sleepless nights, the unsound diet, the virtually unpaid and nonstop work. And all that time his dreams of Africa were dormant but never dead. His prospects had grown dimmer and dimmer each year, of course, but he was only thirty-five, and when he allowed himself the luxury of imagining a life beyond the zoo, he still envisioned the rocky shores of Lake Tanganyika, the verdure of Gombe Stream National Park, or Rwanda's Virunga Mountains. He still pictured himself among his beloved apes in the wild, free from his self-imprisonment, from the cage he'd built himself in Royal. But eventually even his fantasies died, too—with an international scandal tethered to a former zoo employee and one of Dick's closest friends.

—ɯ—

In the early 1990s, a Royal man named Joe Pettijohn, tall and angular and unusually adept at handling the notoriously vexing capuchin monkeys, moved to Oregon and joined Harvestfield Ministries, a tiny Pentecostal church just fourteen congregants strong. Harvestfield apostates, some of whom had sold their homes to support the church, later criticized its preacher, Jonathan Wallace, for his autocratic leadership and apocalyptic worldviews. When he wasn't stockpiling food and water and prepping for the world's end, they said, he was obsessively planning for the church's upcoming mission work in Africa, compelling them to donate every penny to the cause. Pettijohn soon married Wallace's daughter, and in 1997, the church relocated to Lubumbashi, then a war-torn city in the southern Congo, ostensibly to dig wells and distribute Bibles.

Zimbabwean authorities saw it differently. In March 1999, while attempting to board a flight back home to Indianapolis, where the church had again relocated, Pettijohn, thirty-five, and two other male congregants were arrested at the Harare airport. Metal detectors caught a handgun in a coat pocket, several more in their luggage. But the real cache was in the parking lot. When authorities inspected their truck, they found a bona fide arsenal hidden away in secret panels: "two semiautomatic assault rifles, 10 disassembled shotguns and sniper rifles, one machine gun, 19 handguns, 70 knives, silencers, telescopic sights, ammunition, camouflage paint and two-way radios," the AP reported. The so-called "missionaries" were arrested on charges of espionage, terrorism, sabotage, and weapons violations.

Prosecutors claimed the men were funneling arms to Congolese rebels. They claimed the ministry had been spying on both the Congolese government and their allied Zimbabwean troops. And though prosecutors had failed to show proof, they initially claimed a diagram of Zimbabwean president Robert Mugabe's office had been found among their items and that the men were plotting to assassinate both Mugabe and the Congolese president, Laurent Kabila—all of it part of a sweeping Western conspiracy, state-run media claimed, to oust African leaders opposed to American influence. And yet American diplomats in Harare offered no defense for Pettijohn and his crew, and though Zimbabwe rejected the offer, the US government even offered to help investigate the matter.

"We're not gun smuggling. We are not terrorists. We are missionaries who had a few guns," Wallace told the AP.

Back home in Royal, Pettijohn's parents called for prayers for their son.

"God can open doors we can't," his mother said.

Dick wrote letters to his senators, his congressmen, to anyone who might be able to help. "I tried everything to get him out," he says. He even called upon his old mentor Robert Hitchcock, who was then directing a transboundary water management workshop for the Southern African Development Community and the US Agency for International Development. Hitchcock communicated with a host of federal departments—including the US Embassy in Harare, the Zimbabwe Prisons and Correctional Services, and the Ministry of Justice, Legal, and Parliamentary Police—but "virtually all of them said the case was heavily political," he says, and warned him against contacting Pettijohn directly. "I also talked to some of the local nongovernment organizations in Harare who said that they were also trying to find out more about the case, but that they had been warned to stay away from it. It was clearly a complex case.

"I tried to handle the matter judiciously . . . knowing that it was unlikely that this was a church activity: churches do not need large numbers of weapons. All I wanted to do was help Dick, and that is what I attempted to do—carefully, I admit."

For lack of sufficient evidence, all but the weapons charges were dropped. But while awaiting their sentence from the Chikurubi Maximum Security Prison, the Harvestfield men—once facing life in prison—claimed they had been tortured, malnourished, and kept naked in solitary confinement. Shocked with electrical devices. Suffocated. Whipped on the feet with leather straps loaded with lead. Physical examinations later implied as much, and the judge, taking this into consideration, sentenced the Americans to just one year in jail, later reduced to eight months after credit for time served and good behavior. Nevertheless, their explanation for the cache—protecting their family, hunting, simple gun enthusiasts—remained "suspicious," the judge said.

"Quite clearly these are not the type of things one normally associates with missionaries, and a satisfactory explanation was not forthcoming as to why these were found in possession of the accused men."

The men finally flew home in November 1999, each one adamant he'd return to Africa again if it were "god's will." But for Dick, who'd somehow piled months of worry for his friend on top of an already untenable routine, the whole ordeal was too much. Something had to give.

"After that happened to Joe—and it was of his own doing—I just lost all desire to go to Africa. I just decided no. It just wasn't worth it, because I went through hell over that, too, trying to get Joe out of there," he says. "How that ever happened that he was released we'll never know. It was a miracle."

After he'd drawn a few meager paychecks, Dick finally left his parents' home in Royal and moved into a creaking two-story farmhouse fifteen minutes north of town. Owned by his uncle, and his father's uncle before him, it stood on the original homestead of Samuel Haskin, his great-great-grandfather. Dick had visited the homestead, bisected by the crystalline waters of the Verdigris, frequently as a kid, fishing the creek and roaming the hills, often with friends in tow. He felt closer to god in those hills than in any church or cathedral on the planet, but he rarely had time for communion. If he made it home at all, it was to catch a few hours of sleep or warm another can of soup on the stove before rushing right back to the zoo.

But every now and then he'd steal away to the grassy banks of the creek, the sun filtering through to its sandy brown bottom, water rushing through the branches of a fallen cedar, emitting the faintest noise of a waterfall, the valley silent and still. Everything felt like a dream. He played the lead, and yet he had no power to sway his movements, to steer his fate. Had he really spent the last fifteen years building a zoo? Was Reuben really still alone? Was he still alone? And what came of Africa? What came of his future? What came of the kids and the family he'd once dreamed of? His work in Lincoln seemed little more than a distant memory. San Diego, Dian Fossey, the foundation, all of it slipping away. The water kept flowing, swirling the weeds beneath, rounding one bend after another until it dipped beyond his vision. *Is this it? Is this everything I have to show?*

Though Dick refused to publicly vilify the zoo, he often delivered his concerns to the board behind closed doors. He wanted out. They knew he wanted out, he says. They just didn't care. He felt they watched him toil away to skin and bone, and yet they never intervened. They never found him extra help or extra pay, never encouraged a vacation or advertised his position. This was his baby, and they knew he would never abandon it.

"I have terrible feelings for the board members that would allow me to work in that condition. That is absurd. That is totally absurd . . . Somebody should've put a stop to that because it was killing me," he says. "But they knew they had me. They knew the responsibility I felt, that I wasn't just going to walk away. And so I was really my own worst enemy there. I don't want to drag them through the mud, but they did laugh at me. They did use me. They did abuse me. That's a fact. I was their slave and they knew it."

"Dick was stubborn," says Preston Olson, who served a short stint as board president in the early 1990s. "He wanted to do everything himself, you know? He didn't have much help. He was over there all the time, and it just burned him out. You can't work constantly without time off. I said, 'Dick, you gotta just take off for a week, you gotta get out of here.' He didn't trust anybody. Why that was I don't know. All the years I was there I don't know if he ever took a straight week off."

The 1990s passed in a haze of fog and feces. By the end, he'd grown to hate the zoo profoundly, a venom previously unknown. He considered the zoo a "monster," begrudged it for stripping him of his best years, for stealing his youth and his health and his chances for a happy future. For spitting out a total stranger in the new millennium. "I look like I'm on drugs," he says, studying a photo of himself from the end of the decade. A man who knew intimately the nuances of hate, but hardly the broad strokes of joy.

"You need to understand the pain it put me through, the torture I went through there. I was not a free man," he says. "I was one of the caged animals there, and I was treated poorly by the board and by the zoo itself. I just went through hell. It was pure torture. It was like I was a prisoner of war. I just wanted away from that."

For two weeks each December, the zoo featured a light display. Area businesses donated Christmas lights, and the staff shaped them into animals, the whole zoo bathed in their glow, all those reds and greens and blues. "It was awesome," Dick says. "I couldn't believe the attendance." But the construction took weeks and the takedown all winter, and like so many of the zoo's events, the overtime fell on his shoulders. The zoo extended its hours to 9:00 p.m. during the run, and Dick still had to bed the animals and shut off the lights and reconcile the register. He was lucky to finish by midnight. His mornings began at 1:30. Halfway through the run, in December 2000, he rushed to his parents' house for a quick shower. When he finished, he pulled on a fresh pair of jeans, but they wouldn't fit. So he grabbed the pair he'd just stepped out of, and they wouldn't fit either. He'd ballooned from a size twenty-eight to a size forty, he claims, in the span of just a few hours.

"That was fluid. I don't go to doctors, but that had to have been a heart attack," he says. "A few months more and they're gonna pull me out of here in a pine box. I decided, *I gotta get out of here. I don't care. I have got to get out.*"

At the next board meeting, he stood and said plainly: "I've got to go, because if I don't, I'm going to die."

PART II

A ROYAL WELCOME

When forty-three-year-old Dale Bakken, bearded and blunt, accepted the directorship of the Heritage Zoo in Grand Island, Nebraska, edging out fourteen other applicants in March 1995, neither he nor his wife, Sandra, had ever heard of the Northeast Nebraska Zoo two hours north. They'd never heard of Reuben the chimpanzee, and they'd never heard of Royal. Originally from Strasbourg, Saskatchewan, then a town of just six hundred people, Dale had grown up on a farm and previously worked with helicopters as an aircraft maintenance engineer before pivoting to work with animals. He spent around fifteen years working at the Calgary Zoo, serving on the First Responder Task Force, and another four establishing a reptile exhibit in British Columbia. Beyond the job itself, he and his wife—who spent much of her free time back home photographing wildlife at the Algonquin Provincial Park—were drawn to Nebraska, he told the *Grand Island Independent*, by "the openness, the nature and the proximity to the Platte River."

But the Heritage Zoo and the Northeast Nebraska Zoo shared a reciprocity agreement, and thus not long into their tenure, the Bakkens acquired a rough understanding of the Royal attraction. "Royal was considered a bit of a laughingstock in the zoo industry," Dale says, "this guy up there with a chimp and really nothing else." Nevertheless, Dick and the Bakkens developed a limited correspondence, and they met once in person, when Dale and Sandra took a weekend drive to see Reuben. "My impression the very first time was that it seemed kind of like a little roadside menagerie, a zoo with no money," he says. The admissions booth was still in a donated trailer home with cinder-block steps, reinforced corncribs still housed many of the animals, and given the context, the Carson exhibit stood out like a sore thumb—the only formal building on the property. But they liked Dick well enough: scrawny and prematurely bald, talkative and enthusiastic about the animals in his care. Their correspondence continued. Dale loaned Dick a bobcat. Dick loaned Dale a snow monkey. Over the years, Dale began to feel like he knew Dick "reasonably well," and Dick felt the same.

In Grand Island, Dale quietly worked on a new master plan for the Heritage Zoo, which had long been struggling itself, while Sandra, whose bright cheeks and sharp eyebrows italicized her own fiery passions, cared for a small pack of gray wolves, an animal she'd been fascinated by and would later write about in a short book titled *Alone Within the Pack*. And yet, under the impression their work visas only permitted them a three-year stint in the United States, Dale resigned from the Heritage Zoo in May 1998, accepting a position at the Ardastra Gardens, Zoo & Conservation Centre on the island of Nassau in the Bahamas instead. Less than a year later, his replacement in Grand Island drew the city's attention to the zoo's crumbling infrastructure and shaky financial standing, and Sandra, who still owned the wolves on display, began scouting new locations to exhibit the pack. They'd considered other facilities across the state, one in Arizona, too, but "Dick seemed good enough, and the area seemed good, so we just felt Royal was closer to us and easier for us to visit," Sandra says. The Bakkens offered to fund the exhibit, and six months later, Dale flew back to Royal to help build it himself.

"They seemed like nice people," Dick says. "Seemed easy to work with, easy to deal with. In designing and building the wolf exhibit, we'd have differences of opinion, but we were able to talk through it and find a better solution."

Barely a year later, they received an anxious and unexpected call from Dick.

"He wanted out of the zoo business," Dale says. "He wanted me to take over the zoo."

Willing to humor the idea, Dale flew back to Nebraska once again. He met with Dick and the board of directors. He took special note of the facilities, which he viewed as "extremely basic." And he looked over their financial statements, which portrayed a zoo fighting tooth and nail to break even. In 1998, for example, the previous fiscal year, net income totaled just $362, and Dick, their highest-paid employee, made just over $3,500. Nevertheless, Dick insists that Dale combed through the numbers and declared, "There's nothing here that scares me." Perhaps more troubling was Dick himself, who'd gained weight and seemed especially disheveled, drinking alarming amounts of Diet Dr Pepper—"that's probably all he lived on"—and openly admitting he'd burned himself out.

When Dale flew back to Nassau, the blue-green waters mottled by the coral reef below, the sailboats and catamarans bobbing beside the docks, he and Sandra considered the offer, sorry to admit Royal couldn't afford them. They initially passed on the offer, opting instead to leave the Bahamas after less than two years for another gig at the seventy-five-acre Brevard Zoo in Melbourne, Florida, whose brochures emphasized kayak tours and gentle giraffes. But after a brief stint in the Sunshine State, they reconsidered the offer in Royal.

"When we were leaving Florida, we could have moved back to Canada, but there are a lot fewer zoos there. Or we could try our hand at taking the reins of the Royal zoo," Dale says. "Because we'd already moved the wolves there, and we thought more could have been done in Royal, we decided to take on that challenge."

The Bakkens arrived at the Northeast Nebraska Zoo in June 2001, hired by the board of directors for a rumored $45,000 salary, though the terms of the contract remain vague. Dick claims he was never directly part of the negotiation, but that the zoo's financial standing was stronger than it ever had been. The Bakkens refuse to discuss it. Ultimately, it was perhaps wishful thinking all around: Dick anxious to leave, Dale and Sandra itching to get started. The board also provided the Bakkens free housing next to the zoo, a fact Sandra laughs hysterically about today.

"I find that so funny. I'm sorry," she says, catching her breath. "It was very tiny, about eight hundred square feet. The living room was orange colored. The kitchen was red. The bedrooms were bright green. The board bought it for seven thousand dollars. We'd been looking for something else—there was a house outside of town, a small acreage—just so we had more privacy and could get away from the zoo. We never got that far."

The Bakkens expected a challenge, but they quickly realized it would be more than they had prepared for. The zoo housed roughly thirty animals, cared for by Dick, two underpaid staff members—whom they immediately laid off due to budgetary constraints—and whichever board members whimsically decided to volunteer their labor. The entire working budget stood at just under $8,000, and within the next few months, "I realized that pretty much every conversation I had with Dick prior to that wasn't really the truth," Dale says. The Northeast Nebraska Zoo owed thousands of dollars in federal withholding tax. Overdue bills had been piling up for months. And in order to comply with previous USDA inspection requirements, thousands more would need to be spent on maintenance and repairs, including a new eight-foot-tall perimeter fence for the entire seven-acre property. They were especially vexed by Dick's apparent refusal to buy padlocks, opting instead to simply tie the gates shut with baling wire.

"I could probably count the number of padlocks in the place on one hand," Dale says. "I mean it was ridiculous that animals didn't escape or there weren't people breaking in or whatever."

By the fall, the zoo was basically "running on my savings account," Dale says. That November, after he delivered a short diatribe on the zoo's financial peril, highlighting the personal funds he and Sandra had already flushed into nursing the zoo back to a tolerable standard, the board literally passed a hat around the room, soliciting change among their own ranks to pay them back. Dale watched as they slowly filled the hat with a ten here, a twenty there, as if this pitiful collection of alms could put a dent in what they'd already sacrificed. He watched the hat pass from one board member to the next, took stock of his surroundings there in the old Church of Christ, the whining wood floors and the stenciled paw prints scurrying up and down the walls, the cedar trees outside the window, the tin shell of the admissions building, and the silver bullet of propane in between—he took stock of it all and wondered: *What the hell did we get into?*

Just six months after they'd arrived, after a chance run-in with Dick on the road outside the zoo, Sandra raced home to write him a letter, hands strangling the wheel, his easygoing manner now more than she could bear. Though she loved the animals in her care, she struggled to remain optimistic. Try as she might, she couldn't help taking it personally.

"Perhaps because you have been away from the zoo for several months the difficulties of operating this zoo have become faint in your mind. Well, let me remind you of the reality."

She excoriated Dick for "distorting the financial situation in order to coax us here." She claimed Dick had intentionally buried a slew of costly unpaid bills, that he had neglected to face the zoo's fiscal reality himself, that he continued paying employees long after it became obvious the zoo couldn't afford them. And even if the zoo could afford them, she claimed, they seemed to accomplish next to nothing on the job.

Rather than work, it seemed Dick and his staff preferred "sitting around having coffee and chatting in the office." The gate revenue was pitiful, something he neglected to fully iterate, she said, and he'd offered loans to others while taking out loans himself. He failed to replace the furnace in the Carson exhibit while continuing to pay a hefty annual premium to insure the old church for $89,000. And Reuben? Though aggravating, his solitary housing wasn't a surprise. But she claimed Dick had ignored years of USDA citations, a stockpile of warnings that should have compelled him to make improvements to the enclosure.

"Because of your incompetence with the finances there is no money to pay Dale, so we are both working for free. All of these issues are serious ones, and not ones that we would have taken lightly if aware of them prior to our move," she wrote. "You knew we would have turned down the offer to come here if the truth be [*sic*] known about the condition of the zoo, cages, USDA warnings, the lack of operating money . . . to name but a few, that we are now left to pay and deal with."

In a future director's memo, Dale would detail the extent of the debts they inherited: $12,500 in loans; $2,500 in IRS interest, withholding taxes, and workers' compensation adjustments; and more than $21,000 in mandatory USDA repairs.

"We thought you were our friend, but friends don't do this to each other. You lied, deceived and tricked us into coming to this terribly bad situation. So, to sum it up, Dick, we do not want you coming up to us and casually asking how things are going, because you know how they are going!"

As far as Dick was concerned, the letter was "unnecessary."

"When I got out of that stupid zoo, I was sick, I was beyond exhausted, and I really didn't much care if I lived or died," he says. "Then to get that letter? My feeling was, *How much more of this crap can I take?* I had given my whole life for that zoo. I had given my future for that zoo, and this was the thanks I got? If they were having problems, all they would have had to do was ask for my help. Even as bad as my health was at that time, I would have done everything in my power to help them."

The pressure didn't end with the Bakkens. Board president Leroy Hollmann, who had quickly aligned himself with Dale and Sandra, established a formal visitation policy specifically for Dick, limiting his access to that of any other zoo visitor, as if he hadn't spent nearly every waking hour of the last decade and a half inside the gates. "This means no behind the scenes tours, no access to any back areas, diet kitchen, or behind public barrier fences, including no access to any office equipment, files, or documentation," he wrote. After learning about all the unpaid bills, the inadequate record keeping, the apparent dismissal of USDA warnings, Hollman called Dick a "liar," something he later apologized for by offering a second backhanded put-down. "I now believe you just didn't know the adequate business practices needed for the operation of a zoo," he wrote in a letter to Dick in February 2002. "As a board member, I now blame myself for not demanding answers sooner!" But the crux of Hollman's note was to rebuff what he saw as Dick's negativity toward the new management.

"Even though Royal has always had the Hatfields and McCoys feeling to it, all this bickering could stop," he wrote, referring to Royal's litigious reputation. "Right now, it seems the immediate locale of the zoo . . . has a lot of people struggling with your leaving. This was to be expected as these are friends and neighbors and you left big shoes to fill. You and the Bakkens are very different. You are very loud spoken while Dale is very soft spoken. Direct opposites . . . Dick, you didn't want to be a legend to the locals, but you are. Don't destroy what you spent so much of your life doing by running down those who have taken over from where you left off."

After shoring up the immediate concerns of the facility, the Bakkens' first order of business was to remedy Reuben's environment. More than a decade had passed since the premiere of the Carson and Northeast Nebraska Kids Exhibit, and the Bakkens now viewed the building as substandard, a far cry from the environmental enrichment Dick so often espoused. More devastating still, Reuben had lived alone since his arrival in 1986, despite so many warnings against it, and the public seemed either ignorant of or apathetic to the consequences. The Bakkens say the star of Antelope County compulsively tore out his own hair; that his thighs and forearms were nearly bald; and that he acted depressed, frustrated, even psychotic. They soon came to see Reuben as Dick's longtime prisoner, isolated and gravely bored, trapped in Royal to "satisfy the ego of one man," Sandra wrote in *Reuben: The Savage Prisoner*, the memoir of her Royal years, "and that man's urge to have his very own ape bringing notoriety to his life."

"Here's a superintelligent animal living in solitary confinement with very little to play with and very little enrichment items. Reuben took out a lot of frustration by banging on the bars and throwing things at you or spitting at you," Dale says. "He was really a very frustrated chimp, and he expressed it daily."

Dick first expressed his desire to find a female companion for Reuben as early as 1990, and in fact had agreed to adopt a companion under the terms stipulated by the Saint Louis Zoo after the recall threat in 1991. But a companion never arrived. In 1993, the Saint Louis Zoo again pressed Dick to adhere to its plan for socializing Reuben, and again—whether or not he attempted to locate a companion—he failed to follow through. Reuben continued to live alone in the Carson exhibit, his only company that of another species entirely, most of them only passing through and waving from the other side. He often threw dirt through the bars, and at least one visitor claims Reuben habitually pleasured himself in her presence. Perhaps Dick couldn't afford to house another chimpanzee. Perhaps, suffocating under the weight of his other responsibilities, Dick simply lost track of his priorities. Or perhaps, as Dale suggests, Dick "just wanted Reuben to himself."

"That could have been something too," he says. "They had that interaction, the sign language thing, and maybe he didn't want to mess it up with another chimp. When a person sees an animal every day for fourteen years, you know, maybe he doesn't notice this animal is going slightly crazy or losing its hair. Certainly, in his own way, he was close—extremely close. I can see where they went through a lot together and why he'd be dedicated to him. Certainly he sacrificed a lot to keep that animal in his charge. I don't know sometimes what went on in the mind of Dick Haskin."

Whatever Dick's hurdles, the Bakkens managed to secure a second chimpanzee within just six months. After scattering phone calls across the country, Sandra located Jimmy Joe, an eighteen-year-old chimpanzee, in Liberal, Kansas. Like so many captive chimps, Jimmy Joe had been shuffled around like a military brat. He spent his early years in Southern California, living with an eccentric woman who often ushered Jimmy Joe into her convertible and cruised the freeway, Sandra says. He was later transferred and then transferred again, until he finally landed at El Rancho Exotica in Liberal, Kansas, where the owner, Janell Knudsen, hoped he would breed with their lone female, though apparently the two shared little chemistry. When Sandra called several years later, Knudsen saw little point in keeping Jimmy Joe around, and, though she likely could have sold him for at least several grand, Sandra suspects the desperation in her voice tipped Knudsen to offer a deal: she could take him for free.

"The zoological board was ecstatic with the news of getting another chimpanzee," she writes. "They couldn't praise us enough with what they believed was an impossible feat—since Dick had failed time and time again for fourteen years."

To comply with USDA standards and modify the Carson exhibit for a second chimpanzee, the Bakkens reached back out to the zoo's largest benefactor, Johnny Carson, in November 2001. They asked for $9,500, said they'd finally found Reuben a friend but needed extra funding to keep him in the exhibit that bore the entertainer's name. The day after Thanksgiving, they received a handwritten letter from

Carson, accompanied by a check for $20,000—more than doubling what they'd asked for. They stood outside Royal's tiny post office, hoods up, trembling against a frigid winter wind.

"Dear Dale," the letter began. "Enclosed is a contribution to assist in the renovation to house Reuben and his new companion. When it's completed, please send me a photo of the happy couple. Johnny Carson."

According to Sandra's book, *Reuben: A Savage Prisoner*, not long after, Dale drove eight hours south to Liberal, Kansas; waited for El Rancho Exotica to clumsily load Jimmy Joe into his shipping crate; and drove home with an adult male chimpanzee in the back of his rickety old van—tried to, anyway. Halfway home, the alternator died. Dale didn't own a cell phone. They spent hours on the side of the road, waiting for help to arrive. By the time the tow truck delivered them back to Royal, it was nearly 3:30 a.m., and Dale had spent the entire ride spotlighting himself with a flashlight in the back window to keep Jimmy Joe from panicking in the now-empty van. In the pale glow of the porch light, Sandra could only make out Jimmy Joe's broad outline, but even then, she joked, he looked more gorilla than chimpanzee, much bulkier than Reuben, hair thicker and black. After everything Dale had done to keep Jimmy Joe comfortable on the ride home, she knew he wasn't about to leave him alone in the truck until daybreak. She brought out the pillows and a space heater.

"I shut the van door behind him, and peered through the window. What my eyes saw will stay with me for life," she writes. "Jimmy's right cheek was pressed against the bars closest to Dale, and Dale took hold of Jimmy's hand while the night curled up around them."

But their efforts to socialize Reuben didn't end with Jimmy Joe, whom Sandra soon considered a "sweetie" and "a true gentle giant," despite his husky presentation. The following winter, on the day before Christmas, Johnny Carson donated an additional $15,000. The funding allowed them to nearly triple the exterior space of the chimp exhibit and dedicate the full interior, once shared with the capuchin monkeys, solely to the chimps. In September 2003, they adopted two more—brothers Tyler and Ripley—from an animal trainer in California named Bob Dunn, once the entertainment industry's main supplier of great apes and "a legend in the Hollywood animal world," according to the *Los Angeles Times*. Tyler starred in the 2001 family drama *Race to Space* alongside actor James Woods. And Ripley accompanied Jim Carrey in *Ace Ventura* (1994) and Arnold Schwarzenegger and Danny DeVito in *Junior* (1994). He appeared in an episode of *Seinfeld*, too, playing Kramer's antagonist and spitting in his face from behind the bars of his cage. But most entertainment chimps have a "shelf life" of six to eight years, according to the Center for Great Apes. Once they mature, they become too dangerous to work with.

"The sad fact is that for decades these famous simian actors who made us laugh have ended up as experimental subjects in biomedical research," states their website. "Or in deplorable and shabby roadside zoos . . . or in tiny backyard cages . . . or in breeder compounds where their own babies were pulled from them to repeat the whole process of working young apes for entertainment."

By the time Dale and Sandra came to Royal, computer animation had begun to supplant live animals in film. Reacting to the trend, Bob Dunn wanted to scale back, Dale says, and after Tyler and Ripley hit the end of their own shelf lives, the Northeast Nebraska Zoo came calling. The Bakkens drove a rented van to California, picked them up, and turned around. Two washed-up film stars headed for a disappearing railroad town in rural Nebraska. But for Reuben, the additional company was good news.

"Reuben now has a healthier, more normal attitude, a little less insane," Dale wrote in a 2003 director's memo. "He has been forced to be an observer of mentally and socially healthy chimps. Watching them interact without his direct interference has made a huge change of late in his own well-being."

Like it had for Dick, the zoo nearly suffocated the Bakkens. They lived just across the street, within feet of the animals, worked years without a vacation or a day off. In the spring of 2002, Jimmy Joe—merely playing—reached a hand through his enclosure and snapped Sandra's ankle "like a twig," she writes. She wore a bright-pink cast for ten weeks, hobbled around on crutches after that. Not long before, Orion, the male tiger, had sunk his teeth into Dale's hand, anxious to be fed. Bacteria in the tiger's saliva caused blood poisoning, which kept Dale bedridden at the Creighton hospital for a week. The Bakkens literally shed blood, sweat, and tears in Royal.

But it wasn't the animals they blamed. It was Dick, who'd saddled them with debt from the start. It was Jerry Peterson, the former zoo board president, who often stopped by the zoo for no apparent reason beyond singing Dick's praises, once urging Dale to commission a bronze statue of Dick and Reuben for the zoo's entrance—a level of praise even Dick finds peculiar, given their limited interactions. And it was the board, who never tired of contrasting Dick's management style with their own. After explaining all the work they'd put into monitoring Reuben's recent respiratory infection, all the pains they'd taken to administer his medication, Sandra expected praise—at the very least, a thank-you. Instead, board member Carol Schmidt asked why she hadn't called Dick.

"People in the area delighted in reminding us, and reminding us often, Reuben was like a son to Dick," Sandra writes. "After a while I grew tired of hearing it and wanted them to choke on those words, chiefly since Dick hadn't bothered to visit Reuben. Her remarks reconfirmed some locals would never welcome our being there, and we'd forever be under scrutiny with how we ran so-called Dick's Zoo."

Perhaps the only person in northeast Nebraska who loathed Dick as much as they did was fifty-year-old Diana Wavrunek, who never forgot the day they met at the Royal centennial, a garden hose dripping from his hand, Reuben wet and trembling in his corncrib. She'd thought about the zoo frequently in the weeks and months that followed, but it wasn't until eleven years later, in 2002, that Diana noticed an article on the front page of the *Norfolk Daily News* about the zoo's new Bengal tigers. She was in between jobs at the time, and the article extended a call for volunteers.

After introducing herself, Diana immediately began criticizing the way Dick had run the zoo, Sandra writes, adamant that he had long neglected the animals in his care. Rarely had they run across a local who seemed to prioritize animal welfare above their own, and there was no denying they could use the help. Though she lived twenty miles north in Verdigre, the Bakkens hired her on for seasonal, part-time pay as what they called a "relief keeper." But almost as soon as she started, she fumbled, Sandra recalls. Inexplicably, the ten-year-old cougar, Dakota, had escaped during her shift. Dale and Sandra quickly caught him and returned him to his cage, but it was more than enough to sour her involvement. Diana had expressed concerns about working that end of the zoo with such little experience, she says, but Dale had quickly dismissed her. Still, she downplays the incident: the cougar was declawed and defanged, she says, and had been raised from birth as a pet. Regardless, Dale promptly demoted her to the petting animals: no more cougars and certainly no chimpanzees. Later, her hours were cut altogether.

"Rarely in my long years have I come across two more bitter, petty, vindictive people than Dale and Sandra," Diana says.

By December 2003, there was no hiding the Bakkens' resentment. They wore it like a scarlet letter. After incurring a fine from the USDA for just over $1,500, Dale wrote in his director's memo that "we should have instead received a letter of appreciation from them for turning a garbage dump into a zoo in less than two years."

Despite their frustrations, their work didn't go wholly unrewarded. The membership numbers were climbing. Their gate attendance had improved. They paid off the back taxes and loans they'd unknowingly inherited upon arrival, and they happily took credit for achieving the first year of surplus in the zoo's history. And they doubled the number of animals on display, from thirty to sixty, including the addition of two Bengal tigers, several foxes, and an African serval cat, in addition to Reuben's new playmates. "The zoo entered its golden days," says Leroy Hollmann, who served a roughly five-year term as board president starting in the late 1990s, bridging the transition from Dick to the Bakkens. The *Norfolk Daily News* even printed an editorial praising the zoo's progress at a time when other Nebraska zoos were struggling. The Heritage Zoo had just closed down, and the Riverside Zoo in Scottsbluff was scouting a new director for the third time that year.

"Local and area residents should appreciate more than ever the presence of a thriving zoo in this corner of the state," the editorial stated. "Zoo Nebraska is laying the groundwork to become a true regional facility. Royal may not be a very big community, but it's home to an impressive zoo."

If Dick ran the zoo with tunnel vision—and he did, often losing himself in the process—the Bakkens managed with a wide-angle lens, always strategizing new PR campaigns, new business models, new opportunities. They acted, whereas Dick reacted. They planned ahead. They immediately overhauled the zoo's marketing plan, which was basically nonexistent prior to their arrival. To start, they again changed the name of the zoo, this time to the sleeker Zoo Nebraska, which they hoped would erase the perception that it was a regional attraction. They designed new brochures, and they bought a professional-quality sign for the chimp exhibit, which they now called simply the Carson Center for Chimps, dropping reference to the kids whom Dick had so often praised for their efforts to keep Reuben in town. They installed signs on the highway and bought new radio and newspaper ads. They initiated bulk- and direct-mail campaigns. But most importantly, they advertised their memberships online.

Under Dick's directorship, the Northeast Nebraska Zoo had established reciprocity agreements with a number of zoos across the country, including the crown jewel, Omaha's Henry Doorly Zoo. An annual membership to the Northeast Nebraska Zoo granted the cardholder free admission to the Henry Doorly Zoo, and vice versa. It had always been a lopsided perk; memberships in Royal were significantly cheaper than those in Omaha, but director Lee Simmons had long supported the idea of small zoos. When the Bakkens began marketing this perk online, Zoo Nebraska memberships doubled from 2,000 to nearly 4,500, and attendance spiked to nearly 17,500 visitors in 2004.

But what initially proved to be a huge boon to Zoo Nebraska proved the opposite for Henry Doorly, which saw its own numbers decrease in inverse correlation. Citing the same stats Zoo Nebraska had celebrated, Henry Doorly accused Royal of poaching thousands of would-be customers. In 2002, just prior to Zoo Nebraska's online campaign, the Henry Doorly Zoo granted free admission to 1,799 Zoo Nebraska members; in contrast, one year after Zoo Nebraska went online, that number skyrocketed to more than 20,000, according to the *Omaha World-Herald*, an increase of 1,031 percent. Furthermore, 54 percent of Zoo Nebraska members had addresses in the Omaha area. In October 2004, Henry Doorly canceled its reciprocity agreement with Zoo Nebraska, claiming they'd lost thousands of dollars to online "value shopping."

In a letter sent to Zoo Nebraska members in November 2004, director Lee Simmons wrote: "It was evident that cleverness and greed had gotten the best of Royal's management and they had simply figured out how to use the internet to skirt both the legal aspects and the long established spirit of zoo reciprocities."

"I'm sorry to see it come to this, but there seems to be no other choice," he told the *Omaha World-Herald*. "It's not fair that someone who lives right next door to one of our customers, who's clever enough to get on the internet, gets a membership at half price."

Dale couldn't argue with the numbers, but he felt slighted by Simmons for canceling the agreement without warning. And try as he might, it was difficult not to feel victimized, the David to his Goliath.

"Our entire zoo budget was probably less than Lee Simmons's salary as director," Dale says.

That's almost certainly true. In 2003, the Bakkens reported an operating budget of roughly $120,000, a significant increase from what they started with, but a drop in the bucket for the state's biggest tourist attraction. Looking back, Dale sees the breakup with Henry Doorly as "one of the pins that was set up for the downfall of the zoo."

The other, he is quick to point out, was the Jensens.

THE POOR FARM

When the locals shake their heads and roll their eyes, they mean a small white coon dog bays from the hood of a disemboweled school bus. They mean a decades-old refrigerator stands beside it, rusty and sunbaked, brittle like an old tin can. When they ask, *Hell, have you seen their place?* they mean it looks like a salvage yard. They mean it looks like the setting of a slasher film, chains and gates and tree branches tickling sheet metal. Locusts in the bromegrass, spiders in the eaves. Empty corncribs, like the one Reuben used to know. They mean a plastic lawn chair peeks out beneath a rain-specked washbasin, a coil of barbwire rests on a spare tire, twisted handlebars sprout like dandelions from the dirt.

"The hell with them," Marlowe says. "It's ours. We'll do what we want."

The Jensens live in this place, about two miles northwest of Royal. Marlowe and Earleen and sometimes—when his diabetes takes control—their son, Justin, too. They call it *the poor farm*, always have. In town, they call it something else. An eyesore, a blight. Sometimes simply an *oh god*, if they can manage words at all. A narrow dirt lane cuts through the wreckage. An old two-door garage with a tacked metal roof sits on the west side, its white paint stripped and bruised and fading away. Above the doors, a wooden sign announces JENSEN WHEEL SHOP and lists a half-legible telephone number.

The house itself lies opposite the garage, same color, small, squat, shaded by a row of elm trees. An electric cable sags from the peak of the roof. A blue sheet hangs limp from a steel pole outside. If there ever was a lawn, it is gone now, massacred by a jubilee of weeds and vines and thistle and crabgrass. A tall mesh fence guards the front of the house like a prison yard. Were it not for the dog and a relatively new tin roof, the whole property—painted in dust and half-hidden by withering shelter-belts—would seem deserted altogether.

"It's the biggest damn junk pile you ever seen," Marlowe boasts. "You ought to drive by, just educational."

Perhaps, if the disarray stopped there, the Jensens might have curbed their reputation at merely *eccentric*, as they're often called in politer circles. But the junk does not stop there. According to Marlowe, they own more than twenty buildings in town, not counting the caboose and boxcar they bought from the railroad and later marooned in an empty lot just off the highway. And according to most of Royal, all twenty are chock-full of shit, have been for decades, buckling under the weight of a pack-rat ideology they defend as a constitutional right; the right to keep and bear junk—the right to hoard. Of those twenty buildings, only one is inhabited, and, until recently, most would have guessed otherwise. Justin lives in it, and before his third and last wife flew in from the Philippines, dirty plastic sheets obscured the windows and piles of old paperwork and VHS tapes jammed the doorways. When she set about civilizing the place, she found entire rooms filled with clutter, locked away and quarantined.

At one point, the Jensens bought the childhood home of Jeri Southern, a once-famous jazz singer who grew up in Royal. They founded the Jeri Southern Home & Museum Society, Inc., with the express intent to "restore the former home of entertainer Jeri Southern into a public museum," according to the articles of incorporation. They founded the society over a decade ago. Today, the doors droop from their hinges, the shingles peel like pencil shavings, and two train cars sit in the backyard like forgotten toys. There is no museum. There is no historical marker. "It's a laughingstock for us, I guess," says Marvin Young, the last zoo board president. The Jensens suspect the old school building sold for a buck just to safeguard it from their influence.

"The people just don't want everything to turn to crap," Marvin says.

In the last fifty years, the Jensens have built—without qualification—the most inflammatory reputation in town, a reputation so deeply provocative most people think twice before getting started, afraid they'll say too much. Bridge clubs countywide whisper their names at the card table. People who have never met them dismiss them outright. The junk, their supposed legal choreography, their general unwillingness, as many people see it, to leave well enough alone—it's been more than enough to ostracize them from the community. Warranted or not, they've developed a brand name.

"We bought up land when it was cheap, and now they think we ought to sell it cheap. And that burns them up," Marlowe says, adding that what's inside is "none of their damn business."

Marlowe had always considered himself a real tough son of a bitch. As a kid, he carried himself like a bull, loose cheeks and bold black glasses, shoulders thick like slabs of beef. He played center for Royal's six-man football team. He rodeoed. He boxed. In high school, his father bought him a Harley, and he and his friends tore through Royal like knockoff Brandos.

"All through high school, even grade school, I'd get into them [fights]. If they picked on somebody, I'd be right in there," he says. "This old Bill Grubbs, he was celebrating his twenty-first birthday over at Winnetoon one night. And there was two boys over there, Phil and Vern—the McManigal brothers—and they thought they was just tougher than hell. And I was dancing, and all at once I noticed ole Phil and Vern, they had ole Bill over by the door, and they was working on him. I just excused myself from the dance, and I went over and I grabbed ole Vern by the shoulder, and I stuck my thumb clear into him as far as I could, and I said let's go outside, this is bullshit."

He signed up for the army reserves when he was twenty-one years old. He wasn't making a statement. It was simply his duty. He drove to O'Neill to enlist, requested active duty in 1957, and told the recruitment officer, "I want to do it now and get it over with."

If he passed his basic training in Omaha, the officer told him, he'd serve immediately. And because he was a farmer, he'd be eligible for a seasonal occupation release, cutting him loose after twenty-one months. Of course, full of life as Marlowe was, barrel chested and built like an ox, he passed basic training without a hitch, and several weeks later, they shipped him off to Butzbach, Germany, to an American army base just north of Frankfurt. After three months of running medical supplies, they placed him on emergency standby and charged him with helming the ambulance. Some days the fog drew so thick around Frankfurt, Marlowe says, he had to drive with the door wide open just to keep from plunging off the autobahn.

"I worked in the ER. I helped with deliveries. I've started tracheostomies, I've done suturing . . . I mean, oh god. I went through the whole ball of wax."

But he considers himself lucky. He never soldiered, never fired a weapon; hell, he says, he never witnessed a barrack inspection. He wore whites, and he took three months leave to explore Europe with a fellow soldier, a Mormon missionary named Jay Longhurst.

"Back in Barcelona they called me the Banty Rooster," Marlowe says. "I had maroon boots with beige tops on them, short-sleeved shirts with the sleeves rolled up. Jay and I cut quite a path down there in Barcelona. They probably remember us yet."

After twenty-one months abroad, he flew home on his seasonal occupation release, just like the recruitment officer had promised, but machismo didn't feel like it used to. Cockeyed and footloose, he cozied up to the bottle, cut off his sleeves, grabbed Antelope County by the shoulder, and squeezed so tight he just knew it'd squeal. But it never did; in fact, it ignored him almost entirely, and when another lost soul was foolish enough to accept the challenge, Marlowe didn't always land on top anymore.

"I fought a guy over there at Ewing two times one night. Boy, I got my nose broken, everything else. Next week I went up to ole Hoot Gibson, I said I was pretty drunk the other night. I said I think I could make a better showing of myself tonight. He said, 'Marlowe, let's just call it a draw. I couldn't hardly take a breath all week.' He said, 'I thought you broke my ribs.'"

When the dust settled, he packed up his braggadocio like a failed salesman and drove back to the family farm, the one place that hadn't moved on without him. Years later, people would tell him he high centered on the precipice, that the slightest wind could have tipped him either way. Luckily for Marlowe, he met a young schoolteacher named Earleen Schrunk, his bride-to-be.

"When you settle down," Marlowe says, "you want to change your ways and start tending to business that way."

When Earleen was a kid, she used to watch her father on the ranch, mounting his horse and sniffing the wind each morning, she says, "just soaking up the day," before checking the cattle. A stern and quiet man, he owned 3,600 acres, "on paper, a millionaire," she says. He smoked cigarettes like a freight train, a trail of smoke always loitering behind him. He had raised his family Catholic, but during mass one Sunday, a cornhusk shook loose from her brother's pant leg, and when the priest admonished him for his slovenly appearance, her father denounced the church at once, making a clean break and taking his family with him.

"My dad said if the priest can't accept where his wages are coming from then that's it. We quit."

One night several years later, as Earleen lay in bed, a searing pain shot through her ears as if she'd been hooked up to an electric current and jump-started in her sleep. She woke up screaming, clutching her head in her hands, praying for the pain to go away. The next morning her parents rushed her to the audiologist, who delivered a grim prognosis: by her midtwenties, he said, she'd be totally deaf in both ears. Some sort of degenerative disorder, though she can't remember the exact terminology.

Had they still been Catholic, Earleen trusts that would have been the end of the story, the beginning of a long and gradual descent into silence. But they were converts to the Reorganized Church of Jesus Christ of Latter Day Saints—"not the Utah Mormons," she clarifies—and the RLDS church believes in the sacrament of the "laying on of hands." According to the official RLDS website, the sacrament "opens the door to the gift of healing." So the Schrunks drove to the church—her parents, her seven siblings, her extended family, too—their medical resources exhausted but never their faith.

The elders gathered, the ministers, and they gently placed their hands on her head and shoulders. One of them smeared the blessed olive oil across her forehead while the others prayed for Earleen's health, for the degenerative disorder to simply fade away, like breath on a mirror. Earleen prayed, too, knowing her own faith was most important. When the ceremony was over, the organ began to play, and Earleen stepped down from the altar. She returned to her family in the pews, stood between her father and her aunt while the song continued. And then, just like the first time, a blazing pain shot through one ear and came out the other, so fast and so severe, she says, "I thought it hit my aunt."

"And that was it. So when people make fun of my church, I say, *Well, I'm sorry, but I'm supposed to be deaf to this day, and I'm not.* It's a testimony to me that something happened somewhere along the way."

—◊—

Three months after they first met in 1962, Marlowe and Earleen tied the knot. Nobody thought it would last. They knew Marlowe, his boozy predilections, his sharp tongue, his back-alley brawls. They took bets on how long it would take him to self-destruct, for the marriage to crumble; they put money on it too. Their best friends gave it six months—at best. They hit six months, then a year. Then two, three, four. Decades later, little had changed. If anything, they grew stronger, synergized, Earleen always on standby with the name or number Marlowe couldn't remember, both of them defensive and easily distracted.

Not that it was all traditional. Only after they married did Earleen discover the extent of Marlowe's coonhound business. She knew he had several dogs, of course. The first time she visited the poor farm, five wagging tails met her in the driveway. What she didn't know at the time was that he kept most of them hidden away behind the shelterbelt, 123 coonhounds in total. Earleen saw little choice but to roll with it, not that Marlowe needed her encouragement. He found a kindred spirit in regional celebrity Vern Hoscheit, a coach for the Oakland As, three World Series rings to boot, who came back each fall to have Marlowe outfit him with a few coonhounds for his coyote hunt. They used to spend afternoons together in Vern's basement, he says, talking shop and watching baseball.

"I tell you, people don't really understand what a dog can tell you," Marlowe says. "I had that one old coon dog, and he'd go out and he'd tell me every scent that he'd come across. And every once in a while I'd say, *Jeff, you old bastard, I said get your head out of your butt and get to huntin' coon.* He'd let out sort of a chuckle. He'd tell me if he smelled a possum. He'd tell me if he smelled a skunk. I mean, I could tell every damn word he was telling me."

Marlowe and Earleen had two kids. Their first child, Nurita Belin, was born premature. Five pounds, two ounces at birth, a half pound less after six days in the hospital. No eyebrows. No fingernails. They fit her in a shoebox, took a photo with Marlowe's wedding ring around her wrist. That she survived her infancy at all seemed a minor miracle. One night, snowed in at home, Nurita developed croup. Marlowe boiled water and rigged a makeshift tent over the stove, flipping her like an omelet every half hour until the snow cleared and he could rush to Orchard for medicine. Justin came later, and nothing about the two of them fit together.

When Earleen went into labor with Justin in late February 1965, snow covered the back roads of Antelope County, and the family car was, frankly, a piece of shit. The Jensens didn't trust it would start, let alone deliver them safely to the Plainview hospital twenty miles away. So they wrapped themselves in coats and sweaters, fired up the tractor, and drove five miles to Marlowe's father's house in town, where they borrowed his car and sped off to Plainview.

Justin spent his childhood pedaling around town on his bicycle, usually with his best friend, Alan Colson. In the summer, they would ride out to Grove Lake, three miles from town, swim away the afternoons or go hunting in the woods with their Red Ryder BB guns. When they ran out of activities, they walked the railroad tracks on the edge of town, past the crossing, behind the shelterbelt, concocting far-fetched scenarios. One day, Justin told his friend, he was going to marry a girl from the tropics, just like the explorers from the movies.

Earleen and Marlowe handled Nurita like fine china, delicate and precise. But Justin grew up in reverse. At birth everything seemed fine; by age ten he was suddenly passing out cold or growing so manic Marlowe would have to wrestle him to the ground like a rodeo calf.

In second grade, he transferred to a school six miles away. The bus rides grew more painful every year. By the time he was thirteen, he couldn't make it home without having to ask the driver to stop the bus so he could urinate in the ditch. His mouth was always dry. He was thirsty. He was unusually tired. When the doctor diagnosed his type 1 diabetes, Justin broke down in tears, as if he'd just been told to pick out a casket, that he had just days to live. The prognosis was hardly so grim, but in many ways it marked the beginning of a much different life.

Justin was embarrassed by his diabetic fits. He grew dependent on his mother. He'd always been sheltered, his neighbors say, always been a mama's boy, but the diabetes took it all to another level. He struggled to maintain his blood sugar. He often ignored the rules. He ate too much candy. When he felt it climbing, he'd hit the gravel, sometimes running two or three miles, the coon dogs trailing behind, his cold breath rising as he counted the fence posts. He could smell his own body—sweat, but also the reek of alcohol, on his breath, on his skin, sort of fruity, sort of like nail polish, a result of low insulin.

He avoided sports, never much of an athlete. He showed brown-and-white-spotted Jersey cattle in 4-H and became an Eagle Scout at seventeen. But it was art he really excelled at—he loved to draw. He was president of the art club and painted the mascot at center court. As a senior, he competed in the scholastic contest for art design at Chadron State College, a statewide competition for high school students. He drew a series of three-dimensional cubes and garnished it with floating dots. The other students engraved intricate designs in wooden planks. He knew his design was too simple, that he'd lose, but he won and rode home with a scholarship and a gold medal draped around his neck.

"I think Justin knew how to see as the artist sees and could maintain the curiosity that it takes to look at everything that you draw or paint as if it's something brand new," says Deb Fonder, his former art teacher. "He could disassociate his own biases and knowledge of the subject and get right to it. Many times my best bet was to stay out of his way. Justin may not have stood out in a lot of areas in school, you know, but in art he was king."

Unfortunately, at Orchard High in the early 1980s, the title of Art King carried few social privileges. He remembers the day a classmate "knocked me down and rolled me a few times," and he remembers how Marlowe reacted, finding the kid and squeezing his shoulder until he crumpled like a soda can to the floor. He remembers the day he ratted out a few tough guys who were taking kids into the locker room, forcing them to breathe heavy, and then socking them in the gut, hoping they'd hyperventilate. When Justin saw it, he started "screaming like a banshee" until the principal arrived.

"At that point I turned from Justin Jensen, quiet boy, to Justin Jensen, narc."

But his classmates don't remember the snitching. They remember his diabetes. They remember the art. They remember the wide-eyed kid with the goofy laugh who'd sketch their portrait in the span of a conversation. They remember his potential, the doodles that had no place crammed in the margins of a spiral-bound notebook. During his senior year, Justin applied to an art academy in Omaha. Several months later, he tore open the envelope. "Dear Justin," the letter said. "Congratulations!" But his father, Marlowe, couldn't fathom a life in the arts, couldn't trace the line from hobby to career. He told Justin it was a pipe dream, that he'd never make any money as an artist.

"The guy is an amazing artist, and I think he could have done something with that," says Gailen Volquardsen, a former classmate. "Instead he just squandered it away, stayed home with Mom."

Though Marlowe had always been closer with Nurita, it was thanks to Justin that he broke into the wheelwright business. In 1977, on his twelfth birthday, Justin asked Marlowe for a buggy. Marlowe didn't know the first thing about wooden wheels or how to set them. So he started asking questions, visiting blacksmiths all over northeast Nebraska, South Dakota, Iowa. Eventually he blazed south, down to Jamesport, Missouri, where he met an Amish wheelwright who taught him the craft.

And soon enough Justin had a true jump buggy with new wooden wheels. But it didn't stop there. Marlowe kept building contacts in the Amish community, absorbing their expertise in a craft all but forgotten in the modern world. Word carried that a man in Royal knew how to build and repair horse-drawn vehicles, and soon paying customers began showing up at his doorstep. Eventually he opened a buggy shop in Orchard, and until recently, he worked there full time, often with Justin's help. He's sold wheels in thirty-six states, some of them on display in museums and on government lawns.

After more than two decades in the wheelwright business, proficient in the craft and unexpectedly familiar with Amish customs, Marlowe was eating dinner with Earleen at the bar in Royal when a couple dressed in Amish garb stepped through the door. Marlowe introduced himself and Earleen and soon discovered the couple was part of an Old Order Amish community located near Marlette, Michigan. Pushed out by Detroit's urban sprawl, the couple was scouting relocation options in Nebraska. Marlowe suggested they try the land around Verdigre, another small town about twenty miles north. They took his advice, and in 2003, a handful of Amish families moved onto six hundred acres of undeveloped farmland just west of Verdigre. To this day, Marlowe and Earleen keep in close touch, chauffeuring their Amish friends in their gas-powered vehicles when long-distance travel is necessary.

As Justin and Nurita grew older, Marlowe wasn't the only one working outside the poor farm. In 1970, Earleen opened a consignment shop in Royal, Jensen's New and Used. At one point they had nearly 650 consignors, some from as far away as Arizona and Wisconsin. When the store filled up, they purchased vacant homes around Royal and filled those, too, furniture mostly, armchairs and end tables. By the early 1980s, Earleen says, western buyers would visit with trailers so large it took all day to pack them.

But they never turned a profit. She got carried away purchasing items in bulk at the Omaha markets, items she couldn't turn over back in Royal. The store and all the homes they'd purchased bloated with old furniture and knickknacks they couldn't sell. The items accrued, collected dust, eventually obscured the path to the register altogether. The overhead decayed. Finally, in 1991, Earleen closed the store, said goodbye to the few customers they had left. They didn't sell; they simply chained the doors and walked away, like a factory during the Great

Depression, everything arrested in time, waiting for the whistle to blow again. With little else to distract her, Earleen began volunteering more and more of her time at the zoo.

In fifty years, the Jensens have scraped together a history from whimsy and wood glue. Everywhere they look, they see conspiracy, greed, illicit power plays, downright unconstitutionality. In 1986, the village board declared two of their buildings condemnable and slated them to burn. Considering the shape of the other buildings in town, the crumbling post office in particular, the Jensens were convinced of wrongdoing. They believe the town board installed a new sewer system Royal didn't need for a $10,000 bribe from the contractor. They're convinced the board members took the money—all of them but one. The supposed holdout died at the Plainview hospital not long after. The Jensens don't believe in coincidence. The breathing tubes were pulled out, Earleen says, "so everyone knows what happened."

They say the mayor bought a new motorboat after that. One board member built an addition to his home; another bought a new house altogether. The alleged killers bought a new camper trailer. They understate the whole story, as if this were commonplace, or they've told it so many times it's simply lost its flavor.

"The board up here has pulled so many deals," Marlowe says.

Underlying each of their claims is the belief that Royal has corrupted itself and the equally unyielding belief that they are not part of it. If they don't hold their neighbors accountable—or their town or their county, for that matter—they don't know who will. After fifty years, certain patterns have begun to reveal themselves to the Jensens: the town board is in cahoots with the mayor, the mayor is in cahoots with the county supervisor, the supervisor is in cahoots with the county attorney, the county attorney is in cahoots with everyone else. They tried to file harassment charges against the last zoo director, they say, but he was in cahoots with the county sheriff. The way they see it, they're about the last ones in town who aren't scamming the system.

"They're very eccentric. I don't think in their hearts they're bad people, they're just very, very eccentric," says Mike Long, former Antelope County attorney. "But they've caused a lot of problems with the nonsense they've stirred up over the years, harassing some of the people in the area . . . People think the Jensens have a lot of time on their hands. But in their hearts they probably believe in their little town. It's very hillbilly-ish up there, in a way."

EFFECTIVE IMMEDIATELY

The Jensens had been volunteering at the zoo for years, well before the Bakkens flew in from the Bahamas. Despite their reputation and "some problems off and on over the years," Dick enjoyed their company and especially admired Earleen's tact with the schoolkids. They helped clean the cages. They made weekly trips to pick up and deliver feed from corporate donors in Norfolk. They worked the attendance booth. They mowed the lawn. And ever since the Bakkens had arrived, Earleen and Justin had served as members of the board, Earleen as secretary-treasurer. They rarely saw eye to eye with Dale and Sandra, and while they hadn't opposed their directorship, the Jensens now privately believed the couple was responsible for busting the coffers of the Heritage Zoo in Grand Island, which folded around the same time they arrived in Royal, and suspected they might try again.

"Between the two of them being on the board and having more political pull and Marlowe in the background, there were a lot of rumors and innuendo spread around about me," Dale says. "Everything from running off to Canada with half the animals to sneaking off in the middle of the night with all the money and everything else. They were very good. I heard them talk about how they ran a guy out of town, and I could see them doing that."

The way Dale and Sandra see it, once the zoo started showing a profit, the Jensens began scouting their prey, scheming for control. And when the reciprocity agreement with the Henry Doorly Zoo fell apart, the Jensens attacked, using the controversy—which made statewide news—as evidence of the Bakkens' mismanagement.

"I had a conversation with Justin and Marlowe in August or July of 2004, and I remember distinctly Marlowe asking, 'So if the zoo closed its doors and went bankrupt, who would get all this land and all these buildings?'" Dale says. "It's like the wheels were turning, and they wanted to add that to their collection of land. When the Henry Doorly Zoo thing came down, the overthrow was starting. And basically, it took about ninety to a hundred days, the campaign to get me out of there through rumors and innuendo. One by one, the Jensens would piss off a board member until they'd say, 'I can't work with you anymore,' and they'd leave. And then they'd go out and recruit someone they could manipulate down the road. One by one, we saw the core board members drop by the wayside. Most just quit in frustration and left it to the next person to deal with. Each time that happened, the Jensens got more and more and more control. They would come up with someone else that seemed like an unbiased person, but basically that person was just weak and someone they could manipulate."

In 2004, the Bakkens and several other board members—the few who still supported them after the Jensens' supposed campaign for exile—began researching opportunities to relocate the zoo to a larger and more "immediate" population base, perhaps Norfolk or even Yankton, South Dakota. The Bakkens had publicly condemned the lack of support from Royal since shortly after they arrived, and divorced from the Henry Doorly Zoo, they now faced a monumental revenue plunge. Divested of the memberships it previously sold with the reciprocity agreement, Dale estimated an $80,000 loss, more than half of its $150,000 operating budget.

"It's up to the people, really," Sandra told the AP the year before. "They have to decide, is it worth quality of life to have a zoo sort of in their neighborhood, and how much are they willing to support that?"

In the fall of 2004, they met with the Norfolk Chamber of Commerce. The owners of a large pumpkin patch and outdoor activity center south of the city agreed to make arrangements for the zoo, Dale says, and "a considerable amount of progress" was made. And yet by the end of the year, "we knew our days were numbered." In the meantime, they made a habit of locking the gates to keep the Jensens out "because every time they came in that year, it spiraled us into another controversy." And slowly, they took steps to relocate the animals, placing them in more stable environments, in facilities properly funded and detached from what they now viewed as local greed. The Bakkens had already removed the foxes and several of the wolves, and if twenty-six-year-old Erin Loeser, their only paid employee, had her way, the chimps would be next.

Loeser had come to Royal almost a year earlier, responding to a job listing the Bakkens had posted to an online forum for zoo industry professionals. She'd previously been working with chimpanzees at the Primate Foundation of Arizona, her first job since graduating from Colorado State University, where she studied psychology and zoology with an emphasis on animal behavior. But she soon discovered the Primate Foundation had strong ties to biomedical research, which she strongly opposed, and was shocked to encounter such an antiquated facility. The chimp cages, for example, had no drains, and the employees spent as much time scooping out water as they did working with the primates. Still young and admittedly naive, Loeser quit the job, assuming six months of experience would be enough to find another job working with chimpanzees. She was wrong. She scoured the internet for open positions, applied to the relevant listings, but they all said the same thing: she lacked experience. Growing desperate, she ran across a call for a chimp keeper at a small roadside facility called Zoo Nebraska. She'd never heard of it, the pay was trivial, just eight dollars an hour, and the town itself was barely on the map. Nevertheless, she needed the experience, and after she put in a few years, she figured she could pack up and find something better. When the Bakkens offered her the position, she quickly accepted.

Whereas many of the locals found the Bakkens standoffish and impersonal, Loeser found them sincere and hardworking, and though the zoo itself looked more like something from the 1970s, she felt the Bakkens were doing their best to turn it around. But she struggled establishing meaningful relationships with the locals. Outside of the Bakkens, the closest thing she had to a social life was her work with the chimps, and by the time she recognized that a shakedown at the zoo was underway, she considered Tyler, Ripley, Jimmy Joe, and Reuben her best friends. She felt the board cared less about the animals' welfare than keeping them physically in Royal, particularly the Jensens, and she now feared what might happen to the chimps if the Bakkens were to leave. She set to work contacting sanctuaries that would adopt the chimpanzees and wrote detailed letters to activist groups such as the Animal Legal Defense Fund and the Chimpanzee Collaboratory.

After eleven of what she considers the darkest months of her life, Loeser accepted a new position at Chimp Haven, a chimpanzee sanctuary near Shreveport, Louisiana. Even then, she kept tabs on Royal, her concern for the animals only increasing after her departure. Months later, after the zoo passed up several opportunities to place the chimps with reputable sanctuaries, including her own, she wrote a letter to the editor at the *Norfolk Daily News*, criticizing the zoo for showing "time and time again that it is not concerned with the welfare of the animals."

"What possible reason could the board have for denying the chimps a better life? The chimps at Zoo Nebraska need and deserve much more. The offer to put the chimps in the sanctuary still stands," she wrote. "I encourage everyone to urge the board to do the humane thing and release the chimps to a much better institution, an institution that is financially stable, has a staff that is knowledgeable in caring for chimpanzees, and will provide the chimps with the rich social opportunities that are imperative for their welfare."

She'd known them less than a year, but she considered the Jensens "the most insane people I've met in my life—manipulative and nasty." Calculating. Conniving. She and the Bakkens once discussed spaying and neutering a litter of feral cats to keep them from running amok at the zoo. Earleen stood on the periphery without saying a word, Loeser recalls, but decried the expenditure at the next board meeting as a misuse of funds. They just had that mind-set, she says. And after she told Justin he couldn't feed the tigers, that it was unsafe, that he had no formal training and posed a liability for the zoo, Justin "got up in my face."

"So I pushed him. If an adult man is coming at me, I'm gonna push him back," she says. "I knew he had previously assaulted a woman on oxygen who was in her sixties. I was scared and lived by myself. Much later, he called down to Chimp Haven and said that I had assaulted him, which was just so not true. They're very dishonest and very corrupt. I've never met people like that in my entire life."

Early that December, twenty-two area residents signed a petition calling for the Jensens' removal from the board of directors. They stated that they'd be more willing to get involved at the zoo if the Jensens weren't a part of it. But the Jensens predictably refused, threatening to sue the board if it took action. In response, three board members resigned that evening, fed up with the Jensens and with a board seemingly intent on tearing itself apart and dragging the Bakkens through the mud. Many of those who previously supported the petition backed down, afraid to call the Jensens' bluff, well aware of their reputation for legal maneuvering. Even Dick, who sincerely valued their volunteer efforts during his tenure, admits they were strangely defensive of the zoo and its place in Royal.

"They were doing a good job there for me, but you know, I think it gave them an identity at the time. They had something positive they were working on," he says. "And they do have good ideas, like the

Jeri Southern Home. They just need some help to execute those ideas. There's nothing wrong with that. But I wish they would get along with the people in Royal."

On December 27, Jerry Peterson hobbled onto the porch of Dale and Sandra's Ponca Street home, steadying himself with his black wooden cane and clutching a single sheet of paper less than half-filled with text. He knocked several times. Behind him stood several state patrolmen, the county sheriff, and another area cop. Believing Dale to be "an aggressive individual," Jerry had personally requested the entourage. He was afraid the nature of his visit might push Dale into a violent frenzy, despite his having no history of such behavior. Sandra opened the door, "scared shitless" at the sight of the men. She told them Dale wasn't home, but the men stepped inside anyway. They entered her small kitchen, the walls red and closing in. Jerry handed her the letter.

"A majority vote was made by the board of directors of Zoo Nebraska that the director, Dale Bakken, be removed from his position at Zoo Nebraska effectively [sic] immediately," she read. "After this date he shall have no control over any property owned by Zoo Nebraska nor shall he have any authority to take any action for or on behalf of Zoo Nebraska."

The letter was signed, "Jerry Peterson, Vise [sic] President."

"It's such an insignificant little letter to look at," Sandra says. "Vise president? He doesn't even know how to spell *vice*. It has no grounds for termination, doesn't give any reason. It's very vague. Very general."

Jerry told her to vacate the house—paid for by the board—in four days. Sandra hesitated. Jerry countered. *Okay,* he said. *One week. In the meantime,* he told her, *don't go near the zoo office. Don't touch the computers. Don't touch the paperwork.* The board hired a security guard for the week, chiefly to prevent the Bakkens from tampering with the books or embezzling zoo funds, which many members of the board—notably Jerry and the Jensens—now suspected them of doing. Sandra quietly agreed, too shocked to put up a fight, though she'd later wish she had said more, had asked the officers for a warrant, had kept them waiting on the porch under that cold blue sky, four officers and a so-called problem solver, the letter still pinched between his fingers and swaying in the late-December wind.

Before the week's end, Sandra and Dale had returned to Canada, the fate of Zoo Nebraska no longer in their hands. Nevertheless, they continued to make their voices heard from up north. They heaped every scrap of information they could upon their former USDA inspector—primarily that no one at the zoo had any legitimate experience with great apes—hoping it would be enough to revoke the zoo's license. Dale often called Jerry Guenther, whose beat at the *Norfolk Daily News* kept him abreast of the zoo's goings-on, both to inquire about the new leadership and to offer a few leads of his own, some of which Guenther printed. Both Dale and Sandra submitted regular letters to the editor after they left as well. In one of her last, Sandra bemoaned the lack of trained personnel at the zoo, specifically calling out Diana and the Jensens, and questioned how often their temporary replacements were actually on-site in Royal.

"I can only imagine the daily chaos and danger created by the new inexperienced staff trying to work the zoo's four chimpanzees without Erin Loeser or my husband present," she wrote. "There is no one left with any practical great ape or chimpanzee experience, despite what they would have you believe, and that creates a dangerous situation. When will this board come to its senses, and what disaster will unfold first?"

REST

B ack on the homestead, the burr oaks craned toward the stars, their gnarled fingers prattling in the breeze. The Verdigris lassoed the last sliver of twilight as it wriggled its way through the valley, licking the grass at its banks. Up in the old farmhouse, in a second-floor bedroom overlooking a meadow, Dick finally slept, nothing but the wind and the crows to wake him. He slept for days. He slept for weeks. He slept as long as he possibly could, trying his best to catch up, though there is no catching up, really, he says. Smoke trailed from the chimney, the woodstove crammed with logs he'd cut himself. His uncle, who still owned the property, used to plant the meadow with corn. When Dick moved in, his uncle planted beans. Dick needed to see the road, he said.

"I don't need to see that road," Dick told him. "As far as I'm concerned, you can plant corn there every year."

His uncle had assumed Dick would appreciate the reminder: quiet as it was out there, the road to civilization was just outside the door. But Dick was running the other way. That's why he'd moved to his uncle's house in the first place. Every now and then, his distant neighbors insisted on checking in, but he didn't need it, never asked for it. Dick never sought out the limelight. When you move back to the smallest town in your county with an adolescent chimpanzee in your father's pickup truck, the limelight tends to find you. Despite his previous daily interactions with the public—touring school groups through the zoo, talking to reporters, presenting updates to the board—Dick would have preferred working completely behind the scenes, just himself and Reuben, whom he hadn't seen now since the day he left, worried that a visit might agitate him.

"I was staying away for Reuben's sake," he says. "If he'd seen me, even at a distance, he'd have gone berserk."

Dick had lingered at the zoo for roughly a month after the Bakkens arrived, helping to grease the transition. But by mid-July 2001, he'd fully divorced himself from the zoo. He did little but sleep that first year out, often fifteen or sixteen hours a day. His brother-in-law Gary, whom he'd worked hogs with as a kid in Royal, ultimately hired him back to work his ranch, though Dick was always dragging his feet, always sick, always tired, often spacey and despondent, forgetful, and slow to respond.

"During the day, I'd go over to the ranch, maybe get sick, come home and sleep the rest of the day. My brother-in-law understood what was going on. I couldn't have had another job. I'd have lost it," he says. "I needed to heal physically, if possible, but a lot of the damage was done."

Dick was so concerned with distancing himself from the zoo that he'd never stopped to consider his next move. He kept up his part-time work with Gary for two years, but once he started the job search in earnest, he quickly hit a wall. Nobody would hire him, not even for the most menial positions. When he finally called a friend at the potato plant in O'Neill, she said they'd be happy to have him, but he'd likely be insulted by the pay. She didn't know he'd been surviving on canned soup in a drafty old farmhouse heated by a single wooden stove. She didn't know he'd lived most of the last decade with his parents, lucky to earn a thousand bucks a year. She didn't know that he'd lived on cash his entire life, that he'd once been denied a cell phone for lack of credit, that a board member ultimately had to sign for him.

"What do you pay?" Dick finally asked.

"Thirty thousand."

"I've never made that much money."

"You're joking," she said. "We thought you were making, like, a hundred K."

"I think that's what everybody was thinking, that they couldn't pay me [enough] because of that zoo," Dick says. "I was getting a few thousand a year! And it's like, now you're gonna give me thirty thousand dollars a year? I'll take it!"

Dick may have been anxious to leave the zoo behind, to bury his sins and push ahead, but the Bakkens were being hammered by his wake. Try as he might, the bedlam he'd left behind was bound to catch up to him. He'd already been pummeled by Sandra's fuming letter and Leroy Hollman's claims of his ineptitude, not to mention the growing notion—catalyzed by the Bakkens' arrival—that rather than being a deeply committed caretaker, Dick was instead guilty of animal neglect, having isolated Reuben for so many years.

Amid all the chaos, Jerry Peterson had begun to secretly reconnect with Dick. He and the Jensens had been plotting ways to remove the Bakkens from their post, he said, and should they succeed, they felt Dick was the obvious man for the job. As Hollmann admitted, he "left big shoes to fill." And so Dick, though he'd sworn never to return, briefly considered a second dalliance with the zoo. Immediately after the reciprocity controversy, Dick wrote a letter to Lee Simmons at the Henry Doorly Zoo, ostensibly to clear his name.

Well before the Bakkens first visited Royal, he wrote, he had noticed an increase in membership sales to both Lincoln and Omaha himself. But after placing a call to John Chapo, now director of the Children's Zoo, he began to suspect the memberships weren't purchased in good faith, that they weren't meant to support Royal, and thus he ushered into effect a new policy—approved by the board—prohibiting the Northeast Nebraska Zoo from advertising within a certain radius of both Lincoln and Omaha.

"However, Mr. Bakken chose to ignore the policy and began selling memberships in Lincoln and Omaha almost immediately after he was hired," Dick wrote. "When I warned him not to do this, he simply told me I had been holding the zoo back. Needless to say, I feel that you did exactly what had to be done. His actions have been questionable, at best, and dare I say unethical.

"I have been contacted by a couple of the Zoo Nebraska board members. They feel that Mr. Bakken should be fired and would like me to return as director of Zoo Nebraska. If they can succeed in removing Mr. Bakken, I would return to the helm of the zoo in Royal—with provisions. One of the provisions would be that there be a chance of regaining reciprocity with Omaha's Henry Doorly Zoo. Do you think that there would be a chance of this?"

Though warming to the idea of returning to the zoo, Dick was apparently hesitant—despite having hired them in the past—to work with the Jensens. The politics had grown more complicated since he left, and if living in Royal had taught him anything, it was that politics was the Jensens' game, not his own. Filling his truck at the One Stop, Dick voiced his misgivings a bit too loudly, Jerry claims, and in Royal, "you don't dare sneeze, or within twenty-four hours, the whole town knows about it." Once the Jensens caught word of Dick's back channeling, they immediately backed away from the whole idea.

Dick returned to his hermitage, his bachelorhood in the hills, his life among the wild animals, those who knew neither tourist nor trap: the deer and the raccoon, the fox and the coyote, the trout in the creek, and the geese overhead. He kept working at the potato plant, but he had time now to lose himself in the woods. He could retrace his childhood along the creek, leap from one bank to the other, squat in the grass and let his fingers go numb combing the water. He'd return to the house and throw another log in the stove, his mistakes trailing him like a clowder of feral cats. He let the sun come up. He let the sun set.

"I've always learned more from animals than I have people, even as a child," he says. "Animals live day to day. They don't worry about the future. They're not trying to financially get ahead of anybody else, you know. They take things as they come. It's what we do out here. You just let the sun come up. Let the sun set."

A WILDLIFE LEARNING
ENCOUNTER

One afternoon, well before the deputies escorted the Bakkens out of town, a middle-aged couple from Gretna, a suburb of Omaha, appeared in Royal. They introduced themselves as Kip and Stacey Smith, directors of a nonprofit group called Wildlife Learning Encounters, and said they had come to see the chimpanzees. At thirty-eight, Kip was a tall man with Nixonian jowls and a receding hairline. He wore glasses, loose jeans, and plain sneakers. Stacey was much shorter and younger looking, with her brunette hair pulled back in a ponytail. The couple toured the country educating and entertaining the public with a slew of exotic animals, which they housed in a wildlife refuge in their own backyard. In many Nebraska schools, their show was an annual event. County fairs too. They often worked with world-renowned naturalists Jim Fowler and Jack Hanna and sometimes accompanied them on shows like *Good Morning America* and *The Late Show with David Letterman*. The Smiths and the Bakkens quickly befriended one another.

"They were people with exotic animal knowledge—maybe not zoo people—but they knew about marketing, and they knew about dangerous animals," Dale says. "They tended to have a fair bit of money and free time and would kind of throw some things our way. They wanted to help the zoo, and Kip had some connections in Omaha with investors and things like that. It looked like they could help us with future constructions and help keep the zoo progressing."

The relationship evolved during the Bakkens' brief reign at Zoo Nebraska. The two couples used each other as sounding boards for their respective projects and hired each other for contract work. The Smiths even donated the two Bengal tigers to Zoo Nebraska. But eventually, Dale says, Kip and Stacey caught wind of the rumors, of the claims—though unsupported—of skimming money and stealing animals, of the general distrust now settling in at Zoo Nebraska. The Jensens "planted some seeds of doubt in their minds about me," he says, and like so many others, the Smiths grew distant. Late that fall, about a month before Jerry Peterson landed on the Bakkens' doorstep to deliver his letter, the Smiths joined the board.

So when the Bakkens—begrudgingly and against their will—packed their bags and fled Royal, the Smiths offered to sub in as zookeepers until the zoo found a fitting replacement. "Sort of interim director," says Marvin Young, the last zoo board president. They hadn't been around long enough to spoil a reputation, they supported keeping the zoo in Royal, they had already been serving on the board, and they were the only individuals left at Zoo Nebraska with any professional qualifications. The choice seemed clear.

"Kip was kind of our rescue man," Marvin says. "Several people on the board knew him. The Jensens knew him. And he was advising us what to do at the zoo."

But the Smiths still lived in Gretna, 150 miles away, and they still ran their own exotic animal farm back home. They eventually bought a second home in nearby Orchard, Nebraska, but the arrangement didn't last long. The zoo, they soon realized, had major facility issues. They would need more money to upgrade and expand the animal enclosures, and they were short-staffed. In other words, they simply inherited the Bakkens' struggles and Dick's struggles before them.

"I think they quickly realized this was going to be too much of a time commitment for them," says Jerry Guenther, a reporter for the *Norfolk Daily News* who covered the zoo extensively. "It was such a long trip they couldn't really make the journey all the time. And then you're relying on local volunteers. It's really a full-time position with people who are trained, and as small as the zoo was, it was still a huge responsibility."

Kip recruited a local man to help out when he and Stacey were away, a hulk of a man named Ken Schlueter Jr.: thick arms, short neck, fingers fat like Polish sausages. The locals called him Junior, and he ran the used car lot and truck parts store opposite the zoo on Highway 20. He was new to Royal, but he'd shown an interest in Zoo Nebraska, attending a board meeting in early December to voice his support for keeping the zoo in town.

One night early in the spring of 2005, roughly twenty-five people gathered in the old activity center for an open meeting of the board of directors. They sat in metal folding chairs, many of them still wrapped in the scarves and overcoats they had arrived in. The board—Marvin Young, Jim and Lucille Haskin, the Jensens—sat behind a table at the front of the room, tapping their pens, shuffling papers, calling this or that to order. Under Kip and Stacey's watch, the Bengal tigers had recently mated, a fact displeasing to the board, which felt the zoo had overextended itself already. Growing defensive, Stacey fired an insult at Marlowe—he no longer remembers the exact slight—and Marlowe, who so far had remained silent, stood up, arms dangling fat and loose at his sides.

"You know what's sure funny?" he said, turning to face Kip. The onlookers held their breath. "Every time you show up, these young girls show up with short shorts on. They don't come any other time. That can't be by chance."

According to the Jensens, they'd warned Kip before. Several young girls from Brunswick—none of them over twenty-one, Marlowe claims—had been showing up to board meetings, waiting for Kip. They say he was known to womanize, though it hadn't been discussed in public, not so openly, not like this. Before Marlowe could finish, Kip burst from his seat. He sprinted across the room, past the folding chairs to where Marlowe stood in the back. Head down, arms wide, shoulders tight, he bull-rushed him. But Marlowe had been here before.

He ducked Kip's charge, hooked his right arm around Kip's neck, and cinched it tight, the torque of a wheelwright. They shuffled back and forth, back and forth, Kip squirming in vain to pry himself loose, his glasses skidding across the floor, Marlowe tightening and retightening his grip, a knot of pride and provocation. They grunted. The chairs around them tipped over. The screech, the rattle, the metal on wood. Bystanders gaping in a repurposed prairie church. The world dark and cold outside the windows. The animals asleep in their cages. Kip reached back, still struggling, hunting for a limb, incidentally catching his wristwatch on Marlowe's cheek and tearing it forward. The cut grew red; blood pooled up and trickled down his cheek. Junior and two other men tried to cleave them apart, but Marlowe was locked on, locked in, heart pounding, arms throbbing, the specter of his youth, adrenaline and sweat and an audience too. He showed no signs of budging until Earleen hustled forward.

"Marlowe!" she said, grabbing him. "Marlowe, let go. He's turning colors. Let him go."

He slowly loosened his grip, letting the blood rush back to Kip's loose cheeks. Kip coughed and cleared his throat, ripping loose from Marlowe's hold. He found his glasses on the floor, crushed in the shuffle.

"If you want to turn around here and assault somebody," Marlowe told him, still panting, "you're gonna lose your glasses."

At the front of the room, before all those in attendance, Marvin Young, acting as president, rose to speak.

"None of this leaves the building," he said, somewhat shaken. "This goes no further."

It was the last board meeting either Marlowe or the Smiths ever attended.

HIGH AND MIGHTY

Early that August, the board unanimously elected Junior Schlueter—who had just begun working with the Smiths before the infamous boardroom brawl—the new director of Zoo Nebraska, which had reverted once again to an unpaid position. Unlike his predecessors, Junior had no experience managing exotic animals, certainly not for public display, nor had he ever been in the position of managing an all-volunteer staff. He'd first been recruited by the Smiths because he was able-bodied and seemed to have both the interest and the free time, but in truth, the directorship of Zoo Nebraska was hardly a competitive position, stuck in what most consider the sticks, the broom closet of so-called flyover country. That both Dale and Sandra had started publishing letters in the *Norfolk Daily News*, detailing the zoo's malfeasance and their ongoing concerns for the animals that remained, didn't help. If visitors hadn't caught on before to the tempest roiling beneath the zoo, they had now.

Before coming to Royal, Junior had spent twenty years working for a company called Associates Commercial Corp, a consumer finance group "where they finance big wheels and stuff," his sister Kathryn says. He started at the Omaha branch in 1981, later relocating to both Dallas and West Virginia. But in 2001, Citigroup bought out ACC's parent company for $31 billion, and Junior moved back to Nebraska with a pension "you wouldn't believe," Kathryn says. "That kid could live high and mighty. He had money up to no end."

By the time Junior landed in Royal, he'd officially retired. He managed the auto parts store across the highway less for the money, Kathryn says, than to keep busy, a mentality that quickly evaporated after he accepted the position at Zoo Nebraska. The new gig devoured every scrap of free time he had left—and then some. With even less help than his predecessors, Junior found himself scrambling to keep up, pounding the highway to pick up feed, repairing drooping fences, burning through the night to nurse the new tiger cubs. And despite their initial encouragement, Kathryn says, the Jensens now seemed to dismiss Junior's pleas for help.

"Kenneth went to Marlowe all the time, and he just kind of brushed it off," Kathryn says. "He would go in and say, 'Hey, we need this for the zoo,' and they'd say, 'Oh, don't worry about it. We don't need that.'"

But those who still showed up each day to help clean the cages, feed the animals, or take tickets at the admission desk soon discovered Royal's newest transplant wasn't the fix Zoo Nebraska needed.

"He came across great guns until we all agreed for him to be director," says Diana Wavrunek, by then a board member and reinstated as a volunteer. "Which I thought meant he would be running the business end of things but he took to mean he was now dictator, apparently."

By most accounts, Junior Schlueter, well over six feet tall and roughly 275 pounds, was a bully. They say he ignored the board and simply muscled his way through the backlash, that he literally threw his weight around the zoo, awkwardly backing volunteers up against the wall or blocking their exits until they acceded to his demands. They say it worked, that even the biggest among the volunteers cowered, unwilling to test his limits.

"He'd just verbally threaten you, but he's a big enough man, he could kind of scare you," Marvin says. "His exaggerations were just way out of line. It got to the point where you didn't know whether to believe ten percent or zero or forty percent of what he was telling us."

This wasn't the same convivial, animal-loving kid his family seemed to know back in South Sioux City, Nebraska. The oldest of four siblings, Junior—at home they called him Kenneth—played trumpet in the high school band, participated in the drama club, cared for the family animals— the pet pigs and the pet cow too. The type of kid who'd give you the shirt off his back, they say. His mother taught college classes on the nearby Winnebago reservation, made sure he kept a clean report card, straight As and Bs, nothing less. His father worked at the state's missile silos in the 1960s and later at the meatpacking plant in Sioux City. Junior saved his competition for the golf course or the football field or, more to his fancy, the wrestling mat. To this day, Kathryn says, he holds the school record for the fastest pin.

After a summer laying irrigation pipe for his uncle, he enrolled at Wayne State and studied business administration. One afternoon, roughhousing with his friends, he pinned the star of the wrestling team almost instantly. The coach witnessed the whole thing, Kathryn claims, and offered him a full athletic scholarship on the spot.

"What about the other guy?" Junior asked.

They said he'd lose his scholarship. Junior left the offer on the table.

"Kenneth wouldn't do that," Kathryn says.

He excelled academically at Wayne State and later taught several business classes of his own on the Winnebago reservation, the same small tribal college his mother had taught at.

"Kenneth would work night and day with kids to get them to pass their classes," Kathryn says.

But when Junior told his family about the position at Zoo Nebraska, they hesitated. He'd already been collecting a number of pets on his own, penning them up behind his garage: ducks, geese, llamas, donkeys, peacocks, rabbits, chickens, turtles, and more. He had more than enough to care for on his side of the highway, Kathryn says.

"We kind of told him not to. He had a plate of his own," she says. "We knew it was going to be a lot of work. The zoo was a total disaster. The fences were falling down, the pens were no good, rotten and stuff, and the animals didn't look too good. Finally, we said, 'You know, Kenneth, we don't want you to.' But he saw what was going on with the animals, and he didn't like it."

Halfway through his first summer on the job, as wilting crops begged for irrigation and the mercury tore past one hundred, Jerry Peterson and the board of directors invited a local country singer to perform a midmorning show at the zoo. When Junior caught word of the activity, he immediately phoned Jerry, livid they'd scheduled the performance without his consent. Junior tore into him over the phone, he says, shouting profanities like a four-star general. He barked so loud and for so long Jerry's entire body seized up. His teeth clenched and his limbs jerked and a cool, numbing sensation washed over him. Despite the doctors' findings, Jerry believed he'd never fully recovered from his exposure to the trichloroethylene more than a dozen years earlier, and Junior's verbal attack now pushed him over the edge, he claims, inducing a seizure that left him bedridden for three days. When Jerry finally gained the strength to crawl out of bed, he was told that Junior was driving up to meet him in person, and he seized up all over again. "I am very scared of Junior Schlueter," he would later tell his doctor.

Not only did Junior routinely make those around him uncomfortable, but many who worked at the zoo felt his standards were far too low. Some claimed that he seemed to have few qualms about letting the animals go days without fresh water, others that he let them live in their own feces, or let the llamas and goats freely roam the zoo grounds during operating hours, oblivious to clear liability issues. According to both Jerry and Marvin Young, Junior ignored multiple orders to keep the animals penned up, and later that summer, a loose donkey bit a young girl, spooked by a light touch.

"It horrified me," Jerry said. "There she was, crying her eyes out. My wife was running her aid, washing her up. Her arm was bruised, bleeding a little bit. We got it to stop, put a Band-Aid on it. I thought, *Here we go*. I was just waiting for a lawsuit."

As the girl and her mother stood to leave the zoo, Jerry absentmindedly said, "Come back again sometime."

"We won't be back," the mother said firmly.

After the donkey incident, Jerry called Marvin, then the board's vice president, portending disaster if something wasn't soon changed.

"We can't continue this way, letting the animals loose on the grounds," he said. He pictured the small piles of manure now littering the green space like a minefield, the little girl crying and gripping her arm. "Somebody's gonna get hurt. If a llama stomps on a small child and maims [them] for the rest of [their] life, our million-dollar policy won't cover it. It could happen so easy. We've got to do something, Marvin. We've got to get rid of Junior. He's ruining the zoo."

"Yeah," Marvin said. "But we need a director."

"Listen," Jerry said, his voice quiet but sharp. "If you don't go ahead and get rid of Junior Schlueter, I'm going to quit. We can't have this going on anymore. It's scaring me."

Marvin hardly disagreed, but the zoo was already short-staffed, and the chances of finding someone to fill Junior's shoes—no matter how poorly he performed—seemed slim to nonexistent. Nobody would want the job, and even if they did, the zoo was broke and broken. They couldn't afford to hire a new director, and no one could fix this situation without a massive influx of money. Most of the volunteers had already quit. The board had withered to just three or four active members. If they fired Junior, Marvin knew the daily chores would fall on him, and he already had more work than he could handle on his farm outside

Royal: 160 acres of corn and soybeans, more on rented land, 175 cow-calf pairs. At seventy, he simply lacked the ambition to throw himself into more physical labor, into a zoo that, at this point, seemed less like a business than a broken family affair. He had hesitated taking the position in the first place, and he sure as hell hadn't signed up for this. Until they had a backup plan, Marvin decided, Junior would have to stay.

"Junior finished running it into the ground," Marvin says. "We, as a board, should have said, *You're out.* But we had no other director, and nobody wanted to do the work, and there was a lot of work to be done. So he stayed."

True to his word, Jerry resigned from his post as president of Zoo Nebraska just a few days later. He sent his resignation letter by mail, terrified at the prospect of meeting Junior at another board meeting, of slipping into another seizure, stuck for days in bed, afraid to answer the phone, afraid to answer the door. Meanwhile, Justin Jensen, too, had reached his limit. He and his mother, Earleen, had been volunteering at the zoo off and on for nearly seventeen years, before Junior, before the Bakkens, before the donations from Johnny Carson. To Justin, the zoo was "like magic." He'd spent his entire life looking outward, past this sleepy town and over the horizon, imagining what kind of world lay beyond. But the zoo had changed that, at least a little bit. The exotic now howled within earshot, prowled and pounced just down the street. Tigers. Bears. Chimpanzees. Animals he never imagined he'd see in real life. And all the tourists now familiar to Royal—the activity thrilled him, the feeling that perhaps the rest of the world hadn't forgotten about the only place he really knew.

But the magic had faded, and, disturbed by Junior's apparent disregard for the board's authority, Justin no longer wished to associate himself with Zoo Nebraska. He felt Junior's decision to let the pack animals graze outside their pens posed a threat to the public and—echoing Jerry—a huge liability for the zoo. During the first week of

September, Junior arrived at the zoo to find the llamas penned up in the back. Justin stood nearby.

"You put those llamas in?" Junior allegedly asked.

"Yeah," Justin said, already tense and looking toward the pen. "They were out this morning. Somebody's gonna get hurt by those llamas bein' out here."

"You will let them llamas loose."

"Not while I'm on the board. There's too much liability. If one of those llamas runs over a kid or anything like that . . ." Justin said, trailing off. "I'm on the board. I'd be takin' it pretty short here."

"You will let them out!" Junior repeated.

That night, Justin submitted a letter to the board, notifying them of his "undetermined leave of absence."

"After hearing and seeing the present actions of new Zoo Director Schlueter . . . I feel I cannot be a part of the daily volunteer work carried out at Zoo Nebraska," the letter stated. "I believe the liability of loose animals biting, jumping on, and chasing zoo visitors is not something I wish to be a part of, so I am giving my undetermined leave of absence to continue until the zoo becomes an environment that is safe for the public. This is effective immediately September 3, 2005."

The letter concludes in all caps: "I WILL NOT BE A PART OF THIS DAILY WORK AT THE ZOO, BUT I WILL NOT GIVE UP MY SEAT AS A BOARD MEMBER OF THE NORTHEAST NEBRASKA ZOOLOGICAL SOCIETY."

LIMITATIONS

Few were surprised to hear of Justin's haughty departure from Zoo Nebraska. Even fewer cared. Like the rest of his family—save for his sister, Nurita, whom most either exempted or forgot about entirely—Justin had been written off by the community as a misfit with less-than-honorable intentions. Pushing fifty, he was a severe diabetic, type 1, with pale skin, large ears, and a more-than-passing resemblance to Pee Wee Herman, less prim and without the makeup. He spoke in halting starts, and his laugh didn't help, squirrely and high pitched. That he would butt heads with someone as mulish as Junior seemed all but guaranteed.

After high school, Justin had worked a string of odd jobs: a summer at his uncle's service station in Grand Island, two hours south; three years at a Gibson's Discount Center in O'Neill, thirty minutes east; then Lucille Haskin's drapery shop back in Royal, where he helped sew and hang curtains. But by 1992, he was restoring buggies for his father, making chump change and eating cereal for every meal. Everyone he knew had skipped town. His childhood friend Alan Colson had been deployed to Kuwait. He was lonely. He was bored.

"It was just no life here," he says. "So I thought, *I gotta go out and find a life.*"

Despite brief stints elsewhere, Justin had never truly left home, not in his heart. So he packed up—defying his parents, defying

Royal—threw everything he owned in the trunk of his old Buick, withdrew what little savings he had in the bank, and tore off down Highway 20. He felt alive, Nebraska stretching out before him. An hour later, he stopped in Norfolk, Nebraska, the home of Johnny Carson. Compared to Royal, Norfolk was a metropolis, with restaurants, movie theaters, multiple stoplights, a population of twenty-four thousand people, and opportunity thick as mud, or so it seemed.

Still, he had no place to stay. When the sun sank, he found a country road just outside the city limits, parked beneath the stars, and slept the next two nights in his Buick. It wasn't comfortable, but this was the start of something new, something foreign. When the sun rose, he would piece together a new beginning.

And soon enough, he did. He got a job at Jerry's Standard, a filling station, and when they later fired him—Justin claims they mistook a hypoglycemic attack for a symptom of drug abuse—it was Dick Haskin who found him a job in the produce department at the same Pic 'n Save that donated fruits and vegetables to the zoo. Despite all of Justin's idiosyncrasies, Dick had always considered him a friend, ever since Dick moved to Royal and started buying comic books at Jensen's New and Used. He felt no obligation to help Justin secure a job, nor did he feel pressured to carve out a space for the Jensens at the zoo in spite of the many recommendations against them. Whereas many volunteers "just stood around and did nothing" or needed constant supervision, the Jensens simply got to work, no questions asked.

"All three of them enjoyed the zoo and thrived on hard work," Dick says. "Their combined talents and abilities, along with their passion for the zoo, was a winning combination."

Justin soon found an apartment, and over the next six years he patched his résumé together like a crazy quilt: he cooked and cleaned house for the intellectually disabled; he worked in the water treatment facility of a meatpacking plant called Beef America; and he performed nursing care in four different facilities. One night, while working at

Norfolk Veterans Hospital, he lifted a patient from his bed and "it was like black snow coming down from my eyes," he says. He suffered neovascularization, a side effect of having high blood sugar. When he lifted the patient, the vessels behind his eyes ballooned and burst. When he awoke the next morning, he'd lost all vision in his right eye and the shape of a tornado obscured most of the vision in his left. He spent the next year guided by his parents' hands.

After several different procedures, his vision eventually returned. But in the meantime, he'd slipped back into his old routines. Back to Royal. Back to his parents. Back to the long, empty hours of home. He quit work. He applied for disability. He surfed the web. He often looked at the glamour shots of Jeri Southern on his wall—her lips on the cusp of a curl, her far-off gaze—and he envied her freedom. He saw not just a poised and beautiful woman, but an ideal: from small-town Royal to the rest of the world, a Cather novel realized. Now and then he would wonder what he could have become, where he could have gone.

"Too many limitations," he says.

Justin lived alone in a small white house his parents owned in the middle of town, two blocks off the highway. A tall elm tree shaded the front yard, and a dirty plastic sheet covered the living room window. A smorgasbord of planter boxes and coastal-themed lawn ornaments—a plastic seagull, a pair of dock posts—lined both sides of his concrete stoop. Inside, the walls were lumpy and pale green, and piles of junk mail and other debris cluttered every surface. Over the years, one eBay purchase at a time, Justin had amassed what was likely the largest collection of Jeri Southern memorabilia anywhere in the world, the spoils of which were piled up in the corners of his living room and his two small bedrooms and other storage spaces out on the poor farm. He'd tracked down her grade school autograph books. Original sheet music. Magazines. Glamour shots. Vinyl and VHS and V-Disc.

When his health allowed, Justin helped his father with the wheel-wright business, but as far as the government was concerned, Justin existed outside the labor force altogether, neither employed nor looking for work. When his blood sugar spiked, he'd lose control, grow violent, and require physical restraint. He lived off his parents and a monthly $711 disability check. By the late 1990s, he was spending most days indoors with the lights shut off, scouring the internet and flirting with Filipino women in Yahoo chat rooms. Over a period of years, he would marry three of them. All three would return to the Philippines.

It wasn't the way he looked or the way he laughed that exposed him to such disrepute. It wasn't the way he tended to his home or what many considered his "mail-order brides" or his obsession with a hometown hero. It was the scheming. It was the temper.

It was the fight over the gym.

To Justin, it seemed like a simple request: the Amish wanted to rent the gymnasium. They weren't asking for cordoned-off streets or fireworks. Just the gym to host a traditional Amish supper. The mayor had already agreed. And then, two days before the event, the mayor changed his mind, allegedly unsure "what kind of people those Amish are," Justin says. But the Jensens knew the Amish well, helped recruit them to northeast Nebraska, fixed their buggies at the shop from time to time. They had no doubts about their character, and the gymnasium was the only community center in town, built as a gathering place in 1961. If this wasn't a good use of the gym, the Jensens didn't know what was. To Justin, the mayor's decision was yet another example of the "spoiledness of some of the individuals in the area." Big fish in a small pond, he says. An abuse of power. Corrupt politics. The works.

So on the night of January 14, 2004, Justin and his mother, Earleen, walked three blocks south to the mayor's place, stepped onto his porch, and knocked a few times. The porch light switched on, and the mayor, Max Heiter, leaned one shoulder into the doorframe. Justin and his mother stood side by side. They often did.

"Do you think this is right?" Justin asked, and they began to argue, two grown men beneath a porch light. Justin demanded the mayor

157

reopen the gymnasium. Max refused. They spoke loudly at first, then louder. Inside the house, the mayor's wife, Linda, could hear the bickering. She was weak with cancer—the whole town knew. She started flipping the porch light off and on, and when the voices raised to shouts, Linda stepped outside and approached Justin. She stood close, spoke his name, and when Justin did not respond, she placed her hands on his face. Rage washed over Justin. He jerked like a wild animal, grabbed Linda's shoulders, and pushed her away.

Two days later, she filed a restraining order.

"I should have never pushed her away, but it kind of shocked me," he says. "And I should have been focused on her, too, but I thought maybe I could change Max."

When others tell it, they say he pushed her clean off the porch. They say he assaulted an elderly woman on oxygen. True or not, she arrived in court with a walker. Justin calls it a stunt, compares it to the gloves in the O. J. Simpson trial. He filed one motion after another, appealed the guilty verdict—the state charged Justin with third-degree assault, a class 1 misdemeanor—and demanded a jury trial. The whole affair lasted three and a half years, and in the end, he refused to pay the $1,300 fine, opting for a thirty-day jail sentence instead.

"Because I had diabetes, they had to put me in a safe keep down in Lincoln. That ended up costing Antelope County forty-eight hundred dollars," he says. "Well, my fine was only thirteen hundred dollars, and I didn't even pay that!"

They say the mayor's wife lived just long enough to see Justin Jensen convicted. They say a lot of things about Justin Jensen.

With little but his volunteer work at the zoo to occupy his time, Justin's interest in the internet developed into more of an obsession. He'd spend full days online, digging into the history of Antelope County, downloading music by Jeri Southern, researching his neighbors, his friends, his enemies, interacting with strangers. In one of his favorite chat rooms, one devoted specifically to 1950s jazz music, he met Chielo Pacaldo Sumagang.

For the next three years, they talked online almost every day. When Justin returned from his blowout with Junior at the zoo, Chielo suggested they get married. It would take him a year to get to the Philippines. Earleen told him it was too dangerous, said, "People die over there, you know." Justin booked a flight anyway. He visited first for ten days, and later for six months. They briefly opened a sari-sari store on the backside of her house, he says. "That means *knickknack*." They sold booze and fish.

When Justin returned to Royal, Chielo came too. But the American dream was cold as hell. She hated the snow, hated Nebraska. There were no skyscrapers. No flashing marquees. No wealth or abundance. Instead she was met by the lumpy green walls of 304 Ryan Street, piles of old paperwork and eBay shipments climbing toward the ceiling. There was ice coating the windows and wind so strong it seemed the whole house might just tear back and tumble away. Whatever she expected, Royal wasn't it. She grew homesick. The rest is up for debate. Justin says her prescription medication triggered "emotional problems."

"Justin met a gal in the Philippines, and he brought her here," Valda Young says. "A lot of people in town knew they were having trouble, but they didn't want to help her because they were afraid of him. Finally, there was someone who helped get her away, and she went back to the Philippines, but it's sad. It's just sad. He has diabetes really, really bad. He should have gotten away from his mother."

Whatever the case, Chielo did spend time in Norfolk at Bright Horizons, a "confidential shelter facility for those fleeing an unsafe situation," according to their website. After researching her medication,

Justin tried calling Bright Horizons to warn her off the drug, but they wouldn't permit his call, said only a priest or an officer could speak with Chielo.

"Well, I'd already went to my priest, and he wouldn't help. So I sat here for an hour, foolish, dumb me. An officer could talk to her and get her some help? So I call back and I go, 'Yes, is Chielo Sumagang there? This is Officer Price. I'd like to talk to her about this case.' I just made up the name."

The staff at Bright Horizons saw right through it, reported the offense to the county attorney. On June 17, 2008, he stood before the Honorable Donna F. Taylor in Antelope County Court. He pled no contest. The state of Nebraska charged Justin with impersonating a public servant—a class 3 misdemeanor—and fined him $300. Divorced from the zoo and estranged from his wife, Justin had little but idle time. And idle time, it seemed to many, could be a dangerous thing in the hands of the Jensens.

"I shouldn't have lost my head on that deal," he says. "It was stupid."

THANK YOU FROM THE TOWN BOARD

When Diana's position as a relief keeper under the Bakkens ended, the board, hardly working in tandem with its director, promptly asked her to join. She accepted, and when the Bakkens left—though she no longer received even part-time wages—she continued performing her previous duties as a volunteer, driving forty-five miles round trip every day from her home in Verdigre. Four years and several directors later, Diana maintained her commitment to the animals, if not the zoo itself.

She had messy brown hair and small silver glasses, heavy eyes, and the sharp wrinkles of a disgruntled volunteer. She smoked cigarettes, and she sounded like it, her laugh wheezy and hoarse. On the wall in her living room, she hung a framed portrait of all four chimpanzees, some of their original paintings too—a mess of crude and colorful swirls. And like so many others, she despised Junior Schlueter. Despite numerous complaints from the board, Junior had continued to neglect the facilities, she says, continued to run the zoo as if it were his own, as if he had no one to answer to but himself. He'd pick up boxes of dead chicks from the hatchery in Norfolk—food for the birds of prey—and let them stew in the heat until she arrived to stack them in the freezer, too lazy or distracted to do it himself, she presumed. She often found the diet kitchen, where they prepared the animals' meals, caked in dried blood, the floors sticky or wet. And now that Junior had scared Jerry Peterson off the board, he liked to puff his chest and boast about what he would do if Jerry ever stepped foot back on the premises.

"I really don't like talking about Schlueter," says Krista Anderegg, a former board member who taught high school science in Orchard. "I don't know why we had board meetings, because the board would say one thing and he'd just do whatever he wanted. It didn't matter."

Though Diana could have used more help, she was hardly upset to find Justin Jensen's letter to the board; she'd acted more like his babysitter than his equal, anyway, constantly double-checking his work and keeping him focused on the chores still unfinished. Diana often felt like the de facto director, and in some ways, she was. In order to convince the USDA that Zoo Nebraska had proper staffing to care for nonhuman primates following the Smiths' departure, the board listed Diana, whose experience, while limited, could be counted in years if stretched.

"I was pretty much in charge," she says. "I was practically running the place. Junior didn't do anything but cause trouble. He didn't lift a finger over there. He'd help maybe drag a dead pig in for the tigers, but that's just about it."

But while she'd long grown tired of Junior and the board politics and what seemed like constantly rotating "leadership," she still couldn't abandon the animals. She couldn't say goodbye to the chimpanzees, especially Jimmy Joe, whom she now considered her best friend. Over the past four years, she'd grown closer to the chimps each day. She found qualities in them so humanlike they almost spooked her, qualities she couldn't turn away from. After four years, she could identify the distinct personalities of each one, certain she had earned their trust. Tyler loved to play games, loved to be scared, loved it when Diana popped around the corner and surprised him. Reuben seemed more passive than the other chimps, less interested in humans. *If he ever knew sign language, he doesn't seem to know much anymore,* she thought. When she tried to sign with him, he just stared at her, bored and confused.

Like his half brother Tyler, Ripley liked to play, but he was also prone to what Diana called "deep thoughts." Every now and then, something or someone would spark his interest, and without any warning at all, he'd lunge for it. He once grabbed a visitor's hand and tried pulling her into the cage. Another time he caught Diana's coat with two fingers and ripped it to shreds. "And yet he could be so sweet," she says, and she had determined that, of all the chimps, he was the hardest to get a hold on.

Though he terrified the other volunteers, Jimmy Joe was Diana's favorite. Whereas the other chimps warmed up to Diana slowly over a period of months, Jimmy Joe seemed to trust her immediately. He was much larger than the others, so much so that Diana often wondered aloud, only half joking, if he wasn't part gorilla. He seemed built with a much different design, big and bulky, silver down the back. And she liked his quirks, the fact that he refused to allow her to brush his teeth or cut his nails, that before going to sleep each night, he'd primly straighten out his blankets, lie on his back, and wait for Diana to come tickle him. One afternoon, a disgruntled visitor began to yell at Diana, and as soon as Jimmy Joe noticed, he quickly stood up behind them, "ready to take the customer's head off." She considered Jimmy Joe a gentleman.

—⁂—

Diana woke to a cloudless sky on the morning of Saturday, September 10, 2005, a steady southeast breeze rustling the trees outside her window. With the mercury already pushing seventy, it would be a hot afternoon, made even hotter by her rounds at the zoo and Junior's looming presence, his stiff-necked authority, the way he maneuvered the zoo in his golf cart, barking commands and splitting hairs. Like most mornings, Diana skipped breakfast, too busy to cook, too busy for coffee or the morning news. After caring for her pets—seven cats, two dogs, two mules, two horses, and a donkey named Rozee—she got into her 2001 blue Volkswagen Beetle and quickly detoured into Verdigre, where she picked up a birthday cake for a fellow volunteer. She thought it'd be nice to celebrate, to interrupt the daily grind of the past few months, to have a little fun where there had recently been so little.

With the cake in her passenger seat, she turned south onto Highway 14. On a clear, warm day like today, the drive to Royal took less than half an hour, and from the crest of each swell in the road, she could see for miles in every direction, over cropland and open pasture. She listened to Bob Seger and Stevie Ray Vaughan, and like most mornings, she visualized a checklist as she drove, spacing out for miles at a time until she met Highway 20 and sped the last few miles into Royal.

The wind swelled, lifting the flag in the parking lot, and as Diana began her work, an occasional gust would pluck leaves from the trees and sweep clouds of dust from the walking paths. She took a nose count of all the parrots and parakeets in the visitor center "to make sure nobody was on the bottom of the cage," she says, and then headed for the Carson Center near the back of the property, counting the other animals as she passed. Zoo Nebraska had evolved over the years, but it never lost that naturalistic feel, not with its pitiful budget. *All part of the charm,* its advocates insisted, or it used to be, before the donkey riddled the yard with shit and the llamas grazed freely outside their pen.

Attached to the north side of the Carson Center, a large green cage paralleled the fence line, a byzantine jungle of wire mesh and sliding locks and shifting gates. Like the interior, the outdoor exhibit was split in two—one side larger than the other—by a shift gate that keepers could safely open and close from outside the cage. Visitors approaching Royal from the west could drive down Ponca Street nearly blind to the zoo's existence, only to hit the dead end three blocks south and find four chimpanzees hanging from their enclosure just off the road, climbing the old plastic jungle gym inside or, on a more lethargic afternoon, lazing in the sun like hungover socialites. Black rubber tires lay in the dirt, and multicolored fire hoses drooped like party streamers from the ceiling.

Typically, Diana cleaned the larger outdoor enclosure first. When she finished, she and the chimps traded places. Two or three times a week, she and another volunteer would power wash the whole interior, scrub the walls, mop the floors, which was sometimes a four-hour job on its own. But today, Diana had extra hands. Jason Klug and his wife, Fayette, had driven up from Norfolk to volunteer for the afternoon, so they tackled both enclosures at once. Fayette closed the shift gate outside and started on the small side first, while Diana and Jason worked inside the building, sweeping feces and debris toward the drain. Locked outside on the far end, the chimps continued to groom and play, to swing from the tires and roll in the dirt, an eye trained always on their keepers' work.

Meanwhile, board member Eugene Carstens, Fayette's father, manned the admissions desk up by the highway, the large metal entrance gate pinned back like an open kennel. Less than a dozen visitors roamed the grounds, rather slow for a Saturday, the numbers perhaps tempered by an exasperating wind. Frustrated with the register, Eugene moseyed down to the Carson Center around noon. Fayette laid her work aside to relieve her father, following him back to the office and closing the gate behind her. When Jason and Diana stepped outside, they noticed Fayette had left but assumed she had simply finished her work and moved on.

On most days, Diana would have finished up inside, opened the shift gate, and let the chimps roam freely in and out of the building.

She'd then move on to the macaque; then the tigers, bobcats, and din-goes; and then on to the pack animals: the donkey, the llamas, the long-horn steer. She would prep all their meals in the diet kitchen, drag hoses from one exhibit to the next. She would wash the blankets used as bed-ding for Babe and Dakota, the cougars, both now old and rheumatic. And once she'd made all the rounds—clean, feed, water, repeat—she would return once again to the chimps: Tyler, the clown; Jimmy Joe, her gentleman; Ripley, a "deep thinker"; and Reuben, the original star of Zoo Nebraska.

After she opened the gate, the chimps calmly stepped through, all four of them in a single-file line, no rush at all, like children waiting for the school bus. For a moment, Jason and Diana just stood there, cap-tivated by their intelligence, their gangly limbs, coats black as asphalt. Despite all the time she'd spent with them over the past three years, Diana never lost that sense of awe, she says, never settled into the com-fort of familiarity. She and Jason headed for the back door. The chimps lumbered to the other side of the cage, and when they reached the west-side gate, Jason stared in disbelief—momentarily paralyzed—as they simply pushed it forward and stepped on through, the first time the chimps had left the Carson Center since they'd each arrived. Then it hit him.

"Diana, the chimps are out!"

Diana spun around to find all four chimps lumbering freely from the cage, knuckling the earth and craning their heads to the sky. The sun trickled through the elm trees; the grass shimmered like a riverbed. The path unspooled before them, flat and wide and running north toward the highway. The wind split their coats and pressed them forward.

"Get inside," she said. "Now."

She and Jason darted inside, threw their backs into the door, caught the water hose in between. They ripped the hose forward, pitched it aside, slammed the door again, and locked it. Diana pulled the walkie-talkie from her belt, held it trembling to her mouth.

"The chimps are loose!" she yelled. "Get everyone inside."

"The chimps are loose," she repeated, slower this time.

"Hello? The chimps got out. The chimps are loose. Get everyone inside."

Static coughed from the radio. She gave it a few more seconds, and when nobody responded, she remembered the cell phone in her pocket. She pulled it out and dialed the front office, but the call was dropped— no signal. The two huddled in the kitchen for several minutes, hoping the chimps would clear the area, their hearts racing, temples pounding, gravity mounting in shifts, then Diana stepped outside and called again. This time she found a signal. Pacing back and forth and waiting for someone—anyone—to answer, she spotted the chimps farther up the path, halfway to the visitor center, staggering past the dingo enclosure. The dingoes themselves stood at attention, ears perked, heads cocked. When the front office finally picked up the phone, Diana told them to get everyone inside, to lock the doors, and to stay clear of the windows.

She knew the stories of chimpanzee escapes and the attacks that followed. Just that March, two chimpanzees had broken loose from their cage in a California animal sanctuary and pounced on a visiting couple. One chimp bit down on the wife's thumb and tore it away in a single jerk. Then both tackled the husband. They bit off his nose, shredded the skin from his face. They chewed on his feet, on his buttocks, on his skull. They bit off his genitals, tore off his lips and most of his teeth. One of them stuck its finger in his right eye and scooped it out. Only when the owner's son-in-law heard the screams, grabbed his .45-caliber pistol, and shot them both did the chimps let up. Jason locked himself in the small black bear enclosure on the south side of the Carson Center. Diana sprinted to the diet kitchen and grabbed the shotgun.

Within minutes, Junior sped toward her on the zoo's topless white golf cart. She climbed on board without saying a word, hair sweaty and sticking to her forehead, and as they drove farther up the trail, they found Jimmy Joe, always her favorite, her "gentleman," squatting before the cage of the great horned owl, fingers hooked through the chain-link fence. She called out his name, "Jimmy!" and he quickly turned around. Of the four, he was the biggest, roughly 185 pounds, hands that could palm a Frisbee. His mouth hung open. His nostrils flared. He furrowed his brow and cocked his shoulders. She knew he hated guns, the noise, the way the sun wrapped around the cold steel barrel—like most of the chimps, he'd been tranquilized before, transferred from one facility to another. She lifted the shotgun to her shoulder, drew the beads between his eyes.

"He looked me right in the eye, and I swear to god that look said, 'You will never pull the trigger on me.' He was right."

He held his gaze on Diana for a moment longer—a look that would follow her for months and years to come—then turned his back and walked away, shoulders hunched, and headed toward the unfinished tiger pen. They'd lost track of the others, but they kept Jimmy Joe in sight. Nearing the office, Diana leaped off the cart and pushed her shoulder to the back door, praying the tranquilizer gun was in order.

"It's me!" she yelled. "It's Diana. Let me in!"

Junior, meanwhile, kept circling the yard, trying his best to lure the chimps away from the buildings, to coax them "to chase me," he would later write, the only line of defense—though still unarmed—between four unpredictable chimpanzees and the visitors huddled up inside. Up ahead, he discovered a young family strolling the grounds and Jimmy Joe pressing toward them. Too far from shelter to make a run for it, twenty-seven-year-old Dana Olmer turned to face the chimp, his pregnant wife and three-year-old daughter hiding behind him.

"I'm a big guy," he later told the *Lincoln Journal Star*. "I stood there trying to make myself look as big as I could."

Jimmy Joe stood on his hind legs, meeting Dana shoulder high. He tried his best to look away, to avoid eye contact, as if he were dealing with a rabid dog. Jimmy Joe "growled at me," he said, but soon returned to all fours and kept walking. The Olmers rushed toward the office, trying their best to keep low. Another chimp cut them off halfway, but Junior sped between them, distracting the chimp and opening a path to the office. Seconds later, the chimps were upon them once again, pounding on the back door.

"Our little three-year-old doesn't understand," Dana's wife said. "But we do. That could have been our lives."

— ⁓ —

Anna Schaben and Candace Macke, both from Orchard, had just left a jewelry party at the home of their friend Stephanie Hughes when Anna noticed a chimp clinging to the zoo's western fence line. She wondered aloud if this was normal, though she didn't slow down. They'd never considered that the animals might escape; for most locals, the zoo had lost its exoticism years ago, so familiar now it seemed almost normal, the way a Western painter might include the barbwire fence, as if it had always been there, every bit as natural as the bluegrass and the boiling thunderheads above. A howling wolf no longer raised eyebrows. A hooting chimpanzee was as common as the noon whistle. The mother of three kids, Anna had been to the zoo hundreds of times. And so they kept driving, certain a keeper was close behind, that it was just another day at Zoo Nebraska.

When they turned west onto the highway, where the power lines split and the road opened wide, they found another chimp barreling toward Thirsty's Bar, a dark flash beneath a powder-blue sky. There was nothing left to interpret. Anna flipped a U-turn, certain now something had gone awry. She watched in the rearview mirror as the chimp pilfered a plastic chair from the parking lot and let it grind on the asphalt behind him, lazy and loose, like the neighbor's boy tired of shoveling snow. Above him: the sky, sprawling and sharp and completely unobstructed, the sun spreading itself across the pavement like soft butter, no longer sliced and divvied by the wire crosshatch of a cage or the wooden slats of a shipping crate or the water-stained skylight of the Carson Center. Anna sped back to the zoo. They rushed through the gates and rapped on the office door. They heard the lock slide back. The door cracked ajar.

"Hurry up," Fayette said. "Get in."

Inside the admissions building, they joined Fayette and her father and roughly a dozen puzzled customers whom Fayette had ushered inside at Junior's command just moments before. She'd steered them toward the back and away from the windows. Then she'd made three phone calls: to 911; to the vet; and to Marvin Young, the zoo board president. And then she lied: she told everyone this had happened before—several times—that it was no big deal and would blow over soon, that the director would have them corralled and back in their cages in no time flat.

"I didn't want anyone to panic," she later wrote in a voluntary statement for the state patrol. "I talked and calmed the visitors down and everyone was in good spirits . . ."

That was, until a furry black hand punched through the ticket window, showering a fistful of glass on the counter. The front door began to shake, the gold handle twisting back and forth. They could hear the chimps—were there two, three, four?—hooting and slapping, pounding the tin with fists like rubber mallets. Tufts of hair darted back and forth, visible just above the windowpane. The air conditioner began to click and rattle, the chimps' heavy blows ringing inside the metal cage, the whole unit threatening to push through the wall. The families inside gathered tight, parents hugging children to their sides. Anna grabbed

Candace and hid in the bathroom. She locked the door. Like Diana, she knew the chimps' strength, knew they "could rip your arms off." *If they make it inside and everyone bolts,* Anna thought, *hopefully they'll chase the people who run.*

Then came the pounding in the back—and how could they tell, really, if it was man or beast, if that anxious, butterfly beating was an excited chimpanzee or a desperate visitor, though Fayette would later insist "they showed no signs of aggression." For a minute the building calmed. All still outside the eastern windows. All still out front. And then the racket returned, a pounding on the back door, though it seemed somehow steadier this time. Fayette hesitated, but the knocks kept coming, and when she finally cracked the door, a shaken Diana pushed her way inside. She offloaded her shotgun on a visitor near the door, a man who looked like he'd pulled a trigger before.

"If they come around the windows, show 'em that gun," she said. "I don't know what else will stop them. They can go through glass in a heartbeat."

Just moments later, she found Jimmy Joe standing outside the front door, more electric now than he seemed before, as if at any second he might swing those long, brawny arms behind his head and throw them forward through the glass. She stepped behind the door where he could see her and said, as loudly and calmly as she could muster, "No, Jimmy! No, Jimmy!" And like that, he scampered away.

Diana found the tranquilizer gun and the drugs inside the cabinet, and with fingers shaking, nerves sparking like a blown transformer, she began to hastily load the darts and screw in the CO_2 cartridge—she tried, anyhow, but she skipped a step, or she reversed the order, or perhaps she never knew how to handle the gun to begin with. Two recent USDA inspection reports had specifically warned that "currently there is no means [at Zoo Nebraska] to restrain or capture the animals in the event of an emergency. For example, none of the employees knows how to operate the tranquilizer gun." Whatever the case, Diana says, "I really think I kind of lost it at that point."

Outside, Junior had been circling the building, waiting for Diana to load the darts, trying his best to distract the chimps. When she finally delivered the gun out the back door, Junior sped off but returned just seconds later. The gun wasn't firing, he said. She returned to the office and tried again, this time with guest Dana Olmer standing over her shoulder, the air thick and stale, the walls closing in. The CO2 cartridge was empty, he told her. She loaded another and passed it back to Junior, still waiting outside. The shrieking seemed farther away now, and for a moment, the building settled, the only noise the flute of wind through the shattered window. She could feel her heart beating against her chest, like a bass drum beneath her ribs, sure it was soon to punch through.

Oblivious to the escape, a pocket of townies sat around small Formica tables at the One Stop, shooting the shit and drinking cheap coffee from Styrofoam cups. One of those townies was forty-seven-year-old Arvin Brandt, a mustached off-duty cop with the county sheriff's office and Dick Haskin's third cousin, portly and graying at the temples. The men had parked their trucks haphazardly around the old analog pumps, around the single red maple tree in the parking lot. Different sections of the newspaper lay scattered across the tables, Hurricane Katrina still crowding the headlines. Around 12:15 p.m., the conversation choked to a halt when an especially long and hirsute forearm gently opened the front door. Arvin slammed it shut. They locked every door in the station. Arvin's older brother, Duaine, pulled up in his truck, spotted the chimp outside the One Stop, and skidded to a halt. Confused and crowding the windows, the men watched from inside as Ripley—or perhaps it was Reuben, they couldn't be sure—crossed the highway, sauntered onto the Johnsons' front lawn, and began to ride the tire swing.

Framed by two silver maples and a small white home with tidy black trim, the grass cut short, the mailbox rusting beneath the sun, the chimp appeared, if only for a moment, utterly American, suspended in some bizarro Norman Rockwell painting and slowly twisting back and forth, back and forth, back and forth. Then Ripley crossed that blustery hot-plate highway once again, past the buckling childhood home of Jeri Southern, cut through another yard, and sauntered past Bill Mitteis's machine shop.

"[Bill] said he just had a feeling that he should close the garage door, and, as it was closing, he saw a chimp go by," says Steffanie Hughes, who lived two blocks west.

Still idling in the driveway of the One Stop, Duaine raced to the zoo for answers. When he returned, he told everyone to stay inside and keep the doors locked—that all four chimps were at large. The brothers jumped in their trucks, drove to their respective homes, and grabbed their firearms. Arvin loaded his pistol and a shotgun; Duaine, a .22-caliber rifle, typically used for target shooting or small game. Along the way, Arvin picked up his friend Dennis Bridge, a conservation technician for the nearby trout-rearing station, and he called his nephew Justin Brandt from Orchard, who packed two deer hunting rifles and hit the road. Dennis was eating lunch when Arvin pulled up, still unaware of the events unfolding around him. Watching Arvin scurry up the walkway, service revolver tucked into his denim bib overalls, Dennis knew immediately "something was not quite right."

"The chimps are out," Arvin said. "Grab your rifle and get in."

For the next few minutes, the two of them crisscrossed Royal in Arvin's pickup, windows down, elbows out, scanning for sudden movement. When they passed someone on the street or out in their yard, they slapped the truck and warned them back inside. In years past, both men had supported the zoo. Both knew the chimps by name, remembered Reuben when he was still in diapers, the shoddy trailer house Dick had named the Midwest Primate Center. Dennis's own children used to volunteer during their summer breaks at the zoo when Dick ran the show. And both Arvin and Dennis now considered Junior a close friend, sometimes part of the morning crew that joined them for coffee and donuts in the shop. They cared for the zoo and cared for those who looked after it.

But at the moment, none of that mattered. They gave little thought to how this all might look in the weeks and months to come, gun-toting men hunting chimpanzees in the streets of Royal, where it all might settle in the zeitgeist, how it all might filter into the bedrock of the community, the tragedy never quite stripped from the soil. They couldn't have predicted the backlash, the newspaper reports, every know-it-all outsider criticizing their actions, nitpicking the way a tiny farm town handled the escape of four adult chimpanzees. They were the last and only line of defense. Royal hadn't prepared for this, and they saw that all too clearly now. No alarms. No sirens. No established protocol, either in town or at the zoo. Only later did they consider their own safety and how either brave or stupid they'd been.

"You're hoping for the best, expecting the worst," Bridge says. "In the middle of it, you just did what you had to do and didn't stop to think about it. And I'm not bragging, but there was some people that stepped up and literally put their lives on the line for their community."

Only a dozen small blocks, Royal didn't take long to cover. Seemingly quiet, Arvin and Dennis headed back to Zoo Nebraska, desperate for good news. Junior met them at the front gate, still on his golf cart, his thick forehead crinkled and red and glistening with sweat. He said the tranquilizer darts weren't working, weren't slowing them down. He asked to borrow a gun.

"Human safety was the main concern," Arvin would later write in his testimony for the state patrol. "The chimps needed to be brought under control."

—⁓—

Standing on her back porch one block west of the Carson Center, her strawberry-blonde hair lifting against the wind, twenty-six-year-old Steffanie Hughes had just waved goodbye to her friends Anna and Candace when she heard the rising chorus of chimpanzees. She and her young family had volunteered at the zoo off and on for the past six years, under multiple directors, and so she was hardly surprised to hear the commotion, a more or less daily occurrence. Less common was the neighbor's kid, Austin Schleusener, a husky fourteen-year-old boy, screaming, "There's a chimp loose!" and sprinting down the street toward his house, Ripley trailing close behind. Austin thundered through the back door and leaned his weight behind it, but Ripley caught it first, his own momentum crashing forward. Austin and his mother planted their feet and spread their palms flat against the door, and still Ripley—she swears it was Ripley, though others claim it was Reuben—held steady, pushing and jostling the doorknob, a two-inch gap between the door and its frame, a stalemate at 2nd and Fremont.

As Ripley struggled to enter the home, forty-three-year-old Carolyn Petersen, Hughes's neighbor, and her daughter Kristi ripped around the corner in Carolyn's red Ford minivan, honking the horn and screaming, "Get inside!" Up ahead, the pointed cap of the water tower peaked above the trees, still flush with green in September. Distracted by the horn, Ripley surrendered the door and rushed toward the van, knuckles brushing the grass, every muscle shifting and flexing beneath his coat. Still outside despite the warning, Hughes watched from her porch as Ripley, midsprint, effortlessly lifted a gas grill from the yard and hurled it with one arm at the van like a pissed-off baggage handler. When Carolyn accelerated, the chimp lunged at the vehicle and slapped it with his hand.

"Unfortunately, she was driving around looking for them," Bridge says. "She should have been home. Just kind of a busybody—no disrespect intended. I don't think she realized the danger."

Hughes was now the last one outside, despite her many opportunities to retreat. Ripley noticed. He spun around, built up steam. She moved inside. She locked the door. Her five-year-old daughter began to scream "because she knows how dangerous they can be," she says, which riled him up even more. He hooted and paced, shoulders hunched. She sent her kids to the basement. *They can't panic if they can't see him,* she thought, and she prayed aloud "that god would put his hedge of protection around us." Ripley turned away from the door. He played on their swing set, hung off the steel frame. He sat still in their garden. He picked their strawberries. A few minutes later, Ripley heard gunshots in the distance and the screams of the other chimps and ran back to the zoo, leaping over the perimeter fence as if it were no obstacle at all.

"Believe in the power of god or not, that's how it happened," she says.

A single chimpanzee, most likely Jimmy Joe, now lumbered outside the vestibule like a priest with a great weight on his shoulders, worry shifting from knuckle to wrist to shoulder. The others milled about like parishioners after church, loosely assembled in the clearing behind him. At 12:57 p.m., roughly an hour after the chimps first slipped their cage, State Trooper Brian Detlefsen pulled off the highway just as Junior—still in his golf cart—stuttered through a clearing in the trees. Neither one seemed to concern the brooding chimp, who continued his idle pacing until the golf cart cut off his path. When he lunged forward, Junior fired. He didn't sprawl out or spin around, didn't nurse the wound or fold into the church. Instead, the chimp slapped the dirt like an all-star forward, shrieked once, and sprang forward again, chasing Junior's golf cart from behind.

"It looked like the old Wild West," Detlefsen says, "like [Junior] was on a horse shooting over his back."

Lured by the sound of the gunshot, Tyler, just ten years old, rushed toward the action. He ran smack into Junior, who whipped the pistol out from his hip, foot still on the gas, rotated in his seat, took aim, and fired again, striking him in the side. With an earsplitting howl, Tyler leapfrogged off the church and hid briefly in the crook of the vestibule, where Junior found him, shooting him four more times in the chest from ten yards out, until he finally collapsed on a pile of rocks beside the church, choking on his own heavily tranquilized blood.

Meanwhile, Ripley and Reuben retreated toward the south end of the zoo—or perhaps it was just before, or maybe just after, the timeline a swirl of adrenaline and moving parts, four chimpanzees, at least two wounded, a golf cart and a pistol and a congress of conflicting accounts. The chronology would never be fully reassembled. Either way, Jimmy Joe soon dashed toward a large pile of cinder blocks on the eastern edge of the parking lot, a long open sprint to relative safety or, as Fayette would later claim, an act of heroism, "protecting them like he always did" and drawing the gunmen's attention away from the other retreating chimps.

Trooper Detlefsen was still in his patrol vehicle outside the gates. He hadn't trained for this; in fact, the academy hadn't covered animal control at all, so much as he could remember, save for one sage piece of advice: "If it's run over in the road," he says, "get the farmer's permission before you shoot it." It was a tenet he'd always followed, and one he had considered again briefly as he cruised into Royal just moments ago, still expecting a loose steer or a busted fender and a bleeding goat.

But as he watched Jimmy Joe pacing atop the cinder blocks like a depressive on the ledge of a parking garage, gunfire ringing out intermittently from the farthest reaches of the zoo and a derby of dusty trucks whipping past him, that counsel hardly seemed relevant. He stayed in the vehicle a few beats longer, trying his best to assess the chaos, though in his personal estimation he was three links down the chain of command. Arvin was technically off duty, but Detlefsen followed his lead. Arvin knew the zoo. He knew the director. He knew the social blueprint of Royal. Either way, given how much had already unraveled, Detlefsen struggled to envision a happy ending.

Detlefsen was still sitting in his truck when Arvin hustled forward, motioning a pump action with his hands.

"Get your shotgun out," he yelled, barely audible above the wind.

When Arvin's nephew finally hit Royal, he didn't beeline for the entry gate but drove to his sister's house instead, where Ponca Street simply peters out and spits you into a grassy no-man's-land beside the Carson Center. So close to ground zero, Justin worried she hadn't heard, that a chimp might catch her hanging clothes on the line or cleaning up around the yard.

When he parked the car and stepped outside, a shot rang out from the south side of the building. He followed the noise and found Junior in his golf cart outside the zoo, taking aim with a borrowed handgun at a chimpanzee scrambling up the fence. Junior shot him in the back— the heavy metal blast rapping off the Carson Center—and again, and again, at least four to five times by his own count, the chimp finally plummeting to the grass in the shade of a small bush, his right eye swollen shut.

Even then the chimp wouldn't give up. Somewhere along the line, Junior had acquired a second weapon, a .30-06, which he now pressed to his shoulder and pulled the trigger. Standing beside him, Justin raised the barrel of his .223 and shot two more times, finally ending what must have felt like an eternity of struggle, certainly for the chimp, and perhaps both men, too, who would refuse to discuss it for years to come. Guns lowered, they could now clearly identify the subject. It was Reuben. The most famous chimpanzee in Nebraska. He was twenty-two years old, roughly 120 pounds, the adopted son of a man named Dick Haskin. He liked Pepsi and cartoons. Some claim he was simply returning to his cage—that he was going home.

—⁓—

Jimmy Joe calmed himself on the cinder blocks. He could see the small militia now forming in the parking lot, the cache of weapons, Detlefsen's cruiser and the fleet of pickups, a socket of cedar trees, a lone pine, an old red van parked inside the fence, but mostly just the flat earth running deep into the sky and the dust blowing north across the highway. Detlefsen didn't know where the other chimps had gone, but he could hear the gunshots and assumed they were contained. He focused exclusively on Jimmy Joe, who resumed pacing on the blocks. And while all of this was insane—the kind of story his friends back home would find ludicrous—he saw no choice but to proceed as he would with any other questionable suspect.

"If he's just going to stand there not hitting anybody, you treat him like a human being," he says. "But if he wants to be a criminal, then you've got to treat him like a criminal."

Detlefsen grabbed the shotgun and stepped outside as Jimmy Joe dropped from the blocks. Shielded behind the door of his truck, Duaine—even heavier than his brother—planted a foot in the dirt and shot twice with his .22, the rifle tiny against his massive frame, striking the chimp both times in the chest without slowing him down. Hardly defeated, Jimmy Joe took three quick strides, launched over the fence, and promptly disappeared. Arvin nodded at Detlefsen's shotgun.

"You have a rifle?" Arvin asked.

Another shot rang out behind them. Detlefsen jogged back to his vehicle with the gun held out from his side, swapped it out for his Ruger Mini 14, a gun he would keep long after the state patrol transitioned to automatics, "a good reminder of the day," he says. All three men converged in the middle of the lot and slowly approached the blocks.

"All I had was my twenty-two, but he's been hit," Duaine said. "He's somewhere in the area by that van or behind the bricks."

Detlefsen jammed the magazine in his rifle and released the bolt.

"You keep watching 'cause if he comes over that fucking wire, hell . . . ," Arvin said.

"Where's he at?" Detlefsen wondered aloud, nervously standing atop the bricks himself. He inched toward the ledge, found Jimmy Joe behind the wheel.

"He's inside here!" he called to Arvin below.

"He's inside the van?"

Jimmy Joe began to jump and thrash, rocking the van, screaming and tearing up the upholstery, smearing his blood across the dash, as if he just now realized he was trapped inside.

"It was like *Planet of the Apes*," Detlefsen says. "Every time I see that movie, I'm looking around because the scream in that movie is the same one [that came] out of that van."

Duaine reparked his truck parallel to the blocks, creating a make-shift barricade. Two more locals joined the huddle with rifles slung over their shoulders.

"Take him out inside the van?" the trooper asked Arvin.

"Oh, we don't want to break windows, do we?"

"As long as he's in there—"

"If he tries to get out," Arvin called back over his shoulder, "take him."

But the standoff seemed to enter a strange intermission. Fifty-mile-an-hour gusts now whipped the trees like dirty rag dolls, their shadows dark and distended across the parking lot. The flag clanked against its pole. Another truck rumbled past on the highway. The sun bounced off the shiny hood of the trooper's vehicle, the whole scene playing out upside down in its reflection. At least seven armed men now gauged the situation, patrolling the gate or standing behind Duaine's truck, ready to shoot if Jimmy Joe sprang out. Uncomfortable with silence, the men filled it with idle chatter.

"I had one tryin'a get inside my house," one said.

"Well . . . this is too bad of a deal," said another. "Can't overreact."

"At least he's smart enough to hide himself," said a third.

"He's bleedin' pretty good," Detlefsen said.

Through the tinted back window of the van, the men could barely make out the chimp still protesting inside. Two more trucks arrived and helped buttress the barricade. On the other side of the fence, Junior approached the van on his golf cart, cutting behind the trees, maneuvering around a pile of surplus fencing, wooden poles, and metal stakes, unaware of the current standoff. The men in the parking lot yelled, "Don't shoot! Don't shoot!" but Junior couldn't hear them.

"Careful, guys," Detlefsen said, leaning against the hood of the truck. "Make sure if he starts to shoot, you guys get down. He's gonna start shooting, I bet."

Arvin stepped forward and cupped his hands around his mouth.

"The vet is coming!" he shouted over the cab of the pickup, but it seemed as if he were shouting into a cardboard box, his words refusing to carry.

"The veterinarian! Is coming! With some stuff! To knock him down!" he shouted again, louder and slower this time. Junior seemed to catch it. He backed away from the van.

Despite everyone now crowding the scene, no one knew exactly how many chimps were still a threat. *Was there only one in the van, or two? Was the chimp in the van the same as the one on the blocks? Who took care of the one on the south end? On the east? How many chimps were in town, and how many came back?* As the men clumsily tried to piece it all together, Randall "Doc" Pedersen, the local veterinarian, easygoing and semiretired, finally pulled off the highway in his burgundy pickup.

Pedersen's wife, Nancy, had answered the call and then relayed the message to her sixty-eight-year-old husband, who was working cattle roughly twenty minutes away. Pedersen asked her to grab the tranquilizer gun from his office and meet him at the zoo. En route to the standoff, Pedersen called his son, also a veterinarian, who helped him calculate the right dosage for a chimp. He'd long ago memorized how many cc it takes to drop a steer. He'd run a practice in Beatrice, Nebraska, for nearly twenty-five years before easing into semiretirement along the Verdigris. But he had limited experience with exotics, and needless to say, he'd never tranquilized a chimpanzee. He sped east down Highway 20, straining to envision the chaos he would soon be asked to sedate.

"Historically, if one chimp gets out, somebody gets hurt. If two get out, somebody gets killed," he says. "And this time, there were four."

When Pedersen finally arrived, his wife was already there, waiting as promised with the gun, wearing denim shorts and a baggy red shirt as if she'd just stepped away from the garden. She held the gun at her side while Arvin and the trooper apprised him of the situation.

"The one in the van took a pretty good shot to the chest, point-blank," Detlefsen said, breathing steadier now, eyes trained over the doc's shoulder.

"Well, golly," Pedersen said, adjusting his faded ball cap. He wore loose khakis and a casual green button-down. "We got the stuff to do it, we got the gun. Because you could get pretty close to him, couldn't ya?"

"Yeah, I think so . . . By the time I got here, it was just pure pandemonium."

Standing on the periphery, Robert Schleusener, one of the many locals who had since trickled in, interrupted with his own unsolicited testimony, clearly still shaken.

"One came right up—the boy was hanging clothes on the line, he come through runnin' and screamin'. I thought he was chimp meat," he said. "Then he come up tryin' to get in the house. I was outside, boy and my wife was tryin'a hold the door shut."

"Well, we got the stuff," Pedersen repeated. "We got the gun and everything."

Pedersen hardly doubted that Jimmy Joe—or any of the others, for that matter—had already been tranquilized to no effect. Under normal conditions, the tranquilizers would have taken about eight minutes to kick in, "but the more excitable the animal is, the more vasoconstriction you have, and the slower the anesthetic works." The doc would compensate, slightly increasing the dosage of the 5 cc darts he was soon to load into his rifle, though he wasn't convinced it was worth the effort. Even if he made a clean hit, the animal had already sustained several gunshot wounds, "and with the armament they had, it would have been a real tough wound to do much with," he says. Either way, Jimmy Joe's chances were slim.

"He's not going anywhere," Detlefsen said, and just then, as if to prove him wrong, Jimmy Joe shattered the rear window with his fist, the men behind the truck scattering like a host of sparrows.

"Hang on," he said. "Hang on."

"He's coming out!" another man yelled. "What do we do?"

"What do you think, Doc?" Detlefsen asked. "Do you want to tranquilize him?"

"We can try, but if you already shot him with a forty-five . . ." Detlefsen hesitated.

"We can try," Pedersen said again, calmly walking back to his truck. Detlefsen turned back to the other men still awaiting his command.

"He better hurry up," one said.

Krista Anderegg, the science teacher at Orchard High, now joined the circle. Another vehicle. Another body, though one of the few without a gun. She'd taken her life sciences class to the zoo once a year since 1989, and though she admired Dick Haskin and his passion for the animals, she had watched over the years as he slowly worked himself into the ground. She now served on the board and was planning to work that afternoon with the black bear when she encountered a "firing squad" instead. Like the others, she'd never considered a chimp escape. If anything, she would have guessed the tigers, new as they were to the zoo.

"When I figured out what was going on, I asked if anybody had called Dick yet," she says. "Everybody looked at me like, *Why?* I thought if anybody could have done something about it, it was Dick. He has so much experience working with chimps and primates. He would have been the first person that came to mind."

But at the moment, Dick's savvy with primates was merely a distraction. With the help of his wife, Pedersen loaded the darts in less than five minutes. When he returned to the barricade, he and Detlefsen slowly approached the cinder blocks, rifles held out from their chests, followed by an entourage of suntanned farmers and ranchers armed with rifles most of them kept year-round in their trucks.

"You are my protector," he told Detlefsen, his voice gravelly and calm. "If this guy comes over the fence, you've got to take him out."

Pedersen clambered on top of the blocks and dropped to one knee, searching for a clear shot through the fence. He needed to hit Jimmy Joe in the ass, frankly, but he couldn't find the angle, the chimp was facing the wrong direction, he couldn't maneuver any lower. Detlefsen covered the doc from below, safety off, his rifle tight against his shoulder and sighted on the shattered window, spitballing ways to lure Jimmy Joe in the right direction.

"Arvin, get everybody with their guns facing this way," he said, calculating on the fly, as much for himself as for Arvin, "and have somebody stand down there to distract him; that way he's looking out the windshield, and Doc can get a shot at his butt."

Nancy stood motionless back at the pickup, watching her husband steady himself on the blocks. Jimmy Joe shrieked again, and the troops, edgier now, pulsed back. But Jimmy Joe stayed inside the van. Pedersen knelt a second time as another patrol car entered the parking lot, one more vehicle in this surreal country parade. Knees throbbing, the doc resumed his aim, steadying his rifle for another four long minutes, Jimmy Joe crying all the while, shrill but more rhythmic now, almost birdlike in its consistency.

"Come on, you asshole!" one man yelled.

And so Jimmy Joe took flight. He sprang from the broken window like an Olympic swimmer just off the block, head down, arms outstretched, back slightly bowed. He looked like he might never land, like he might shoot straight up into the clouds and spin the earth in his wake. He looked, in that fleeting moment, free as a chimpanzee ought to be. There, in the zenith of his flight, ready to grab the fence and jump again, Detlefsen, fifty feet away, curtly raised his Ruger and pulled the trigger. Jimmy Joe's body folded into itself, hands to feet, collapsed like a pizza box, and crashed into the fence. He landed on his back less than ten feet from the doc, and then he tried, in vain, to scramble back to the van. Justin Brandt, who had placed the final bullet in Reuben less than forty-five minutes before, stepped forward and shot again, pinning him to the dirt. Jimmy Joe cried out a few more times, each cry fainter than the last, his blood painting the crabgrass, until finally he let go.

"Thank god no one was hurt," Justin would later write in his voluntary statement. "All shots were kill shots on the animals."

—⁂—

For nearly an hour already, Diana had been trembling with the rest of the evacuees inside the admissions office. She stepped outside just in time to watch them "gun Jimmy down in the back."

The levee burst. The tears spilled out. She grew weak and her knees buckled. And then, as if someone had flipped a switch, she turned livid. Her sorrow boiled to a rage that she dumped on Arvin, who was standing nearby. Her wailing was deep and punctuated with hiccups of terrible silence, so utterly wrecked her body seemed too weak to release the full horror of her cry.

"You killed them, Arvin!" she sobbed. "You can't kill them . . . no, no . . . not Jimmy . . . no."

Still jittery himself, Arvin let her cry, let her say what she needed to say, tried his best to console her, though of course her pain would linger for years to come. She would replay that final shot over and over and over again, until it ravaged her dreams and ripped her awake in cold sweats. Soon her husband, Dean, would arrive to load her up and take her back to Verdigre, to her quiet home along the creek, though Arvin had already called her an ambulance. She waited two days before completing her witness statement, her grief in the moment all encompassing.

"I remember trying to interview her. She was just—nothing," says Trooper Bill Price, slicing a hand through the air. "She was just gone."

Price had arrived just a minute before Detlefsen pulled the trigger to find "twenty to thirty people running around crazy with rifles," and after the shooting, he walked out to meet the group in the middle of the lot. Still under the impression a fourth chimp was missing, they began to deploy again when Price stopped them.

"Why don't you guys get a plan before you just roll over the monkey," he said.

"We didn't have time to get a plan," Arvin snapped back. "Don't come in here and just start telling us we're doin' everything wrong."

"I'm not tellin' ya you did anything wrong. I'm just sayin' you got everybody runnin' around with guns—"

"If we can tranquilize them, that would be the best," one woman said.

"I realize that," Arvin said calmly. "We had chimps try to break into peoples' houses . . ."

"I know, I know," she said.

"We had them break into the station. We're doing the best we can. It's not obviously good enough, but we're trying."

"It doesn't look like your plan is going real well, though," Price said.

Before the pissing match could escalate, word trickled back that the last chimp had already been killed, that Reuben was dead in the southwest corner of the zoo, that at some point Ripley had voluntarily returned to his cage, slipping in where he'd first slipped out, and that Junior had locked him in. The men began to relax, "literally high fiving," Price says. They started to load up and go home when Price stopped them again. The guns. The animals. The chaos. Everything was "totally outside the norm of life," he says. He wasn't about to let the witnesses and active participants just hop back in their trucks and drive home, though their diesel was already burning in the parking lot. They couldn't bungle this one—the press was sure to pounce on it. He and Detlefsen would need to handle the escape as if it were a crime scene: call the supervisor, gather witness statements, photographs, interviews—all of it.

"He just came right at the doc here," Detlefsen said, still processing his own role.

"You're fine. You're justified in what you did," Price said. "But if you shot, we need to get a supervisor up here."

Price sent Detlefsen back to the cruiser to secure his weapon, one less gun on the scene. Arvin approached Detlefsen from behind.

"Thank you from the town board," he said. "We appreciate everything."

"I'm sorry."

"Well, I don't like what we had to do either, but under the circumstances, I don't see where we had much choice. I mean, the doc never got a shot off, and the chimp was trying to climb the fence, so what the fuck you supposed to do?"

While Detlefsen took statements in the church, Price took photos of the kill zones: of the broken windows; of Jimmy Joe sprawled in the grass, his nose pressed in the dirt; of the open padlock at the Carson Center; of Tyler at the base of a cedar tree, head resting on his arm, rocks scattered beneath him; of Reuben already loaded into the back of the utility vehicle, the white tarp slopped with bright-red blood; of the dented red minivan, whose driver didn't trust her insurance company would believe her; of the injured whitetail deer that Junior had seen lifted by a chimp like a strongman and lobbed through the fence. Junior said the chimp then beat his chest and jumped in with the Bengal tigers, who quickly chased him off. Junior said he'd thrown a hammer at one of the chimps from the golf cart before he was properly armed. He said the chimp threw it back.

"When I called my captain, I said, 'Captain, you are not going to believe what I'm about to tell you, and you'll never get a phone call like this again in your life.' Who would have thought in the middle of nowhere, Nebraska, that these monkeys would get out and this would occur? The news was going to love it."

But the press arrived late. The local news station supposedly drove its van to Royal, Iowa, instead, three hours east, which gave the troopers time to work without the gaze of a camera over their shoulders. When they finished gathering testimony, the troopers would drive back to their small office in downtown Neligh. They'd write up their official narratives, and Detlefsen would fill out his firearm discharge report. He would keep the dashcam video close to his chest at the behest of his superiors—who also advised him to lie low for the next few days—but after the six o'clock news, Detlefsen's mother would call to say she'd seen him on TV. And if his mother already knew, why delay the gratification of sharing the tape with his friends and colleagues?

Eventually, the academy started using the video in training. Every time Royal popped up in conversation, Detlefsen says, his colleagues across the state would look at him and say, "Hey, you're the monkey guy!" or simpler still, "You're the *guy*."

Before the troopers left Royal, they found Dick Haskin at the gate asking what only the science teacher seemed to have considered: "Why didn't you call me?" Six months earlier, he'd started a new job as the business manager for Building Blocks for Community Enrichment, a nonprofit that helps recruit and license foster homes across northeast Nebraska, but he often still slept through the day if he wasn't on the job. That Saturday, he'd run a few quick errands in town and been back in bed by noon. His father, Jim, let himself inside shortly after one o'clock.

"You're not gonna sleep after what I tell you," he said, standing over Dick's bed.

"What?"

"Reuben's dead. He was shot," Jim said. "They escaped, and he was shot."

Dick didn't wait for more. He brushed past his father, jumped in his old Chevy Blazer, and "floored it," he says. He found the patrol cars in the parking lot and the ambulance outside and Diana in the grass beside it, now fainted or looking like she had. Like Diana, Dick had never forgotten the day she found him spraying Reuben down at the centennial, how she'd ripped him up and down as if he knew nothing at all about this animal he'd devoted his life to. And through the grapevine, he'd since heard about her incident with the cougars and how the Bakkens had subsequently let her go. All of which left him with "a healthy dislike for her," he says. And so, in passing, he couldn't help but flippantly dismiss her breakdown. A few weeks later, after he learned Diana had played a role in the escape, he would fight the urge, day after day, to call her and ask a simple question: "Well, a water hose or a rifle?"

But for now he kept on walking. When he reached the gate, Sheriff Hamilton blocked the way.

"You can't go in there, Dick; it's a crime scene."

"Darrell," he begged. "Darrell, I've got to—"

"You can't go in there."

There was no argument, no punches thrown, before Dick broke down. He simply turned around, slumped against the fence, and buried his face in his hands. So this is how his grand, cursed experiment would end: locked out of a zoo of his own creation, three dead chimpanzees inside, all of it just a few hundred yards from the classroom where he first learned what it meant to dream—*really* dream—to feel that calling in his marrow, to slip that pale skin and rise from that old wooden school chair and transport himself to a world so green he lusted for it, an adventure so raw and so real he could practically feel the dew on his fingertips. Now he felt nothing but dirt and the sun burning the nape of his neck.

"What are you doing out here?"

Dick lowered his hands to see Arvin standing above him in overalls.

"You need to be in there."

"They won't let me," Dick said, wiping back tears.

"You're going in."

"Why wasn't I called?" Dick said again. "Why wasn't I called?"

Arvin led Dick to the golf cart, and they slowly drove toward the Carson Center, the first time he'd seen it up close in years, the few remaining wisps of his hair trailing in the wind. Arvin was shaken but strong, sitting upright in the cart. Dick was little more than a sack of skin and bones, arms dangling at his sides, both weightless and a million pounds.

"Why didn't they call me?" he said, as if the record were skipping. "Why didn't they call me?"

Dick stepped off the cart, walking past Ripley, the lone survivor. It didn't take much to empathize, both of them lonely and suddenly missing a few parts of themselves. Ripley needed to be relocated, needed to be resocialized after enduring such hell, he said to no one in particular, still standing outside the cage. He thoughtlessly began adjusting his movements, his postures, his expressions, the same way he always had around Reuben, the same way he always had with Kumi and Cousteau and Chewy back at the Children's Zoo so many years ago. Though the two had never met, Ripley turned his back in reply, an act of submission, Dick says. A nearby volunteer said that Ripley never acted that way around strangers, but most strangers, Dick said, "don't know how to communicate with him."

Dick says that afternoon is a blur, but he remembers Ripley, and he remembers the blood on the fallen chimps and on the hands of all those still cleaning up at the zoo. He was concerned about potential zoonosis, diseases easily transferable from animals to humans, about herpes and shigella. He told everyone they should all go in for testing, though no one seemed to listen.

"There was blood everywhere and blood on everybody," he says.

Arvin stopped near the back gate, where the old trailer used to sit, where Reuben used to show off inside, still an adolescent. In the back of a small utility vehicle, a black tarp wrinkled itself around a body. Arvin nodded at Dick, who stepped down and slowly pulled it back, white on the other side, save for the scarlet ribbons of blood, not dissimilar to the chimpanzee paintings Diana had framed on her wall at home, trivial loops and scribbles. Reuben's body lay in a crumpled mess, hair slick with blood, his right eye crusted shut, chest and neck swollen from what the necropsy would call "subcutaneous emphysema." Dick stood there in the shade of the trees, looking down at his next of kin. His breath shortened. He wiped his eyes again. The wind ruffled the tarp.

"Why didn't they call me?" he asked Arvin again, staring down at his mistakes. "Why didn't they call me?"

"Why didn't they call me?"

"Why didn't they call me?"

"Over the years, the zoo took most everything from me," he would write in a personal letter more than a decade later. "Reuben's death took whatever was left. My family thought that I went through a depression after I got out of the zoo. I don't think I did. But I do know that after Reuben died, I lost the will to live. I didn't care about anything anymore. I had no hobbies. I had no interests. I really didn't care about anything."

From that day forward, Dick says, he merely existed.

After all the testimonies had been recorded and all the chimps were wrapped up in tarps, Junior returned to those who remained in the activity center. He told them to go home, Fayette says, "because the international press was coming to crucify each of us." When Jerry Guenther, a reporter for the *Norfolk Daily News*, arrived a few minutes later, Junior gave him several shaky minutes but little more. The rest clammed up.

"Here's this huge event that happens at the zoo. Three chimps shot, running all over town. How much hotter can it be? And the fact nobody got hurt, that's just amazing," Guenther says. "What I thought was really weird was how nobody would talk. People at the convenience store, nobody wanted to give a comment. In fact, everybody wanted to pretend it didn't happen. Everybody in Royal wanted to keep that zoo so bad as an attraction for northeast Nebraska that maybe they thought, *Oh, if we just don't say anything, nobody will find out about this.* Everybody was so reluctant to say what occurred. I remember at the time thinking that was a little odd, and when I look back at it, it truly was odd.

"That's Royal, I guess."

The next morning, an anonymous critic would paint "Reuben Killer" on the windows of Junior's machine shop, and the carcasses of all three chimps would be delivered to Omaha, where they'd sit in a refrigerator overnight, awaiting a flight to Saint Louis for their necropsies. They would arrive in the same tarps they left in, their hair "coated in green/black altered blood," according to the report, their tissues "generally in a suboptimal state of preservation." In their stomachs, the pathologists would find monkey chow, liquid paste, and strawberries—their last meal.

In nearby Plainview, the gas station advertised its new lunch specials outside the building: Chimps & Dip. A Reuben sandwich.

In Royal, they wept.

PART III

THE AFTERMATH

The entire Jensen family was 140 miles south of Royal the day the chimps broke loose, exhibiting their work at the Old Trusty Antique and Collectors Show in Clay Center, Nebraska. When they returned the next evening and heard the news, Earleen immediately called Jerry Peterson, who'd resigned from the board presidency just one week before, still incensed about the free-roaming animals. When Jerry heard the news around midnight Sunday, he hung up the phone and lay down in his bed, the room dark and quiet all around him, his head sinking into the pillow. He'd watched his own father die of congestive heart failure in a hospital bed. His grandmother had passed away suddenly of a heart attack when he was twelve, and his mother died in Royal, all alone, of the same.

"But with Reuben the chimpanzee, when I found out he was killed, that's gotta be one of the most saddest days of my life. Because I know it could have been prevented."

The Jensens caught wind of certain rumors, whispered curses suggesting they were somehow responsible for the escape. It irked them, though they weren't surprised, by now intimately aware of how the rumor mill could churn against them. But the rumors didn't last long. Instead, the grapevine circled back to Dick Haskin, whether he could have saved them, whether he should have been called sooner, whether the chimps—high on adrenaline—would have listened to anyone at all.

It was a question initiated by Dick and one he would forever answer with a resounding *Yes, I could have,* though, like so many other catastrophes in Dick's life, he would ultimately blame himself, always questioning what he could have done differently, climbing every link down the chain of reactions until he found himself again. He was angry with those who participated in Reuben's death, but he understood that most locals were only trying to help, that the whole disaster "shouldn't have been put in the people's laps there in Royal" to begin with.

"My heart still aches for Reuben each and every day. I still have nightmares about that day. I am still very bitter at the incompetence that caused the event. I am still angry with Junior, Diana, and the individuals that were part of the zoo board," he later wrote in an email. "But most of all, I am angry with myself because I should have done more to get those chimps removed from the zoo. I knew it was a dangerous situation. And I am angry with myself because I feel that if I had stayed involved with the zoo that none of this would have happened."

In fact, the night before the escape, Dick says, he received a call from Valda Young. Her husband, Marvin, who rented some pastureland from Dick, had recently been roped into accepting the position of zoo board president. She called with questions about the rent, but the conversation quickly turned to the zoo. Dick had expressed concern for the chimps and encouraged her to have them relocated. Especially with Kip and Stacey out of the picture, the zoo didn't have the right personnel to handle four chimpanzees. Junior, whom Dick had met just once, may have loved animals, he told her, may even have had some limited experience with exotics, but that hardly qualified him to work with chimps.

"We've got Diana," she told him.

"What?"

"She's got two years' experience working with chimps."

"Where'd she get the training?" Dick asked. "I know two people in Nebraska that are qualified to train people to work with chimps. I didn't train her, and I think the other one ain't even in zoo work anymore."

"Well, I don't know."

"Valda, you've got a bomb waiting to explode. You really need to do something now."

Trooper Detlefsen's dashcam video would eventually find its way into Dick's hands. He studied it the way he studied his own videos back at the Children's Zoo, analyzing body language. Dick watched the chimps trailing Junior on the golf cart and wondered why he didn't simply drive back down toward the Carson Center. They weren't *chasing* him, Dick says, they were *following* him—the golf cart brought them food. If it were a chase, they would have caught him in a heartbeat. Chimpanzees are capable of running nearly twenty-five miles per hour. To Dick's eye, they weren't showing any aggression until Junior hit one with the golf cart, though, of course, the video is hardly high resolution, the chimps little more than a few blurry pixels. Junior and many others would fiercely disagree.

"If Dick would have been there, he would have been minced meat," Bridge says. "Those chimps were in a mode that they weren't going to listen to anybody. Dick would have gone in there figuring he could have put a stop to it, and he would have been the first casualty. In his mind—I've talked to him—he figures he could have done something. I've talked to his dad, too, and he says he could have done the same thing. I basically looked them both in the eye and disagreed. There is no question in my mind. If you could have seen what the rest of us saw—uh, no. I wholeheartedly disagree."

Had Dick been called, he would have kept the cage open even after Ripley returned, he says. He believes Reuben, shot in the back while climbing the fence near the Carson Center, was on his way home. And Reuben, he says, would have been his biggest issue. By 2005, Dick hadn't seen Reuben in four years, and "When they see somebody they know, that they loved, they just go berserk," he says. "He would have killed me." So instead, he would have focused on the other two first, and if Reuben was still out, he would have coached someone else on how to get Reuben to safety.

"If that didn't work, I would have done it myself because I would have willingly given my life to save his," Dick says. "But Reuben would have been my problem. The other two, they didn't know me. They weren't going to be a problem at all. Junior had never seen me work with chimps. Junior's got that attitude that he knows everything about everything."

Despite their at times strained relationship, Jim always came to his son's aid in public matters. A much older man by 2005, he'd come to believe in Dick's authority, so much so that he'd begun to stretch his credentials.

"He was the only primatologist this side of Omaha. Why didn't they call him?" Jim asked. "Pride gets in the way. That's all it was: pride. I've never felt good about it because I wasn't even called. They knew damn well if I was called, I'd get Dick up here right away. All they had to do was leave that enclosure open. They would have come back in! On their own! They didn't have to chase them. That was stupid. Reuben had been out before, and he'd come back. And, of course, one of them [Ripley] did come back. Dick taught Reuben sign language and other stuff. He could have called him back in."

By Monday, every major news outlet in the state had covered the shootings, most of them recycling the same information: failure to close a padlock, three chimps dead, visitors barricaded in the office. A local editorial cartoonist illustrated a diapered chimpanzee in glasses and a necktie teaching a class called "How to Operate a Padlock 101." The text read: "In an effort to prevent similar chimpanzee escapes in the future, officials at the Royal Zoo implement a new training program for employees." The letter to the editor that ran beside stated, in part, "The people of Royal must all be a bunch of ignorant wimps who are afraid of their own shadows, and it's too bad that Johnny Carson threw away so much money on a zoo such as this." Even the *New York Times* ran an AP brief the following Tuesday: NEBRASKA: CHIMPS ARE KILLED AFTER BREAKOUT.

> Three chimpanzees from Zoo Nebraska in Royal (population 75) were shot and killed after escaping their enclosure, the zoo director said. The animals fled on Saturday when a padlock was not completely closed after a cleaning, the director, Ken Schlueter Jr., said. He used a deputy's service revolver after a tranquilizer gun did not yield results. Employees moved visitors to an office, and the chimps tried to enter the building, Mr. Schlueter said.

The following Monday night, the community gathered in the zoo's activity center. Dozens of muffled voices now filled the old church as friends and neighbors attempted to piece the events back together, as they hugged and thanked god everyone was all right. They knew they were lucky. Some came for answers, some to pay respects, some merely to gossip. Diana sat in the back, holding her tongue.

"We could never get anybody in Royal interested in getting involved," she says. "But the meeting right after the chimp deal, the whole town showed up. All of a sudden, they're interested. They yammered away [that night]. I wanted to scream at them. One of them asked if everybody involved with the escape was here tonight. I thought, *Why are you here? You just want to know who you can point fingers at.*"

The sun set behind the building, and the wind calmed down. The first faint stars emerged, and soon the light inside the school would spill out into the darkness. Dick, too, returned for the meeting, though "it was obvious I wasn't welcome," he says. He only had one question.

"Why wasn't I called?"

They briefly discussed the future of the zoo, whether it should stay open or close down, though they reached no conclusions. Business seemed somehow inappropriate at a time like that, all of it still so raw. Instead, they mourned.

"Kind of like a funeral," Doc Pedersen says.

Several days later, Dennis Bridge stood in the back of the One Stop, eavesdropping on a passerby as he condemned the town's response.

"Were you there?" Bridge asked the man, stepping forward.

"No."

"Were you there?" Bridge asked again.

"No."

"Well then, shut the hell up because until you realize what we saw firsthand, you have no opinion," he said.

At the time, few Royalites understood the danger posed by four loose chimpanzees. The flight response was slow to trigger, the instinct dulled by a false understanding. The townspeople were less threatened than confused. *What's Reuben doing out of his cage? Why's Ripley on the highway?* The reality didn't truly set in until the shots cracked through town and blood stained the dirt. For Dennis, it came two days later, while steering the mower at the trout-rearing station. Clouds suddenly blocked the sun, and he began to lose himself in the afternoon. The station fell away, the green lawn and the concrete shoots, and he saw himself back at the zoo, barricaded behind the trucks. He watched Jimmy Joe fly from the minivan, heard the shots ring out, smelled the smoke lifting in the air. His knees began to shake, his legs weak, his arms loose. He felt so dizzy he shut off the mower and just sat there, dazed, until he could pull himself together.

"My knees just kind of turned to water," he says. "I thought, *Jeez, I might really not be here today if things had been different.* The day after the shooting, I went back up there with some other people, and we were just looking around, and I realized how close we were. You realize just what a close call you'd had."

On September 13, 2005, three days after the escape, People for the Ethical Treatment of Animals filed a complaint with the USDA, requesting they revoke Zoo Nebraska's federal license, a punishment supported by longtime state senator Ernie Chambers, a vocal animal welfare advocate.

"I think that any license this outfit has should be revoked immediately," Chambers told the *Lincoln Journal Star*. "It's regrettable that three animals had to die due to the stupidity of human beings."

Just as the Bakkens and Erin Loeser had been urging for months prior to the escape, they also compelled the USDA to relocate Ripley to a federally recognized chimpanzee sanctuary where he could integrate with another group. Instead, Junior transferred Ripley to Savannahland, a privately funded zoo near Pleasant Hill, Missouri—another unaccredited tourist attraction. Junior called it "a beautiful facility." Lisa Wathne, a captive exotic animal specialist at PETA, called it "basically a roadside zoo" and found it "unconscionable that Zoo Nebraska took this action." In addition to PETA, the Saint Louis Zoo, the Jane Goodall Institute, and others specifically recommended the Center for Great Apes in Wauchula, Florida, which already housed Ripley's father, daughter, and several siblings, in addition to a number of other retired entertainment chimps. Junior wouldn't budge. Ripley would remain at Savannahland until Zoo Nebraska could find a buyer.

"We would have to give away the chimp, which has a clear cash value to us," he told the *Lincoln Journal Star*.

PETA also called for criminal prosecution. Following the AP release, representatives spoke with Antelope County attorney Mike Long, urging him to investigate the matter, to press charges for animal neglect.

"I was pretty clear up front with the folks it was not a criminal matter. I reviewed the video and talked to the officers, but there was no evidence," Long said. "The only criminal complaint was from PETA. The people with personal knowledge—Royalites—none of those people were making complaints.

"I had PETA call me on another case when there were some drunks in Neligh who shot a cat on top of a car with a crossbow. They wanted us to investigate. I charged the guy with a misdemeanor on animal cruelty. That was the situation that occurred a couple years before. They were insistent. I just said this is the charge, the facts. The guy didn't have a record. It was nothing I'd charge a man with a felony over. I said this is Nebraska, an animal state, a ranching state. We care for our animals here.

"They actually do; they find it horrible when somebody does abuse an animal. On the other side, they're somewhat practical about it. They're not going to prosecute somebody for killing a cat. I took the chimp thing as not so much *PETA wanted a story*, but they're zealots. They truly believe what they're advocating and espousing for."

Though Zoo Nebraska was never criminally prosecuted, the USDA did perform a routine inspection the Monday after the escape, citing a slew of federal violations. It noted that a drug called Xylazine had been used on two of the chimps "and may not have been the drug of choice for effective sedation or was not properly administered since it did not affect the two animals." The report also stated that "the person using the gun had not received formal training in the use of chemical immobilization and had never used chemical immobilization. The facility did not have a person adequately trained in immobilization and tranquilization that ultimately resulted in the death of three chimpanzees." And tapping the root of the matter, the USDA noted that Zoo Nebraska lacked "an adequate number of employees to carry out this level of husbandry and care" and that "the supervisor on premises . . . had no or limited background, knowledge, and experience in the proper husbandry and care of nonhuman primates."

Despite all this, Zoo Nebraska remained open. The following January, Junior announced that Ripley would not be returning to Royal and that, in fact, Zoo Nebraska would no longer feature chimpanzees—its main draw—at all. He said safety was his chief concern, that the zoo couldn't afford to purchase another chimpanzee, and that housing

Ripley alone would be unethical. Following another brief stint with a breeder in California, Ripley would ultimately end up at the Center for Great Apes, the facility PETA and others had originally recommended.

"Even though our facility has the same standards as everybody else, it's just very difficult to take care of them," Junior told the *Lincoln Journal Star*.

He resolved, however, to keep the zoo running. For the first few weeks, it seemed like things might return to a new normal. Families from the surrounding communities came to show their support, and attendance remained steady if not exactly strong. But without the chimpanzees, attendance soon withered, and the tourists stopped coming. For nearly a year and a half, Zoo Nebraska held on, until finally, on May 31, 2007, the USDA—presenting violations bridging the terms of all four directors—denied their application for a new license, returning the zoo's ten-dollar filing fee.

"The Northeast Nebraska Zoological Society, Inc. has continually failed to provide minimally adequate husbandry and care to its animals despite receiving repeated written notice from the Department describing the Zoo's deficiencies and opportunities to demonstrate or achieve compliance . . ." wrote Robert Gibbens, director of the USDA's western region. "The Zoo's history of compliance with the AWA reveals a consistent disregard for, and unwillingness or inability to abide by, the requirements of the AWA and its regulations and standards . . .

"For the reasons described above, we have determined that Northeast Nebraska Zoological Society, Inc. is unfit to be licensed and that the issuance of a license to the Zoo would be contrary to the purposes of the Act."

Earlier that month, Bruce Curtiss, an attorney who'd been practicing in Plainview for more than thirty years, received several unexpected phone calls from both Junior Schlueter and the Youngs. They said the zoo needed help, that the USDA had filed a federal complaint and hoped to shut them down. The whole thing was a mess: a mountain of federal violations, each one punishable by a civil penalty that grew larger every day; a history of noncompliance and "lack of good faith"; a board he'd been forced to partition in his mind between "fellas I took to be a little more rational in their approach," such as Marvin Young and Doc Pedersen, and the "renegades," like Junior and the Jensens. Ideally, they all would have liked to keep the doors open for Royal and northeast Nebraska, but Curtiss struggled to see the potential.

"After I looked at the charges and looked at the history and determined what would be proven if we went to trial, I came to the conclusion that there was no saving to be had," Curtiss said. "The potential penalties were enormous, and whatever we worked out, we needed to get those penalties waived or absorbed . . . They couldn't have survived the penalties."

Citing multiple violations of the AWA, the USDA levied a $25,000 civil penalty on Zoo Nebraska, which it agreed to wipe clean—thanks to a deal negotiated by Curtiss—unless the zoo continued to operate without a license or violate any terms of the AWA. Furthermore, the zoo agreed to relocate all the animals to secure facilities.

"There was just no salvaging the zoo in my opinion," Curtiss said. "The earlier violations and the earlier warnings had all been much the same, and here they were again. I didn't see any way to avoid being convicted, if you will, and that's why I told them a settlement was really necessary. I don't like to push my clients to litigate for no purpose. They would have lost, and they would have suffered the penalties."

Less than a week after the zoo shut down, the state of Nebraska repealed its nonprofit status for "nonpayment of biennial fees," and for the next two years, the Northeast Nebraska Zoological Society, Inc. remained officially inactive in the eyes of the state. The gates remained closed, and the board no longer met, though initially, most of the animals remained, cared for by Junior and a few holdout volunteers reluctant to leave the animals behind. Junior fed the animals mostly on his own dime and the generous donations of area farmers: old dog food, baby food, dented canned goods, discarded organs from local butchers, now and then a donated cow carcass. He kept his eye on the local auction barns, searching for cheap old hogs. When PETA offered to relocate the animals themselves, Junior rejected the offer on principle, morally opposed to PETA's philosophy, though he had already tried and failed to relocate the tigers and other exotics himself.

Finally, in early November 2008, the USDA arranged for the Wild Animal Sanctuary in Keenesburg, Colorado, to offload the remaining animals. Arriving with four employees and two rescue trailers, the sanctuary adopted eighteen of the zoo's largest and most exotic—and therefore most difficult to relocate—animals: thirteen wolves, two tigers, a lion, a black bear, and a coyote. According to the sanctuary's director of development and public affairs, the two tigers were underweight, and their veterinarian doubted they would have survived another winter at Zoo Nebraska.

And so the wolves howled one last time in Royal. Few but the camel remained, silently chewing its cud on an unusually warm November afternoon.

A LAUNDRY LIST OF
RANDOM COMPLAINTS

I f the rest of Royal had given up on Zoo Nebraska, cut its losses, and moved on, the Jensens never did.

Without informing the board, Earleen paid a ten-dollar filing fee and reinstated the zoo's nonprofit status in April 2009. She also filed a "Change of Agent" request with the secretary of state's office, replacing the name of the last official zoo proxy—Kip Smith—with her own. Two months later, alleging that Junior had quietly been expressing interest in privately owning the zoo, Earleen and Jerry Peterson filed a motion for injunctive relief against not Junior or the board, but president Marvin Young, hoping to prevent any further sale of the zoo's assets.

In the eyes of many, it was a typical Jensen move: refusing to leave well enough alone, swooping in to rattle the cage just when it looked like the hellish epic of Zoo Nebraska might finally come to an end. As far as most board members were concerned, the nightmare was over. The animals had been relocated. The gates were shut. Maybe Junior ended up with a few animals he hadn't paid for, some equipment nobody really wanted, but it was a small price to pay for peace of mind. But not the Jensens. And not their friend Jerry Peterson, whom many considered their lackey, perhaps even their financier. There was money yet in that zoo, Jerry and the Jensens insisted. There was potential for something more—at the very least, for something else. Unlike the board's attorney, they found plenty to be salvaged.

The Jensens' motion, submitted to the Antelope County District Court nearly four years after the chimps were shot, was a bush-league maneuver, clearly executed by a party with scant legal understanding—what Marvin's attorney would call "a laundry list of random complaints against a 'director' who, notably, is not a named defendant." Nevertheless, it was enough to jam the gears. The motion criticized Junior for his "physical and verbal abuse" of employees and board members, for refusing access to the zoo records, for letting the zoo's various operating licenses expire, for letting the pack animals graze outside during business hours, for using donated hay to feed his own animals and the animals of his friends, and several other counts of mismanagement and neglect. They also accused Junior of meeting covertly with the county assessor "about putting the zoo back on the tax rolls," which they viewed as a move to run the zoo "for personal gain," and finally of stealing Earleen's secretarial paperwork while she was out of town. Rarely do the Jensens forget.

Only twice did the motion address anyone but Junior. Referring to the brouhaha between Marlowe and Kip Smith, they stated that a board member had attacked a "guest" at a board meeting in 2005 and that the acting president, a.k.a. Marvin, "did not remove the member on the spot." Perhaps more importantly, they claimed that "the board engaged in a gross abuse of authority or discretion with respect to the corporation, which resulted in a great loss of revenue." But they'd mistakenly filed the petition against Marvin Young personally, not the board, and even then, it was hardly clear whether Junior was considered a member. Either way, Marvin had no choice but to hire a lawyer.

"Even assuming all of Plaintiffs' allegations are true," his dismissal states, "the Plaintiffs have completely and utterly failed to show they have any clear right, irreparable damage, or that other remedies are inadequate to prevent a failure of justice."

In other words: *So what?* This wasn't their fight to pick. But Earleen's move to reinstate the zoo's nonprofit status had automatically triggered the state's involvement. As a result, the attorney general's office was considered a proper party to the affair under the state's Nonprofit Corporation Act. In petitioning the district court for the right to intervene, the AG's office studied what remained of the zoo's slapdash records and argued the legal standing of both the zoo and its leadership were ambiguous at best.

"Upon information and belief," the AG's petition states, "Jensen and J. Peterson were dissatisfied with [North East Nebraska Zoo's] operations, and therefore reinstated the corporation . . . in an effort to take over its assets."

The AG asked the court to consider the zoo's reinstatement and change of agent invalid, to declare the zoo administratively dissolved, and to appoint a custodian to liquidate the remaining assets. In the meantime, the AG requested a temporary restraining order against the board to prohibit them from acting on behalf of the zoo without the legal authority to do so. The court ruled against the motion for a restraining order, citing insufficient evidence, but agreed to appoint a temporary receiver to sell off the remaining property.

Lobbing a Hail Mary, Marlowe Jensen applied for the position. It was a bizarre appeal, but for those who knew him, perhaps not that surprising. "I feel qualified because as a volunteer in several capacities (maintenance, mowing, trimming, planting, building enclosures and shelving) in the last 15 years I know the assets that should be on the zoo grounds," he wrote. To no one's surprise, the judge denied that request; Marlowe had no certified legal experience and clearly represented a conflict of interest. Instead, the judge opted to appoint a polished attorney from Norfolk named Mark Fitzgerald, a man he thought capable of handling complex litigation. He spoke with a faint rasp, and compared to most Royalites, he dressed like a senator: suit and tie, pleated slacks, sporty black shades when he left the office.

"After 2007 or so, the directors said, 'We don't know what to do next, we don't know where to turn, and everything here is hard and full of legal issues,'" Fitzgerald says. "They just had stopped working. They volunteered to be on the board of directors of a nonprofit organization, and all of the sudden they had major, time-consuming work to do. I'm a lawyer, so I can read my way through the statutes and understand the legal direction of the USDA, but for them, they had to hire a lawyer with no funds, follow USDA directives without legal direction—so I understood they tried their best."

Fitzgerald remembered taking his own kids to the zoo when they were young, pulling off Highway 20 after a day trip to the fossil beds farther up the road. He remembered taking his father, too, who'd grown up in Boston.

"I remember him as we walked through there, saying, 'This is a zoo?' It was never a zoo by Henry Doorly standards, but it was kind of quaint, and it was sort of neat to see how hard they were working in its prime to make it work."

After he was appointed to the case, Fitzgerald sent a new associate at the firm, fresh out of law school, to evaluate the condition of the zoo.

"He was amazed at how dilapidated and terrible it was and gave us the impression there wasn't anything of significant value in the zoo at all."

Fitzgerald assumed they were dealing in scrap metal, valuations so small they were hardly worth counting.

"So it was sad, but it had long since ceased to be operational."

Judge Kube also ordered Fitzgerald to determine the current status of the zoo and its members, to verify—as the AG had implied—that the board was no longer functioning. He started with the board minutes but found them haphazard and disorganized, scattered across the county and many of them missing altogether. He found letters of resignation from various members, only to find those same members listed in the roll call weeks later, as if their complaints had simply been ignored or they had suddenly changed their mind. Fitzgerald started making trips to Royal, but the board members themselves had trouble answering his questions, most of them wishing—even before the chimp disaster—they'd never signed on in the first place. In the end, after piecing together what little evidence remained, Fitzgerald listed the following names as the last members of the zoo board: Marvin Young, Doc Pedersen, and a woman from Creighton named Bev Schwindt. Judge Kube summoned each of them to appear before the court.

ALL RISE

On the morning of Tuesday, March 23, 2010, a small cluster of the zoo's interested parties gathered before the Honorable Judge James B. Kube on the second floor of the Antelope County Courthouse in Neligh, Nebraska. In contrast to Royal, Neligh is the prototype of small-town Nebraska, at least on the surface: a well-defined Main Street buttressed by a floral shop and a bank and a greasy spoon, a pharmacy and the newsroom for the local weekly, all of it capped by the courthouse on one end and the historic Neligh Mill on the other, the two most prominent buildings in town, the mill squatting beside the Elkhorn River running wide and shallow around the bend.

Built in 1894, the courthouse stands three stories tall and radiates with history. Redbrick, white molding, a golden antelope perched on the crown. It's connected to a blasé one-story annex built in 1966. Sidewalks circumscribe and crisscross the lawn, and taken all together, it serves as the de facto town square, shaded by stately old trees and often buzzing with activity.

The last few days had lived up to Nebraska's reputation for extremes, plummeting to a mere sixteen degrees that Sunday before hitting seventy the following Monday. A flat marble sky now dulled the streets outside, and a cool northern breeze coursed through the trees. The courtroom itself lacked the commanding presence of the exterior, the old wooden floors muted with a dull gray carpet on top of which sat twelve long wooden pews. The ceiling hung low, and a soft light filtered through closed blinds in the back that one could part to gaze over the highway at the Methodist church and the old county jail. In one corner, a cheap plastic shrub adorned a single antique display case filled with dusty legal volumes, lending the courtroom a sterile and contrived quality.

The Jensens filed in, followed by Junior Schlueter, Marvin and Valda Young, and the rest of the remaining board members, all of them together for the first time in years. Perhaps the only noticeable absence was that of former board president Jerry Peterson, the only one who actually lived in Neligh and who, coupled with Earleen, had triggered the whole judicial affair by filing the original motion. Notifying the court beforehand, he sent a note from his doctor (and the letter he wrote his doctor to receive it), hoping to justify his absence.

> *I am very scared of Junior Schlueter. I have been seizure free for four years and I don't want to get them started again. This Junior Schlueter is just a Big Bully. He has caused a lot of board members and workers to leave. Even to go into court, I am afraid the stress it puts on me would put me into a very bad seizure. I am asking you to write a letter to the courts stating that I am not able to appear because of serious health problems.*

The doctor's note confirmed Jerry's seizure disorder and also mentioned his chronic depression.

Standing behind a wooden table fitted with several microphones and a box of tissues, Mark Fitzgerald and Abigail Stempson, the assistant attorney general, prepared their notes for the proceedings. At 10:50 a.m., Judge Kube struck the gavel and opened court on *State of Nebraska v. Northeast Nebraska Zoological Society, Inc.*, one of just a handful of nonprofit dissolutions in Nebraska history.

A tall, clean-cut man with a receding hairline, strikingly dark eyebrows, and a slightly upturned nose, Kube had practiced law in Norfolk for over fifteen years before his appointment to the bench just the previous year, and in all that time, "this was unlike anything I've experienced," he says. "More of a mess." He wore small rimless glasses and the customary black robe. The state and American flags hung limp behind the bench, framing him in his seat.

"This comes on for hearing on the state's motion for judicial dissolution and request for further relief. Is that correct?"

"Correct," replied Stempson.

"I would also note before we get to that, there is a motion to extend that's been filed by Earleen Jensen and Jerry Peterson. Are they present in the courtroom today?"

Earleen stood up, glasses pressed tight on the bridge of her nose, her skin taut and a shade darker still in winter, part Delaware Indian, she says, on her father's side. Justin and Marlowe sat on the bench beside her, each of them having donned his Sunday best: blue jeans and button-downs. Their nylon jackets whispered with every nervous fidget.

"Would you like to be heard on your motion?" Kube asked.

"There's been new evidence discovered as of last night, allegedly more fraud," she said, skipping ahead, her naturally meek voice barbed with righteousness. "And we do not think that the camel should be awarded to the person that used the zoo money to buy the camel and then given to him because of the wrongdoing that's come forth. So we are trying to get legal counsel to—"

"When did that information come forth to you?"

"Last night about nine-thirty. We didn't know about the van being sold for two hundred fifty dollars and that the check was made out to Junior Schlueter privately. It was zoo property. And the E-Z Go and the other golf cart were to be sold to the same person that bought the van. He wanted to buy the golf cart and the E-Z Go for a hundred and twenty-five dollars apiece, and also a walk-in cooler valued at nine hundred fifty dollars, and when we went to get them, Junior said no. He sold them to another person, and these are also zoo property and supposedly put in his private funds."

"You're asking for an extension because you want to acquire legal counsel?"

"Yes. Jerry and I together."

"Why do you think you need legal counsel?"

"To prove all the fraud that has been done," she said matter-of-factly. "And by giving the camel to Junior, that's rewarding the wrong-doer. And also, when I filed for the five-oh-two, all the things I filed for, I don't feel that was illegal because I'm a lifetime member of the zoo."

Earleen had previously submitted a copy of her lifetime membership card, accompanied by a photocopied page of the dictionary with the term *membership* highlighted and circled in pen. In compliance with the Jensen family brand, she'd always been stubborn. But unlike Marlowe and Justin, she followed her convictions quietly. Of the three of them, she spoke the softest, and though she rarely let a grudge expire, she preferred to retaliate indirectly, behind closed doors, bypassing the wrongdoer to head straight for the courthouse.

Once Earleen made up her mind about something, had faith in it, there was little anyone could do to shake her. When she believed, she really believed, and now more than ever, she believed in her lifetime membership at Zoo Nebraska. She believed in her right to act on behalf of the zoo. She truly believed in her claims of corruption and misman-agement, and she believed wholeheartedly in her responsibility to take whatever steps were necessary to keep the attraction in Royal.

Judge Kube called her to the stand.

"I've explained to you before in court, or at least explained to your husband, that we want to move quickly here with these items," Fitzgerald said. "Is that correct?"

"Yes."

"You understand?"

"Yes."

"So let's do it in that manner then," Fitzgerald said, and proceeded to question her about the location and ownership of a long list of zoo assets Earleen had previously called into question: the E-Z Go golf cart, the Deutz-Deines mower, the walk-in cooler, three propane tanks, and more. The value of the items grew smaller as Fitzgerald continued, the list devolving into a bill of goods they'd be lucky to pawn off at a Salvation Army: a rusty cast-iron cauldron, a broken popcorn machine, a toaster oven.

"Blankets—you're just talking about blankets?" Fitzgerald said, slightly confused. "Like something you would buy at a discount store?"

"Yes. The chimps had to have blankets all the time," she said. "And we had a big fund-raiser, and they gave a lot of blankets."

"Are they still on the property?"

"I don't know."

"They wouldn't be worth much if they were, would they?" he asked.

"Well," she said, stiffening her neck, "to the chimps they would be."

The list kept going, bird cages and fencing panels and pancake grills and catch nets.

"What's that?" Fitzgerald asked.

"That's to catch animals with."

"Do you know whether or not those are on the property?"

"We borrowed one one time to catch a dog and then we took it back. I don't think they are on the zoo property," she said. "I think they are in Junior's building."

"Why?"

"I have no idea."

"You don't know one way or the other on that, do you?"

"I don't know why they were over there."

"The popcorn machine," he continued, and the sun climbed higher beyond the windows. The cheap blinds cast striped shadows across the carpet, and the attendees shuffled impatiently in their seats.

"I feel like we're in a divorce trial going through the property list here," Fitzgerald said, netting a few laughs from the gallery. "Now we get to an item that most families don't have: fainting goats. What's that?"

"There's a little goat that when they get nervous, they drop over."

"And snow monkeys?"

"Our son took care of a lot of snow monkeys," she said. "And where they went?" She tossed her hands in the air. "They were zoo property."

"How many snow monkeys were there?"

"Four," she said, looking toward Justin. "Seven."

When Fitzgerald inquired about a pile of cinder blocks, the same pile Doc Pedersen had kneeled on to set Jimmy Joe in the crosshairs of his tranquilizer gun, Earleen said they were owned by the zoo, that Junior had recently sold 750 of them to northeast Nebraska's Amish community, but that most of them still hadn't been relocated.

"Do you know what happened to the money?"

"It was deposited in Junior's bank account in Norfolk," she said.

Near the end of Earleen's direct examination, Fitzgerald asked her about the land, if she hoped to buy it. She did, she said, and hoped to devote it to another nonprofit, the plans for which she did not divulge but which she and Jerry Peterson had been discussing for months. They called it the Northeast Nebraska Fun Park, and they'd already pieced together a board of directors: Earleen, Jerry, Justin, and two women from the nearby Amish community.

In private, though, Earleen's and Jerry's dreams for the Fun Park diverged. The Jensens pictured a small petting zoo—something for the kids to interact with, without the danger posed by the exotics. Beyond that, they pictured a multipurpose civic center. They pictured flea markets, of which they'd long been enthusiasts, and big Amish suppers like the kind she and Justin tried booking at the gymnasium before the mayor and his wife stepped in. They pictured Girl Scout campouts and country music shows and community barbecues. They saw a local museum where the chimp exhibit used to be. They saw merry-go-rounds and tube slides and "other fun things like that," Earleen later said.

Jerry, on the other hand, envisioned a tourist destination, something grander and—most would say—flirting with the insane. He'd drawn up plans mimicking Zoo Nebraska, a park that displayed life-size stuffed animals in all the old cages, an idea he was somehow convinced could win back the rural children who used to come here for the real thing.

"We was gonna put these things in the cages and put a sensor so when you get close, it turns on a recording," he said later. "And the chimps squawking, I got recordings of that on my videotapes."

On his diagram, he sketched all fifty state flags posted at the entrance to the Fun Park. He scribbled small flowers all over the zoo. He cut out photos of stuffed animals from different magazines and glued them to the page, each one named after its former real-life counterpart: the Bengal tigers, Orion and Jevick; the mountain lions, Dakota and Babe; the fox, Cocoa; the great horned owl, Hootie; and, of course, the chimpanzees too: Reuben, Jimmy Joe, Ripley, and Tyler. He imagined big, huggable versions of the chimpanzees in the old Carson Center and a guide posted near the cage to tell the children stories. In fact, he said, he wanted to commission a bronze statue of Reuben for the kids to touch. He called it a "healing," like a laughing Buddha or a weeping Virgin Mary. And as if that weren't enough, he hoped to haul in truckloads of sand and build a landlocked "beach" for sunbathing.

"It's out there where the sun gets to it," he said, "and people could go out there and lay in the sand and put their feet into it. How warm and how nice! A place to relax."

But until the state finished its liquidation of the zoo, the Northeast Nebraska Fun Park remained a foggy hypothetical.

"It's your intention, and the reason that you took action here with regard to trying to revive the zoo, was you would like to have . . ."

Fitzgerald now paused. "You would like to maintain some sort of non-profit entity in Royal for the benefit of the community?"

"Yes," Earleen said, "because we have Grove Lake and Ashfall, and it's a good area, and everybody has encouraged us to do something and keep it together."

According to the zoo's original bylaws, if the zoo ever closed, all the remaining assets were to be transferred to another nonprofit organization. Without the mandate, they couldn't receive tax-exempt status from the IRS. Of course, always keen to legal opportunity, the Jensens quickly picked up on the provision. *If the zoo has to close,* they thought, *why not at least keep the assets in Royal?* Why not transfer them to what they hoped would come next: the Northeast Nebraska Fun Park. And if that never came, they always had a backup in the Jeri Southern Home & Museum Society, Inc., the only other registered nonprofit in town. What they hadn't considered was whether the zoo would have any assets left to give after paying off Fitzgerald's swelling retainer fee and a list of creditors that had been growing for years. All the maneuvering seemed premature but also highlighted a fact few were likely to admit: the Jensens and Jerry Peterson were the only parties pushing to keep Royal alive, to keep the commerce in town, the only ones hoping for the future, as twisted or selfish as it might seem.

"That's all the questions I have of Earleen Jensen at this point, Your Honor," Fitzgerald said.

"Do you have anything else you'd like to say to the court at this time?" Judge Kube asked, facing Earleen.

Throughout the proceedings, Justin had been prodding his mother to speak up, to contest the way certain items had been presented. He whispered in her ear, nudged her to stand even when she wasn't giving testimony—all of which Judge Kube quietly noted from the bench. Earleen now hesitated before answering. She looked again to Justin, who was mouthing to her about the licenses.

"Just look at me," Kube snapped. "I don't care what your son wants. I want to know if you want to say anything else to me."

"I would like to say that when I filed for the license through the secretary of state, that I asked them ahead of time, you know, what could be done. So I was going on their recommendations when I renewed those that I did have the right to do that, but that, you know, remains to be seen."

"So you're disputing Mr. Fitzgerald's finding? You're claiming you did have authority?"

"Yes," she said. "As a lifetime member, and with the advice of the secretary of state, they told me how to do it and guided me through it. Because I didn't realize it could be done and the biennial report could be renewed. I was going on their recommendations."

"All right. Thank you. You may step down. Mr. Fitzgerald?"

"I would like to call Junior Schlueter," Fitzgerald said.

Junior rose slowly from a wooden bench near the front of the gallery, passing the Jensens without comment, and carefully took his seat on the witness stand, steadying himself with two hands on the railing before him. The previous October, Junior had suffered a heart attack and undergone quadruple bypass surgery, only to suffer a second heart attack just two weeks prior to the hearing, all of it stress induced, according to his sister.

"Can you hear me all right?" Fitzgerald asked.

"Yes," he said faintly.

"Maybe you can speak up a little bit."

"Maybe not," he said. "I'm trying. Some of the medications make me very hoarse."

"Mr. Schlueter, are you the Junior Schlueter identified as a respondent in this action?"

"Unfortunately."

"Who owns the camel that formerly belonged to the zoo?"

"Me."

"The zoo was prohibited from selling any of the animals. They had to donate them to other zoos or similar entities, is that correct?"

"Correct."

"And the camel was *not* donated, is that correct?"

"Correct."

"And you own the camel, you think, because of your service?"

"Well, not because of my service. They had to be given away, and we had to find somebody that would take a neutered male. Most people that want a camel want one for breeding purposes. So I took him and continued to feed him. He was about twenty-seven hundred pounds. He ate a lot."

"Did you demand, in June of 2009, to the board of directors that they give you the camel?"

"I don't recall it being a demand," Junior said, furrowing his brow, the light catching on his glasses.

"I'm showing you now what I understand are some zoo minutes from June 3, 2009," Fitzgerald said, holding up a small stack of white legal paper. "It says, 'Future of the camel. Junior wants him, feels he deserves him because of all he has done for the zoo. Junior very adamant about wanting him.' Is that true?"

"Yes," he said. "I agree with that."

"Did you understand, at that point, they gave you the camel?"

"Right. If we had to give him away to somebody, why not me rather than somebody that hasn't done anything for the zoo?"

"Have you been caring for that camel since that time and maybe even before?"

"Before and after, and then I had to give him away."

"Where is the camel now?"

Junior hesitated. He shifted in his seat, cleared his throat, stared down at his lap.

"He's at a good place," he said, nodding.

Fitzgerald turned to face the judge.

"Your Honor," he said, "would you instruct the witness to tell where the camel is?"

"Tell us where the camel is," Kube replied curtly.

"Your Honor, because of the way the Jensens treat people and calls and letters and harassment they receive, I need to decline. I don't want to put somebody through that. The camel is still mine, and I can get him back."

"I understand your concern," Kube said, "and I will direct that the Jensens not make any contact with the people with the camel, but I want to know where the camel is."

"He's in Wayne. Outside of Wayne, there's another gentleman that has other camels."

"What's his name?"

"I don't have that with me right now. I honestly don't know his name. I can get it for you."

"Thank you, Your Honor," Fitzgerald said.

As he had with Earleen, Fitzgerald questioned Junior on the where-abouts of a long list of assets, if they were sold, if they remained on the property, if Junior pocketed any of the money himself. Some of it, he said, he probably did. He said the fainting goats had always been his—he'd simply put them on display at the zoo—and the snow monkeys were given to Kip Smith to integrate with his own pack of snow monkeys back in Gretna. He said the board let Diana Wavrunek keep the parrots and that all the parakeets had died, frozen to death in a makeshift atrium when the propane ran dry.

After further questioning, Abigail Stempson stepped in for a cross-examination. She, too, questioned Junior about the assets, specifically the Gator, a small utility vehicle used around the zoo. Junior admitted to using it for personal work after the zoo closed but felt it was fair. He'd paid for the repairs, after all.

"I put in three years of being on call twenty-four hours a day, seven days a week, taking care of the animals. There was no compensation. Them animals had to be fed and watered and cared for every day. And from the time I became the director, I have not been able to miss a day. With the tigers and lion and bear, some of them were dangerous enough—even though we had Jennifer [a volunteer] there for a while working, she was never allowed a key to take care of the animals. I still had to be there. If there was somebody called at night, if the animals were making noise or wound up, I had to get up and go over and check the zoo and go through and take care of the animals. A lot of the work that went with the zoo wasn't just that the animals were fed and watered every day, but the enclosures had to be cleaned out and power washed, the chemicals that you need to clean them, the soaps and stuff you had to have to do it . . . and any day, the USDA could walk in and see how the animals were maintained and taken care of. So we had to buy the stuff and come from somewhere with no income."

Junior claimed the zoo owed him nearly $43,000—that he'd taken care of the animals and maintained zoo property for years without compensation, that he often purchased supplies and paid for necessary services with his own money. And though Fitzgerald found no evidence to support his claim, Junior insisted the board of directors approved his expenditures and agreed to reimburse him.

"It was just very loosely documented and inappropriate, really," Judge Kube said later. "He just came in and said he did that stuff out of the kindness of his own heart, but in a situation like that, you better have good documentation of exactly what you did and why you did it, and he didn't have that."

The further Stempson pushed him, the less Junior's argument held up. Already physically weak, his attitude began to wane, less defensive than pitiful and victimized.

"Mr. Schlueter, I just have one more question. In regard to the camel . . . the minutes the custodian showed you earlier stated that there was a zoo in Arizona that was willing to take the camel, as well as a ranch by Niobrara. Why did you feel it was better not to go to another zoo?"

"Well, it became a pet," he said. "To give him off to somebody else—from my standpoint, if Northeast Nebraska Zoo could get nothing for it, why not allow me to have him instead of somebody else?"

"Do you understand that nonprofit assets are basically public assets and they are to remain for the public benefit?" she asked.

"Yeah, I guess."

"So do you feel that it was serving the public for the director to receive private inurement for receiving the camel? Let me rephrase that. Is it proper, do you feel, that once a nonprofit may be going under and needs to get rid of assets, to simply give it to those that are directors?"

"I guess with the expenses and money and time I put in there, yes," he said. "I got involved in this because it was good for the community and the Jensens pushed me to help, so I went ahead and did it. And if it stayed open for the schools and surrounding area it would have been fantastic—"

"Mr. Schlueter, we are getting off topic a little . . . How much did you get for him?"

"I got two thousand dollars."

"Do you understand that your own articles of incorporation say that upon dissolution all assets must go to a 501(c)(3) entity?"

"No."

"Have you read your articles of incorporation?"

"No."

"Yet you were a member of the board of directors as you testified?"

"I don't know that anybody read them," he said.

"They are on file with the secretary of state."

"No, I have not."

"Your Honor," she said, "I'm done with this witness."

After a brief lunch recess, the court reconvened and called Doc Pedersen and later Marvin Young to the stand. Neither one had much further to say, but when given the opportunity for last comments, Marvin felt compelled to explain how it had all come to this, how the zoo had crumbled to such an impotent and infantile state.

"When I got on the board at the end of oh-five, one thing I said I wanted was peace among the board members, you know, because in the past twenty years, the zoo always had problems. But that didn't work either," he said, his voice phlegmy and sincere. "And it was probably my fault because I was the president—I should have made it happen. But things don't always work that way, and Junior was not cooperative in any way with the board, and things got worse and worse. And that's it."

"Did the board ever take any action to remove Mr. Schlueter as director?" Judge Kube asked.

"No, they didn't."

"Why was that?"

"Well, part of it was we had nobody to do the work. We fire him, who is going to do the work? Me and Doc Pedersen? Neither one of us had time, so we let things slide is about what it amounts to. He just—some of the female people that worked there, he was very rude to them or whatever. Down the road, they ended up quitting. And it's basically—they couldn't work with him."

"Thank you," Kube said. "You may step down."

The court adjourned a little after 2:00 p.m. By then, the clouds had scattered, and the sun shone bright on the red bricks of the courthouse. A harsh glare shot off the golden antelope, its head and antlers facing westward, overlooking Main Street. The respondents said little to each other as they left the building, each of them anxious to return home.

Three days later, Judge Kube issued his findings, agreeing almost entirely with the attorney general's original report. He ruled Earleen Jensen's latest actions on behalf of Zoo Nebraska null and void. He declared the zoo administratively dissolved as of June 2007, when the board first stopped paying its dues to the secretary of state. And he ordered the zoo be judicially dissolved following the sale of its remaining assets, noting the zoo was "no longer able to carry out its stated and intended public purpose" and calling the dissolution a "matter of public interest."

"Somebody should have said, *We need to look at this a little better*, and maybe that was the federal government," Kube says. "If you're going to give somebody permits to have exotic animals, maybe you better be damn well sure they know what they're doing and that the business plan behind it is going to work so you don't have a situation like they had up there, which was just a disaster for everybody. In the end it's those animals that took the beating, and the community too."

Finding much of Junior's testimony unreliable, Kube ordered him to return the proceeds he'd pocketed from the sale of the camel and other assets—a total of $2,747.50—within thirty days. If Junior failed to do so, he noted, he would be found in contempt. In order to liquidate the remaining assets, including the land, he instructed Fitzgerald to organize the public auction. As for Junior's claim that the zoo owed him nearly $43,000, Kube dismissed it with little credence, almost as if he'd never made the claim at all.

Thirty days passed, but Junior never paid up. True to his word, Judge Kube found him in contempt, ordered him to pay fifty dollars a month throughout the summer, and summoned him before the court once again that August. The medical bills following his heart attacks had bled him dry, he explained. He suffered nerve damage and could no longer feel his hands and many of his toes, and now his kidneys were failing.

"They go in and out," he said. "My blood fills with enzymes, and I go and get IVs or water pills to take the fluid off because I balloon up and gain twenty-five or thirty pounds in a week."

Sympathizing with Junior's dilemma, Kube allowed him to continue paying just fifty dollars a month until the end of the year, at which point the remaining lump sum would be due. But when the end of the year came, Junior told Fitzgerald he could no longer afford to pay the monthly fee. By deferring his medical bills, he'd accrued $600, which he offered to hand over immediately if the court agreed to waive the rest of the fine. Considering how long the case had been active, Kube restlessly declared it "unfruitful to keep this open" and agreed to drop Junior's remaining $1,700 bill.

"At some point you just have to stop, cut your losses, take what you can, and move on," he says. "I mean, how much blood can you squeeze out of a turnip?"

By the time all the litigation ceased, after all the assets had been sold and the creditors paid off, those still following the saga of Zoo Nebraska had witnessed a once-endearing public attraction collapse upon itself, a nonprofit board divorced and shut down and guided like children by the hand of the state. They had witnessed, nearly twenty-five years ago, the birth of an opportunity and the power of one man's obsession, the unlikely rise of a full-grown zoo in "the middle of nowhere, Nebraska," in the words of Arvin Brandt. And later, the waning of support and the rust of its facilities; the loss of volunteers and the succession of too many unlikely and unprepared directors; the USDA violations and the claims of customer poaching; and that fateful day in September 2005, the day the shots rang out, a day that meant very little to the outside world but, to Royal, meant the end of something much more, something it couldn't quite define. They'd witnessed the greatest attraction Royal had ever known reduced to a bad courtroom drama, a dream divided and now judicially dissolved.

"As silly as it sounds, Reuben wasn't just an animal to me or those from the area. He was a symbol of what can come out of a small community when someone has a vision and puts forth the effort to make it a reality," wrote journalist Carrie Pitzer in the *Norfolk Daily News* three days after the shooting. "There's no reason a village the size of Royal should have a zoo, but it did. And it was something to behold. It was never flashy like you'd see in a city, but it was still something to be proud of, and we were proud of Reuben. We always will be."

REINCARNATION

Two years before the shooting, Dick took the first few timid steps toward writing a book. He'd always been gripped by the history of the valley, of the homestead, of the old wagon ruts that would carry him all the way to Norfolk, his uncle used to say, if only he chose to follow them. The history of Mars, the first white settlement in the valley, founded by his great-great-grandfather Samuel Haskin in 1879, the old dugouts buried now beneath decades of dirt and debris. As a kid, still jumping from steel bridges over the creek and cleaving fossils from the cliffs, Dick never paused long enough to consider his own family in the same light as Daniel Boone or Old Jules or any of the other adventurous pioneers he loved to read about. But now that he was older, now that his days weren't mired in the shit of too many animals and too many responsibilities, he'd begun to reconsider. He dove into the research, established a family website, watched his history swell as his cousins and distant relatives added their own stories.

"This is important out here. It's part of the state's history. It's part of Royal's history. I would hope that Samuel and all of them will be remembered for years to come, because they did something extraordinary," he says. "I did nothing extraordinary. I made a bad career choice and made bad decisions that created a monster that destroyed me. I'm nobody."

Eventually someone said he should write all the history down, capture the whole thing in narrative. He agreed with the sentiment, but he was hardly a writer—he had hated English in grade school. Hated it in college too. He tried to pawn off the work on his cousin Mark Sanders, an award-winning poet, but Sanders declined. He told Dick he didn't have the information and that even if he had, this was Dick's story to tell, "his inheritance," he says, while Dick is still living in the valley, still intimately connected to his roots. And so Dick finished the research, compiled everything he'd found, and sat down to write. Thirteen months later, he struggled to finish chapter 1.

After Reuben died, Dick lost all interest in the book, at least for a time. He lost interest in everything. He just "gave up," he says. He spent hours at a time just staring at the creek, watching it carry the detritus of the plains off and around the bend. He still worked for the foster-care agency Building Blocks, and several months later, perhaps in a subliminal attempt to distract himself from the pain, he agreed to serve as a foster parent himself. A childless bachelor, he spent the next four years raising a high schooler, "the worst in the system at the time," Dick says. The other foster homes the teenager had been placed in hadn't stuck. He was a troubled kid, but the solitude on Dick's homestead was therapeutic, and "there was nothing he could do to me that those chimps or the orangutan hadn't already," Dick says. He spit tobacco juice on the walls. He kicked the electric fan across the kitchen. He punched holes in the bedroom wall. When he really lost it, Dick would simply leave the house and walk down to the creek. It wouldn't take long for the boy to follow, to join him in the stillness.

"I think he saved my life," Dick says. "I could concentrate on him and not have to think about those events at the zoo and what the zoo had done to me over the years."

The boy stayed on the homestead until his senior year, when he moved back in with his father, leaving Dick to his thoughts once again.

And so Dick returned to his book, determined to give it another shot. He stuck to a writing schedule of four hours each day, and thanks to his old friend Bob Gearhart—the same friend who used to film him at the Children's Zoo, who had since become a history teacher in New Mexico—he refused to let himself get bogged down in the quagmire of conflicting narratives, an element that had dogged his first efforts. As Gearhart explained, "History is the perspective of the person that writes it."

This time everything clicked. When the narratives forked, he followed Samuel's perspective. He wrote in his living room, between the stairwell and the kitchen, crouched over a small desk beside the woodstove, his old *Chicago Manual of Style* on one side, a can of Dr Pepper on the other. He wrote during the day, but if an idea spawned at night—and they often did—he'd race downstairs in his sweatpants and threadbare T-shirt and write until the inspiration petered out, the stove glowing red beside him. In fact, after several months of focused writing, the history began to pervade his dreams, the characters making strange cameos, until one night the decades collapsed like an accordion fan, and he met his great-great-grandfather face-to-face, still tossing and turning in his sheets.

In the dream, Samuel Haskin sat upright in a wooden chair in a small room at the end of a long and narrow corridor, "like a rest home, but it wasn't a rest home," he says. There was no bed. No desk. No furniture of any kind. There were no windows, no lamps, only light. An imposing figure with ghostly white skin and an untamed beard, Samuel intimidated Dick. He wore all black: black boots, black pants, a black vest, and a dusty black town coat. But more than anything, it was his eyes. They pierced right through Dick. He didn't know how or why, but Dick knew his time with Samuel was limited, that already the clock was ticking. He had so many questions, but Samuel was stuck on the genealogy. *How were they related?* They volleyed names back and forth like retirees at the dinner table until it dawned on Dick that Samuel had died before his last three grandchildren were born, the youngest of whom was Dick's grandfather. Now reconciled, Samuel proceeded to ask Dick a series of questions, and Dick proceeded to answer them—he lived on the homestead, he rented the pastures—as quickly as possible now, certain his window was soon to slam shut.

Finally Samuel paused, pulled the pipe from his mouth, and Dick blurted out the question that had long been hindering his research: *But what was your second wife's maiden name?* Samuel had just begun to answer when Dick felt himself being pulled away, as if harnessed to some invisible line above the stage. The room distended, and Samuel seemed suddenly distant. Dick panicked. He began to scream, "No, no, no!" louder and louder until he found himself clutching his bedsheets and screaming "No, no, no!" at the bedroom walls, sweat trailing down his pale forehead. He'd had realistic dreams before, he says. But this felt different. This didn't feel like a dream at all.

Barely a week later, Dick found himself again in that little room inside the rest home that wasn't a rest home at all. Samuel sat across from him just like before, and this time he recognized his great-great-grandson. In the intervening week, Dick had located the maiden name on an old marriage certificate, but the marriage had ended in divorce, and Dick was eager to know why. Samuel told him she couldn't handle the frontier, that she deserted him after realizing the extent of his expectations for a farm wife. At the divorce hearing, she accused him of "beastly cruelty," he told Dick. It was hardly a term Dick could forget, and so not long after, when he found the divorce record at the district court clerk's office, the phrase *beastly cruelty* clearly stated in the text, he nearly fell over.

"That was not a dream. I went somewhere and met him. I want so much to meet him again. I have more questions now. But that was 2009; it's been eight years. I don't think I'm going back. I wasn't pulled away from him so abruptly that second time. I asked him, 'Am I going to see you again?' All at once, we are out of that room, and we're up above here somewhere, and we're looking down on the hills of Mars, and he says, 'Look at these hills. When you look at these hills, you are looking at me.' That was his way of telling me, *No, this is the last time, but I am still with you.*"

Whatever the case, whatever the astral plane, the meeting with Samuel Haskin and his subsequent terrestrial discoveries galvanized Dick's ambition to record his family's legacy. He wrote with confidence, losing track of time as he tracked his great-great-grandfather across the page, his face illuminated by the blue light of his computer screen, his ancestry now palpable in the room, the house, the stand of cottonwood along the road and the big bluestem in the meadow and the brown trout in the creek and the owl perched in the gnarled trunk of the bur oak on the shore. He flew past chapters 2, 3, 4, and before he knew it—he really couldn't explain how, as if he'd suddenly emerged from some fever dream—he punctuated the last line, ". . . and the hills of Mars would echo his name for generations to come" and sent it to print under the pseudonym D. R. Haskin.

The man formerly known as Dick Haskin, of course, bled out at the front gate of Zoo Nebraska a little past one o'clock on the afternoon of September 10, 2005. That was another man, he says. Another time. His author bio makes no mention of the zoo or Reuben or the Midwest Primate Center, though it does note his education at UNL, as if the twenty-some years between college and his new life as a writer and financial manager never existed at all.

"Everybody knew the name Dick Haskin. Most people figured Dick Haskin was responsible for the death of the chimps, that I was still at the zoo at that time. Most people didn't realize I'd gotten out of there in 2001," he says. "I did not want that negativity in trying to preserve what my ancestors and the other settlers had done here. They sacrificed so much.

"I've tried to redefine who I am—*what* I am," he continues. "The past is gone. That person needs to die. The zoo died, and it needs to stay dead. The thing is . . . the spirit of the zoo? That thing is a monster. It destroys the people it touches."

D. R. Haskin published his first book, *The Hills of Mars*, in July 2009. It's now in its fifth printing, a local bestseller, he says, a history that both predates and parallels the history of Royal. Though his needs as a bachelor in the sticks of Antelope County are admittedly minimal, he lived off the proceeds of the book and its sequel for the next four years. He loaded the books in his car and schlepped them around like a traveling salesman from one small-town library to the next, all over northeast Nebraska, Iowa, South Dakota, Missouri, Wisconsin. He formulated a marketing plan, contacted historical societies and nursing homes and elementary schools. The next summer, he began to excavate Samuel's dugout up the road. Though it resembled little more than a naked hillside, he charged a two-dollar admission fee to look at the dig site, a little more for the full tour of Mars, a town so ghosted not even the bones exist in testament.

"Take a tour through the hills of Mars and stand in Samuel Haskin's dugout, walk along the wagon trails, stand on top of the Mars Stable, and relive the history," he advertises in the back of his books. He lists his personal phone number.

In Samuel's day they used to picnic down by the river, in a clearing beneath the oak trees. At one point, D. R. presumes, it was considered the city park. In the intervening century, nature took its course, the nettles and the grass and the gooseberries encroaching on the park until one could barely find it. But in 1996, D. R.'s relatives returned for a family reunion and helped him clean it up again. He's since added nineteen electrical hookups for RVs and pop-up campers. He calls it the Historic Mars Wildlife Area and Campground, and though part of it resembles a backwoods commune—a few rustic outhouses posted beneath the trees, some rusty playground equipment, signs carved in the bark—it is also genuinely serene. Birds chirp overhead. The Verdigris slithers below. From the house in the summer, D. R. can often hear the kids playing in the water a few hundred yards away.

"That's my favorite sound," he says, "hearing kids play in the creek."

In 2011, D. R. began to honor Samuel's birthday, May 19, by hosting a large celebration at the campground over Memorial Day weekend and charging the public five dollars to attend. He books local songwriters to play music, blacksmiths and muzzle-loading groups to give demonstrations. He organizes hayrack rides and a short theatrical performance.

D. R. Haskin wrote the script, but Samuel delivers it. For months, D. R. grows out his hair and his beard. Before the show begins, he stands beside his unintentionally low-flow toilet, staring at himself in a toothpaste-speckled mirror. He's wearing a $900 costume purchased online to perfectly match Samuel's outfit "in both the 1865 and 1890 photographs," he says. Everything Samuel wore in the dreams—or as D. R. would have it, the visitations—plus a black bowler hat, a wooden cane with a gold handle, and a smoking pipe. He uses a colored hair spray to blacken his hair and beard. With a makeup pencil, he fills in his mustache and his eyebrows and draws wrinkles and blemishes onto his skin. The routine takes forty-five minutes. The light filters in through the window screen. He can hear children down at the creek.

When he leaves the house, he walks with a limp and speaks with a rising patriotic timbre. He gestures with the script in his hand, though he never looks at it, doesn't need it. Just like the Samuel from his dreams, he guffaws at a good joke but often turns pensive, peering off into the distance, musing on the past and the present and all the changes "this land" has witnessed. Now and then, he'll reference a series of books written by his great-great-grandson, D. R. Haskin, and call its credibility into question; it's a bizarrely meta performance.

In May 2013, nearly 170 people flocked to Mars for Samuel's birthday, most of them friends and foliage on the Haskin family tree. Shafts of light filtered through the leafy canopy above while campers moved in and out of their trailers below, all nineteen hookups booked solid through the weekend. Never stopping anywhere too long, Samuel hobbled along the trails, greeting visitors, shaking hands, checking on the status of the hayrack rides or the sound equipment or the ticket takers at the gate. In the late afternoon, after a young woman sang and played a solo country set on her guitar, after a two-man performance of the life of outlaw Jesse James, Samuel emerged from the gathering and stood just below the stage. A large crowd gathered around him, repositioning their camp chairs and fanning themselves with paper plates. He paused for a moment, and with the program notes he'd rolled up in his fist, painted the hills behind them.

"Look at these hills. When you look at these hills, you are looking at me," he said, repeating the same soapbox statement from the dream. "The life that was made in these hills is a result of my sweat and my blood. Many families sacrificed, and some gave the ultimate sacrifice, to build Mars. But Mars is more than just the buildings and the crops. Mars is the people and their determination to make a better life. It's their willingness to help each other at all times. That, my friends, is the true spirit of Mars, and that spirit will not be destroyed. The spirit of Mars will continue for generations to come. Many hardships were faced to make a life in these hills, and many hardships are still ahead. Fires, blizzards, floods, droughts, and even war will persist throughout the ages. Yet the true spirit of Mars, the true spirit of the Nebraska pioneer, will always prevail and stand victorious. God bless Mars, and god bless America!"

He says the immersion is uncomfortable. He says he occasionally comes out the other end with no memory of the presentation at all. He says they have told him he is perhaps channeling Samuel himself, and of course, D. R. isn't the type to dismiss a sentiment like that out of hand. But eventually his cousins pack up their tents. The RVs pull out. Those youthful voices on the river drift away, and that stillness returns to the campground. Samuel pulls his face up from the sink to find D. R. Haskin in the mirror. He lives alone in a nearly one-hundred-year-old farmhouse six miles north of the smallest town in Antelope County. He hopes to be buried here.

Try as he might to ignore it, when his back locks up, or the headaches return, or his short-term memory fizzles out, he remembers everything he's tried to forget. He remembers the zoo. He remembers the board. He remembers Reuben. Before it all went south, the Bakkens bid him farewell with a framed drawing by Reuben. At the bottom, it said, "Thanks for our years together. Love, Reuben." It now hangs on D. R.'s living room wall alongside one of Reuben's paintings, the only two keepsakes he openly displays. The painting is a green-black blob, Reuben's heavy hand visible in the wide brush strokes, a tiny hint of yellow and red. A Rorschach test. A scribble of joy. A twister of contempt. Always a contradiction. D. R. doesn't celebrate Reuben's birthday. To remember Reuben is to remember the monster, too, and still, every day, his resentment threatens to consume him.

"Reuben is always a part of me," he says. "Yet he is a huge void in my heart."

D. R. sits at his kitchen table. A log shifts in the stove. He's wearing an old black sweatshirt with a moonlit eagle on the front. He sips a root beer.

"Sure, I had a dream . . ."

AUTHOR'S NOTE

The first time I met Dick Haskin he was sweating on Mars, his ill-fitting blue jeans covered in dirt, his scalp turning deeper shades of crimson in the afternoon sun. We were surrounded by cornfields, in a narrow pocket of trees that he assured me was the site of a pioneer settlement founded by his great-great-grandfather well over a century ago. A large sifter stood on wooden legs between us, and a grid of yellow ropes cordoned off inconspicuous patches of dirt, like empty frames on a wall. The cicadas droned on overhead.

I was sweating, too, though less from the heat than my nerves. Dick had been ignoring me for months, but he'd finally responded when I left a voice mail expressing interest in his dig site. I drove three hours northeast from Lincoln the very next day, a list of questions typed and folded neatly in my back pocket: a few about Mars, a few dozen about the zoo. Less than five minutes after my arrival, while I was still gathering my bearings and exchanging pleasantries, Dick peeled off his gloves, wiped his forehead, and looked me dead in the eye.

"I'm just gonna tell you right off the bat, I will not answer any questions about the zoo," he said. "None."

I walked back to my car and drove home, certain I'd blown my only shot. Over the next seven years, I kept researching Royal and the zoo, doing my best to work around Dick's absence. I interviewed his father, his classmates, his old boss at the Children's Zoo, his college mentor, volunteers, customers, and mere acquaintances—anyone I could find who might shed some light onto who he was and how he'd landed back in Royal with an adolescent chimpanzee named Reuben. It was tedious and incremental work, and it took me in directions I wouldn't have veered otherwise. But every year or two, I would reach back out to Dick, usually by email—one time with a handwritten note—asking him to reconsider. He responded only once, with a five-page, single-spaced letter.

"Everything I am about to tell you is confidential and strictly off the record," he began in bold and underlined text. He then proceeded to narrate his life story, answering everything I had planned to ask him that day in Mars: his college years, the Folsom Children's Zoo, the murder of Dian Fossey, the final shooting, the "monster called 'The Northeast Nebraska Zoo.'" In a short postscript, he told me that my previous letter had "brought a flood of unpleasant, painful memories," and that he'd been unable to sleep for several nights afterward.

I read the note with trembling hands. Perhaps because I was finally learning Dick's story. Perhaps because I'd put years of work into a book he was now compelling me to drop. Perhaps because I suddenly understood so much more but couldn't use any of it directly. The note shook me, but I kept working, trying my best to find other sources to verify the bones of Dick's letter. Oftentimes I got there. Other times I did not.

My luck changed on October 24, 2017. Just a few hours after sending what I had determined would be my last follow-up, Dick responded, "Yes, I will agree to an interview. Could you please send me a list of questions that you will be asking so that I can be prepared?" Two weeks later, I was parking my travel trailer in Dick's riverside campground, just a few hundred yards from his house. Though I'm still not entirely sure what changed, indeed, he seemed prepared—not as if he'd been thinking of what to say, exactly, but figuring out how to steel himself for the pain. Bracing for the toll it would take to rehash a period of his life that still threatened to consume him whenever he thought about it for a second too long.

Dick spoke on the record for more than twelve hours throughout the course of the weekend, most of it at his kitchen table, some of it with tears streaming down his cheeks or a fist pounding the table, the woodstove crackling in the next room. It didn't end there. I spent the next year rewriting the book and incorporating new material. During that time Dick answered every follow-up question I sent, often writing me several times a day to help fill in the gaps. I'm eternally grateful to Dick for the candor and generosity he ultimately showed me, and for the hospitality during my stay at the Historic Mars Campground.

Unfortunately, I cannot say the same for every subject in this book. On the day of the zoo auction, I stopped by Ken Schlueter Jr.'s machine shop. He declined to be interviewed then, and he declined several other times over the years, though not without first asking to see what I had already written and preemptively rejecting what he assumed others had told me. Kip and Stacey Smith also refused to participate, despite repeated attempts to reach them. In each of these cases, I've relied instead on local newspaper reports and personal interviews with other parties to these events and, when relevant, any documentation on file with the state of Nebraska.

This is a book of narrative nonfiction, or literary journalism, and as such I've relied solely on verifiable information, using only real names, dates, and events. Some quotes were lightly edited for clarity. Nevertheless, every story has multiple angles, and many of my sources for this book—as readers will note—contradicted one another. I've attempted to let those contradictions stand, to let my sources speak for themselves, but also to shape their many voices into coherent events by prioritizing the details that overlapped or could be confirmed by a more objective source. For example, in writing about the chimpanzee escape, I relied heavily on Freedom of Information Act materials received from the Nebraska State Patrol; in re-creating the scenes from the district court, I quote directly from court transcripts. I also utilized inspection reports from the USDA and case summaries from the Nebraska Judicial Branch, and I referred often to early coverage of these events in both local and state newspapers.

It is not my intention as a writer, nor my role as a journalist, to assign guilt or innocence or to pass judgment on anyone depicted in this book—not that I would have much success if I tried. After studying Royal and the events surrounding the zoo for almost a decade, I've come to the conclusion that everyone involved lands somewhere in the middle; that intentions were often pure but expectations rarely fulfilled; that "to err is human," as Pope so elegantly put it, but "to forgive, divine." More importantly, I've come to see hints of Royal—both hope and struggle—in small towns everywhere, or, perhaps more accurately, hints of every small town in Royal.

ACKNOWLEDGMENTS

In the summer of 2010, I fell in love with my college girlfriend and agreed to a long weekend at her parents' farm near Plainview, Nebraska. She used to adore the trout hatchery down the road, she told me, how the fish swarmed to the pellets and brought the surface to a boil. We re-created her childhood the next day, fueled by nostalgia. We fed the fish. We hiked around Grove Lake, raced up the chalky bluff they used to call Chalk Mountain. We ate peach pie at Green Gables, a seasonal restaurant housed in an old barn near the fossil beds. Heading home again, we passed through a town called Royal on Highway 20 where a train car lay forsaken in an empty lot and a single buffalo grazed behind the One Stop. About ten seconds later, she pointed out the window and said casually, "That's where Reuben got shot."

I wrestled with this book off and on for just shy of a decade, trying to answer the deluge of *whys* and *hows* that sprang from the brush like a bouquet of spooked pheasants. Driving home from the auction later that summer, the water tower still visible in my rearview mirror, the sun melting over Highway 20, I felt the sort of electricity a reporter rarely feels, a journalistic high I've been chasing ever since. I wasn't yet sure what the story was, *exactly*, but I knew it was there, *approximately*, in the skeleton of the old zoo, in the way the auction goers seemed to clam up at the sight of my recorder. I called my girlfriend and then my parents, too, yammering away about this strange little town and its strange old zoo, how everyone I spoke with had a story about the chimpanzees that used to live there, how the first director ignored my calls, and how the last director kicked me out of his garage, a cigarette still smoking in his ashtray.

What I gave them wasn't so much a story as a vomit of *maybes* and *what ifs*, but already they stood behind the project, asking more questions, encouraging me to return again. From the very beginning, my family and friends have been my staunchest supporters, often supplying enthusiasm when my own ran out or when I felt too confused or defeated to continue. I owe them all a serious debt of gratitude, but especially Mel, who not only took me back to the farm but agreed to marry me too. She is my wife, my first reader, my editor, my sounding board. And especially my parents, who have never once questioned my choice to become a writer, despite the many delusions and insecurities of this long and shaky pursuit. And to my in-laws, as well, my liaisons to the area, for keeping me abreast of all the goings-on in northeast Nebraska, and for the home base and home-cooked meals they provided during my repeat visits to Royal.

Professionally, I'll be forever indebted to author Joe Starita, my former professor, who read the first inchoate chapters of this book when it was still my undergraduate thesis at the University of Nebraska–Lincoln and who helped me shape it into a proposal years later. Joe taught me not only how to write but how to take my writing seriously. More broadly, I owe a thanks to Scott Winter, Charlyne Berens, and many other professors from UNL's College of Journalism and Mass Communications for their early encouragement of this project.

Zoo Nebraska followed me from UNL to the University of North Carolina Wilmington, where I completed the first draft in pursuit of my MFA. I'm particularly indebted to authors David Gessner and Philip Gerard, who served on my thesis committee and encouraged me to think of this project not as the final step toward another degree but as a book with serious potential. I'm equally grateful to my closest friends in Wilmington, who read early portions of this book and agreed to hear even more, given a few beers and a pool cue at the Blue Post.

For the encouragement and journalistic insights, I owe a special thank-you to Don Walton, Jordan Pascale, and Zach Pluhacek. For the encouragement and fine tequila, I owe a dizzy thank-you to Ted Genoways and Mary Anne Andrei—both stepped into my life at a critical juncture for this book and through their own creative and journalistic pursuits, inspired me to keep reaching. For the Individual Artist Fellowship and accompanying funds, I'm grateful to the Nebraska Arts Council, and for the continual distraction during crunch time in Omaha, I'm grateful to the Dive Bar Club. For seeing this book for more than a few chimpanzees, thank you to Ross Harris, my agent, and Laura Van der Veer, my editor.

Last, but certainly not least, my sincerest thank-you to the people of Royal and northeast Nebraska at large. I asked many of you, time and time again, to replay and therefore relive one of the darkest chapters in your lives. I'm forever grateful for the lessons you've taught me in community, intentionally or otherwise. In December 1935, rejecting the accusation that she had written *Old Jules* to vent her bitterness toward her father, Nebraska author Mari Sandoz wrote, "I looked around me for the most promising material and I saw rather early that it was unquestionably Old Jules and his community. That in itself should indicate my respect for the man and his ambitions." It goes without saying that the events of September 10, 2005, sparked my interest in Royal. But what kept me coming back was not the novelty of a chimpanzee escape in rural Nebraska. It was the sense that Royal represented more than itself; that there was something utterly human in the zoo's humble beginnings, and perhaps even more so in its ultimate demise.

ABOUT THE AUTHOR

Photo © 2018 Mary Anne Andrei

Carson Vaughan is a freelance journalist from central Nebraska who writes frequently about the Great Plains. His work has appeared in the *New York Times*, the *New Yorker*, the *Atlantic*, the *Guardian*, the *Paris Review Daily, Outside, Pacific Standard, VICE, In These Times*, and more. *Zoo Nebraska* is his first book.